READINESS FOR READING
WITH i.t.a. AND t.o.

READINESS FOR READING
WITH i.t.a. AND t.o.

A Comparison Between the Read-
ing Readiness and Early Reading
Progress of Children Learning to
Read with the Initial Teaching
Alphabet and of Children Learn-
ing to Read with Traditional
Orthography.

D. V. Thackray, B.Sc. (Econ.), M.A., Ph.D.

GEOFFREY CHAPMAN
LONDON   1971

Geoffrey Chapman Ltd
18 High Street, Wimbledon, London SW19

Geoffrey Chapman (Ireland) Ltd
5–7 Main Street, Blackrock, County Dublin

SBN 225 65930 1

Submitted as a thesis
in fulfilment of the
requirements for the
degree of
Doctor of Philosophy
University of London
1969.

To Frances and Teresa

PRINTED IN GREAT BRITAIN
BY LOWE AND BRYDONE (PRINTERS) LTD., LONDON.

Preface

The research here reported represents the outcome of approximately nine years of study in the field of reading readiness and early reading progress.

The main i.t.a. experiment which began in 1961 has, without doubt, aroused more interest, and has had more widespread influence on the classrooms of the world, then any other experiment in reading. For this reason a research which makes a comparison, over a period of three years, between children learning to read with i.t.a. and t.o. in the normal school situation is very timely.

In particular this research looks very carefully at the concept of reading readiness and the differences between the reading readiness of children learning to read with i.t.a. and t.o. In this respect the research reported breaks new ground.

The author wishes to acknowledge the invaluable help given to him by Dr John Downing and Mr William Latham, formerly of the Reading Research Unit of the University of London; Miss M. Kaye, Adviser to Primary Schools; and the heads, class teachers and children of the schools used.

He is particularly grateful to Alan Alexander, Educational Editor of Geoffrey Chapman Limited, who has worked much beyond the call of duty to bring the research into published form.

Above all the author wishes to pay tribute to his wife for the preparation of all the drawings used, and for being a constant source of inspiration, encouragement and active help in every way during nine years of research.

D.V.T.

Contents

PART I   REVIEW OF THE RESEARCH RELEVANT
TO THE INVESTIGATION

Preface   v

Introduction   2

CHAPTER 1 *A Summary of the Research into the*
Main Aspects of Reading Readiness   7

Definition   7

Development of the concept   8

Factors involved in reading readiness 9

The physiological factor   11

The intellectual factor   15

The environmental factor   18

The emotional and personal factor   19

Sex differences in reading readiness and
early reading   21

The appraisal of reading readiness   22

CHAPTER 2 *A Re-examination of the Concept of*
Reading Readiness   27

The minimum mental age controversy 28

Discussion of the evidence concerning
delaying formal reading   36

Discussion of the perceptual abilities
required by children for successful reading   43

Discussion of new methods of teaching
reading   45

CHAPTER 3   *A Brief Description of the Initial
Teaching Alphabet (formerly called
Augmented Roman) and a Discussion
of the Relationship between i.t.a. and
Reading Readiness*   52

i.t.a. in historical perspective   52

Brief description of the Initial Teaching
Alphabet (i.t.a.)   58

Visual discrimination and i.t.a.   63

Auditory discrimination and i.t.a.   64

Problem solving in learning to read
with i.t.a.   64

CHAPTER 4   *A Critical Appraisal of the Design of the
Main i.t.a. Experiment*   74

Discussion of the variables   75

Methods of teaching reading   79

The 'Hawthorne Effect'   83

The quality and amount of teaching given   90

CHAPTER 5   *A Discussion of the Results of the
Main i.t.a. Experiment*   92

Can children learn to read more easily
with i.t.a. than they can with t.o.?   92

Can pupils transfer their training in
reading in i.t.a. to reading in t.o.?   98

After the whole process of beginning with
i.t.a. and transferring to t.o., are reading
attainments in t.o. superior to what they
would have been without the intervention
of i.t.a.?   103

Will the children's written composition be
more fluent with the simpler i.t.a. code for
speech?   107

How will children's later attainments in
t.o. spelling be influenced by their earlier
experiences of reading and writing the
different spellings of i.t.a.?   109

CHAPTER 6   *An Appraisal of the i.t.a. Experiment*   112

Discussion of the statistical techniques
employed in the i.t.a. experiment   112

Discussion of the main conclusions from
the i.t.a. experiment   117

Discussion of the wider implications of the
i.t.a. experiment   121

PART II   THE INVESTIGATION

Introduction   132

CHAPTER I   *Discussion of the Testing Measures
Selected and Constructed (I): Tests of
Specific Reading Readiness Skills and
Reading Achievement and Progress*   137

Harrison-Stroud Reading Readiness
Profiles   138

Visual Discrimination of Graphic
Symbols Test   143

Auditory Discrimination of Sounds in
Words Test   148

Measures of reading achievement   152

CHAPTER 2   *Discussion of the Measures Selected
and Constructed (II): Measures of
General Ability and Home
Environment*   157

General ability   157

Home environment   161

Measures of physical, social and
emotional factors   164

CHAPTER 3   *Discussion of the Children and
Schools Selected*   166

Number of children and the timing of the tests   166

Selection and matching of the schools   167

Description of schools selected   169

Testing techniques with young children   175

CHAPTER 4   *Discussion of the Results obtained by the Statistical Methods Selected (I): Tests carried out in the Children's First Term at School, and the matching of the i.t.a. and t.o. Groups*   177

Measures of visual discrimination   178

Measures of auditory discrimination   181

Measures of general intelligence   183

Measures of home background   184

Measures of physical, social and emotional factors   188

The matching of the i.t.a. and t.o. groups   190

CHAPTER 5   *Discussion of the Results obtained by the Statistical Methods Selected (II): Tests carried out in the Children's Third Term at School*   193

Measures of visual discrimination   194

Measures of auditory discrimination   195

Measures of reading achievement   196

A study of the relationship between the earlier reading readiness results and the later reading achievement results   198

A comparison of the reading readiness levels required for children to learn to read successfully using i.t.a. and t.o.   201

A comparison of the minimum mental age levels required for learning to read successfully with i.t.a. and t.o.   209

CHAPTER 6   *Discussion of the Results obtained by the Statistical Methods Selected (III):*

Tests carried out in the Children's Fourth Term at School   211

Schonell Graded Word Reading Test   212

Neale Analysis of Reading Ability   212

A study of the relationship between the earlier reading readiness results and the later reading achievement results   215

A comparison of the reading readiness levels required for children to learn to read successfully using i.t.a. and t.o.   217

A comparison of the minimum mental age levels required for learning to read successfully with i.t.a. and t.o.   230

CHAPTER 7   *Discussion of the Results obtained by the Statistical Methods Selected (IV): Tests carried out in the Children's Sixth Term at School*   235

Schonell Graded Word Reading Test   236

Neale Analysis of Reading Ability   236

A study of the relationship between the earlier reading readiness results and the later reading achievement results   238

A comparison of the reading readiness levels required for children to learn to read successfully using i.t.a. and t.o.   239

A comparison of the minimum mental age levels required for learning to read successfully with i.t.a. and t.o.   252

CHAPTER 8   *Discussion of the Results obtained by the Statistical Methods Selected (V): Tests carried out in the Children's Ninth Term at School*   255

Schonell Graded Word Reading Test   256

Neale Analysis of Reading Ability   256

A study of the relationship between the earlier reading readiness results and the later reading achievement results   257

A comparison of the reading readiness
levels required for children to learn to read
successfully using i.t.a. and t.o.   258
A comparison of the minimum mental age
levels required for learning to read
successfully with i.t.a. and t.o.   268

CHAPTER 9   *The Comparison of Boys' and Girls'*
Performances on Reading Readiness
and Reading Achievement Tests, and
a Study of the Reading Progress of
Children from the Different Schools   271

Reading readiness scores   272

Reading achievement scores   273

Reading progress in different schools   275

CHAPTER 10   *Summary and Conclusions*   281
Final note   293
Appendix   295
Bibliography   296

Tables

1. Showing the comparison between the mental
   ages of 179 children and their reading
   achievement and progress.   35

2. Adapted from Downing (1967a), showing
   progress in reading basic reader series and
   percentage frequency distribution of reading
   primer reached.   93

3. Adapted from Downing (1967a), showing
   results for Schonell Graded Word Reading Test
   after 1⅓ years (given in i.t.a. to i.t.a. groups and
   in t.o. to t.o. groups).   95

4. Adapted from Downing (1967a), showing

results for Neale Analysis of Reading Ability measuring Accuracy, Speed and Comprehension in fifth term (given in i.t.a. to i.t.a. groups, and in t.o. to t.o. groups). 95

5. Adapted from Downing (1967a), showing the transfer of learning from i.t.a. to t.o. in Accuracy, Speed and Comprehension as measured by Neale Analysis of Reading Ability in experimental (i.t.a.) groups only, i.t.a. and t.o. test results of same subjects; fifth term. 98

6. Adapted from Downing (1967a), showing the transfer of learning from i.t.a. to t.o. in Accuracy, Speed and Comprehension as measured by Neale Analysis of Reading Ability. Only the scores of experimental (i.t.a.) group subjects transferred to t.o. books at least 6 weeks prior to testing, are included. 99

7. Adapted from Downing (1967a), showing the transfer of learning from i.t.a. to t.o. as measured by Schonell Graded Word Reading Test given in i.t.a. in fifth term, and in t.o. in seventh term. i.t.a. and t.o. results of same subjects. 99

8. Adapted from Downing (1967a), showing the transfer of learning from i.t.a. to t.o. as measured by Schonell Graded Word Reading Test. Only the scores of the experimental (i.t.a.) group subjects transferred to t.o. books at least four months prior to Schonell Test in t.o., are included. 100

9. Adapted from Downing (1967a), showing reading in t.o. at mid-second year in Accuracy, Speed and Comprehension as measured by Neale Analysis of Reading Ability Form A. Experimental and control groups both tested in t.o. 104

10. Adapted from Downing (1967a), showing word recognition in t.o. at beginning of third year as measured by Schonell Graded Word Reading

Test. Experimental and control groups
tested in t.o.   105

11. Adapted from Downing (1967a), showing
reading in t.o. at end of three school years in
Accuracy, Speed and Comprehension as measured
by Neale Analysis of Reading Ability.
Experimental and control groups tested in t.o.   105

12. Adapted from Downing (1967a), showing silent
reading comprehension in t.o. at end of third
year as measured by the Standish NS45 Test.
Experimental and control groups tested in t.o.   105

13. Showing Stanford Achievement Test Paragraph
Meaning raw scores of six studies comparing
i.t.a. and t.o. taught populations after one year
of instruction.   107

14. Adapted from Downing (1967a), showing part
of the Staffordshire study of written
composition results of word analysis.   108

15. Adapted from Downing (1967a), showing t.o.
spelling in experimental (i.t.a.) and control (t.o.)
groups as measured by Schonell Graded Word
Spelling Test.   109

16. Adapted from Sceats (1967), showing the
number of children in the First Enquiry
entering Junior classes still reading in i.t.a.
in September 1965.   126

17. Adapted from Sister John (1966), showing the
number of children in each group who were
above the mean on each of the three tasks of
Matching, Recognition and Auditory
Discrimination.   142

18. Showing a comparison between the mean scores
of the i.t.a. and t.o. groups on the author's
Visual Discrimination Test given for
the first time.   179

19. Showing a comparison between the mean scores
of the i.t.a. and t.o. groups on the Harrison-

Stroud Visual Discrimination Test
(i.t.a. version).   179

20. Showing a comparison between the mean scores
    of the i.t.a. and t.o. groups on the Harrison-
    Stroud Visual Discrimination Test
    (t.o. version).   179

21. Showing a comparison between the mean scores
    of both i.t.a. and t.o. groups (238) on the i.t.a.
    and t.o. versions of the Harrison-Stroud
    Visual Discrimination Test.   179

22. Showing the distribution of the standardized
    scores of 238 children on the author's Visual
    Discrimination Test (Mean 100,
    Standard Deviation 15).   180

23. Showing a comparison between the mean scores
    of the i.t.a. and t.o. groups on the author's
    Auditory Discrimination Test given for
    the first time.   181

24. Showing a comparison between the mean scores
    of the i.t.a. and t.o. groups on the Harrison-
    Stroud Auditory Discrimination Test.   181

25. Showing the distribution of the standardized
    scores of 238 children on the author's
    Auditory Discrimination Test (Mean 100,
    Standard Deviation 15).   182

26. Showing a comparison between the mean scores
    of the i.t.a. and t.o. groups on the Wechsler
    Scale of Intelligence (Verbal tests only).   183

27. Showing a comparison between the mean scores
    of the i.t.a. and t.o. groups on the Goodenough
    Draw-A-Man Test.   183

28. Showing a comparison between the mean scores
    of the i.t.a. and t.o. groups for mental
    ability as estimated by the class teachers on a
    five point scale.   183

29. Showing a comparison between the mean scores
    of the i.t.a. and t.o. groups on the
    author's Vocabularly Profile.   184

30. Showing the distribution of Social Class in i.t.a. and t.o. groups according to fathers' occupations. 185

31 Showing a comparison between the mean scores of the i.t.a. and t.o. groups for accuracy of speech as estimated by the class teachers on a five point scale. 186

32. Showing a comparison between the mean scores of the i.t.a. and t.o. groups for extent of vocabulary as estimated by the class teachers on a five point scale. 186

33. Showing a comparison between the mean scores of the i.t.a. and t.o. groups for extent and quality of play as estimated by the class teachers on a five point scale. 186

34. Showing a comparison between the mean scores of the i.t.a. and t.o. groups for experiential background as estimated by the class teachers on a five point scale. 186

35. Showing the distribution of the standardized scores of 238 children on the author's revised Vocabulary Profile (Mean 100, Standard Deviation 15). 187

36. Showing a comparison between the mean scores of the i.t.a. and t.o. groups for ability to listen as estimated by the class teachers on a five point scale. 188

37. Showing a comparison between the mean scores of the i.t.a. and t.o. groups for attitudes to books and learning to read as estimated by the class teachers on a five point scale. 188

38. Showing a comparison between the mean scores of the i.t.a. and t.o. groups for readiness to read as estimated by the class teachers on a five point scale. 189

39. Showing the numbers from each pair of matched schools. 191

40. Showing a comparison between the mean scores

of the i.t.a. and t.o. groups on the author's
Visual Discrimination Test given for the
second time. 194

41. Showing a comparison between the mean scores
of the i.t.a. and t.o. groups on the author's
Auditory Discrimination Test given for the
second time. 195

42. Showing a comparison between the mean scores
of the i.t.a. and t.o. groups on the Schonell
Graded Word Reading Test given for the first
time (given in i.t.a. to the i.t.a. children;
given in t.o. to the t.o. children). 196

43. Showing a comparison of the correlations,
calculated for the i.t.a. and t.o. groups
separately, between the initial tests of
reading readiness abilities and the Schonell
Graded Word Reading Test given for the first
time (given in i.t.a. to the i.t.a. children;
given in t.o. to the t.o. children). 200

44. Showing a comparison of the mean scores
attained on the Schonell Graded Word Reading
Test by sub-groups of i.t.a. and t.o. children
who attained similar levels of performance on
the author's Visual Discrimination Test. 202

45. Showing a comparison of the mean scores
attained on the Schonell Graded Word Reading
Test by sub-groups of i.t.a. and t.o. children
who attained similar levels of performance on
the Harrison-Stroud Visual Discrimination Test
in i.t.a. 202

46. Showing a comparison of the mean scores
attained on the Schonell Graded Word Reading
Test by sub-groups of i.t.a. and t.o. children
who attained similar levels of performance on
the Harrison-Stroud Visual Discrimination Test
in t.o. 203

47. Showing a comparison of the mean scores
attained on the Schonell Graded Word Reading

Test by sub-groups of i.t.a. and t.o. children
who attained similar levels of performance on
the author's Auditory Discrimination Test.   204

48. Showing a comparison of the mean scores
attained on the Schonell Graded Word Reading
Test by sub-groups of i.t.a. and t.o. children
who attained similar levels of performance on
the Harrison-Stroud Auditory
Discrimination Test.   204

49. Showing a comparison of the mean scores
attained on the Schonell Graded Word Reading
Test by sub-groups of i.t.a. and t.o. children
who attained similar levels of performance on
the Wechsler Scale of Intelligence for Children.   206

50. Showing a comparison of the mean scores
attained on the Schonell Graded Word Reading
Test by sub-groups of i.t.a. and t.o. children
who attained similar levels of performance on
the Goodenough Draw-A-Man Test.   207

51. Showing a comparison of the mean scores
attained on the Schonell Graded Word Reading
Test by sub-groups of i.t.a. and t.o. children
who attained similar levels of performance on
the author's Vocabulary Profile.   208

52. Showing a comparison between the mean
scores attained on the Schonell Graded Word
Reading Test, given for the first time, by sub-
groups of i.t.a. and t.o. children with similar
mental ages.   209

53. Showing a comparison between the mean
scores of the i.t.a. and t.o. groups on the
Schonell Graded Word Reading Test given for
the second time (given in i.t.a. to the i.t.a.
children; given in t.o. to the t.o. children).   212

54. Showing a comparison between the mean
scores of the i.t.a. and t.o. groups on Reading
Accuracy as measured by the Neale Analysis of
Reading Ability (Form A) given for the first

time (given in i.t.a. to the i.t.a. children; given in t.o. to the t.o. children). 212

55. Showing a comparison between the mean scores of the i.t.a. and t.o. groups on Reading Comprehension as measured by the Neale Analysis of Reading Ability (Form A) given for the first time. 213

56. Showing a comparison of the correlations, calculated for the i.t.a. and t.o. groups separately, between the initial tests of reading readiness abilities and the Schonell Graded Word Reading Test given for the second time (given in i.t.a. to the i.t.a children; given in t.o. to the t.o. children). 214

57. Showing a comparison of the correlations, calculated for the i.t.a. and t.o. groups separately, between the initial tests of reading readiness abilities and Reading Accuracy as measured by the Neale Analysis of Reading Ability (Form A) given for the first time (given in i.t.a. to the i.t.a. children; given in t.o. to the t.o. children). 215

58. Showing a comparison of the correlations, calculated for the i.t.a. and t.o. groups separately, between the initial tests of reading readiness abilities, and Reading Comprehension as measured by the Neale Analysis of Reading Ability (Form A) given for the first time. 216

59. Showing a comparison of the mean scores attained on the Schonell Graded Word Reading Test by sub-groups of i.t.a. and t.o. children who attained similar levels of performance on the author's Visual Discrimination Test. 218

60. Showing a comparison of the mean scores attained on the Schonell Graded Word Reading Test by sub-groups of i.t.a. and t.o. children who attained similar levels of performance on the Harrison-Stroud Visual Discrimination Test in i.t.a. 218

61. Showing a comparison of the mean scores attained on the Schonell Graded Word Reading Test by sub-groups of i.t.a. and t.o. children who attained similar levels of performance on the Harrison-Stroud Visual Discrimination Test in t.o.   219

62. Showing a comparison of the mean scores attained on the Schonell Graded Word Reading Test by sub-groups of i.t.a. and t.o. children who attained similar levels of performance on the author's Auditory Discrimination Test.   219

63. Showing a comparison of the mean scores attained on the Schonell Graded Word Reading Test by sub-groups of i.t.a. and t.o. children who attained similar levels of performance on the Harrison-Stroud Auditory Discrimination Test.   220

64. Showing a comparison of the mean scores attained on the Schonell Graded Word Reading Test by sub-groups of i.t.a. and t.o. children who attained similar levels of performance on the Wechsler Scale of Intelligence for Children.   222

65. Showing a comparison of the mean scores attained on the Schonell Graded Word Reading Test by sub-groups of i.t.a. and t.o. children who attained similar levels of performance on the Goodenough Draw-A-Man Test.   222

66. Showing a comparison of the mean scores attained on the Schonell Graded Word Reading Test by sub-groups of i.t.a. and t.o. children who attained similar levels of performance on the author's Vocabulary Profile.   223

67. Showing a comparison of the mean scores attained on Reading Accuracy as measured by the Neale Analysis of Reading Ability by sub-groups of i.t.a. and t.o. children who attained similar levels of performance on the author's Visual Discrimination Test.   224

68. Showing a comparison of the mean scores

attained on Reading Accuracy as measured by
the Neale Analysis of Reading Ability by sub-
groups of i.t.a. and t.o. children who attained
similar levels of performance on the Harrison-
Stroud Visual Discrimination Test in i.t.a.   225

69. Showing a comparison of the mean scores
attained on Reading Accuracy as measured by
the Neale Analysis of Reading Ability by sub-
groups of i.t.a. and t.o. children who attained
similar levels of performance on the Harrison-
Stroud Visual Discrimination Test in t.o.   225

70. Showing a comparison of the mean scores
attained on Reading Accuracy as measured by
the Neale Analysis of Reading Ability by sub-
groups of i.t.a. and t.o. children who attained
similar levels of performance on the author's
Auditory Discrimination Test.   226

71. Showing a comparison of the mean scores
attained on Reading Accuracy as measured by
the Neale Analysis of Reading Ability by sub-
groups of i.t.a. and t.o. children who attained
similar levels of performance on the Harrison-
Stroud Auditory Discrimination Test.   227

72. Showing a comparison of the mean scores
attained on Reading Accuracy as measured by
the Neale Analysis of Reading Ability by sub-
groups of i.t.a. and t.o. children who attained
similar levels of performance on the Wechsler
Scale of Intelligence for Children.   228

73. Showing a comparison of the mean scores
attained on Reading Accuracy as measured by
the Neale Analysis of Reading Ability by sub-
groups of i.t.a. and t.o. children who attained
similar levels of performance on the
Goodenough Draw-A-Man Test.   228

74. Showing a comparison of the mean scores
attained on Reading Accuracy as measured by
the Neale Analysis of Reading Ability by sub-
groups of i.t.a. and t.o. children who attained

similar levels of performance on the author's Vocabulary Profile. 229

75. Showing a comparison between the mean scores attained on the Schonell Graded Word Reading Test given a second time, by sub-groups of i.t.a. and t.o. children with similar mental ages. 231

76. Showing a comparison between the mean scores attained on Reading Accuracy as measured by the Neale Analysis of Reading Ability given for the first time, by sub-groups of i.t.a. and t.o. children with similar mental ages. 232

77. Showing a comparison of the correlations, calculated for the i.t.a. and t.o. groups separately, between the initial tests of reading readiness abilities, and three measures of reading achievement, given in the children's fourth term at school. 233

78. Showing a comparison between the mean scores attained on the i.t.a. and t.o. versions of the Schonell Graded Word Reading Test by 50 i.t.a. children who had not transferred to t.o. 236

79. Showing a comparison between the mean scores attained on the i.t.a. and t.o. versions of the Neale Analysis of Reading Ability, Form B (Accuracy) by 50 i.t.a. children who had not transferred to t.o. 236

80. Showing a comparison between the mean scores of the i.t.a. and t.o. groups on the Schonell Graded Word Reading Test given for the third time (given in t.o. to both i.t.a. and t.o. groups). 237

81. Showing a comparison between the mean scores of the i.t.a. and t.o. groups for Reading Accuracy as measured by the Neale Analysis of Reading Ability (Form B) given for the second time (given in t.o. to both i.t.a. and t.o. groups). 237

82. Showing a comparison between the mean scores of the i.t.a. and t.o. groups for Reading Comprehension as measured by the Neale Analysis of Reading Ability (Form B) given for the second time. 237

83. Showing a comparison of the correlations, calculated for the i.t.a. and t.o. groups separately, between the initial tests of reading readiness abilities and the Schonell Graded Word Reading Test given for the third time (given in t.o. to both i.t.a. and t.o. groups). 238

84. Showing a comparison of the correlations, calculated for the i.t.a. and t.o. groups separately, between the initial tests of reading readiness abilities and Reading Accuracy as measured by the Neale Analysis of Reading Ability, given for the second time (given in t.o. to both i.t.a. and t.o. groups). 239

85. Showing a comparison of the mean scores attained on the Schonell Graded Word Reading Test by sub-groups of i.t.a. and t.o. children who attained similar levels of performance on the author's Visual Discrimination Test. 240

86. Showing a comparison of the mean scores attained on the Schonell Graded Word Reading Test by sub-groups of i.t.a. and t.o. children who attained similar levels of performance on the Harrison-Stroud Visual Discrimination Test in i.t.a. 240

87. Showing a comparison of the mean scores attained on the Schonell Graded Word Reading Test by sub-groups of i.t.a. and t.o. children who attained similar levels of performance on the Harrison-Stroud Visual Discrimination Test in t.o. 241

88. Showing a comparison of the mean scores attained on the Schonell Graded Word Reading Test by sub-groups of i.t.a. and t.o. children who attained similar levels of performance on the author's Auditory Discrimination Test. 243

89. Showing a comparison of the mean scores attained on the Schonell Graded Word Reading Test by sub-groups of i.t.a. and t.o. children who attained similar levels of performance on the Harrison-Stroud Auditory Discrimination Test. 243

90. Showing a comparison of the mean scores attained on the Schonell Graded Word Reading Test by sub-groups of i.t.a. and t.o. children who attained similar levels of performance on the Wechsler Scale of Intelligence for Children. 244

91. Showing a comparison of the mean scores attained on the Schonell Graded Word Reading Test by sub-groups of i.t.a. and t.o. children who attained similar levels of performance on the Goodenough Draw-A-Man Test. 244

92. Showing a comparison of the mean scores attained on the Schonell Graded Word Reading Test by sub-groups of i.t.a. and t.o. children who attained similar levels of performance on the author's Vocabulary Profile. 245

93. Showing a comparison of the mean scores attained on Reading Accuracy as measured by the Neale Analysis of Reading Ability, by sub-groups of i.t.a. and t.o. children who attained similar levels of performance on the author's Visual Discrimination Test. 246

94. Showing a comparison of the mean scores attained on Reading Accuracy as measured by the Neale Analysis of Reading Ability, by sub-groups of i.t.a. and t.o. children who attained similar levels of performance on the Harrison-Stroud Visual Discrimination Test in i.t.a. 246

95. Showing a comparison of the mean scores attained on Reading Accuracy as measured by the Neale Analysis of Reading Ability, by sub-groups of i.t.a. and t.o. children who attained similar levels of performance on the Harrison-Stroud Visual Discrimination Test in t.o. 247

96. Showing a comparison of the mean scores

attained on Reading Accuracy as measured
by the Neale Analysis of Reading Ability, by
sub-groups of i.t.a. and t.o. children who
attained similar levels of performance on the
author's Auditory Discrimination Test. 248

97. Showing a comparison of the mean scores
attained on Reading Accuracy as measured by
the Neale Analysis of Reading Ability, by sub-
groups of i.t.a. and t.o. children who attained
similar levels of performance on the Harrison-
Stroud Auditory Discrimination Test. 248

98. Showing a comparison of the mean scores
attained on Reading Accuracy as measured by
the Neale Analysis of Reading Ability, by sub-
groups of i.t.a. and t.o. children who attained
similar levels of performance on the Wechsler
Scale of Intelligence for Children. 250

99. Showing a comparison of the mean scores
attained on Reading Accuracy as measured by
the Neale Analysis of Reading Ability, by sub-
groups of i.t.a. and t.o. children who
attained similar levels of performance on the
Goodenough Draw-A-Man Test. 250

100. Showing a comparison of the mean scores
attained on Reading Accuracy as measured by
the Neale Analysis of Reading Ability, by sub-
groups of i.t.a. and t.o. children who attained
similar levels of performance on the author's
Vocabulary Profile. 251

101. Showing a comparison between the mean
scores attained on the Schonell Graded Word
Reading Test given a third time, by sub-groups
of i.t.a. and t.o. children with similar
mental ages. 252

102. Showing a comparison between the mean scores
attained on Reading Accuracy as measured by
the Neale Analysis of Reading Ability given for
the second time, by sub-groups of i.t.a. and t.o.
children with similar mental ages. 253

103. Showing a comparison of the correlations, calculated for the i.t.a. and t.o. groups separately, between the initial tests of reading readiness abilities, and the two measures of reading achievement given in the children's sixth term at school. 254

104. Showing a comparison between the mean scores of the i.t.a. and t.o. groups on the Schonell Graded Word Reading Test given for the fourth time (given in t.o. to both i.t.a. and t.o. groups). 256

105. Showing a comparison between the mean scores of the i.t.a. and t.o. groups on Reading Accuracy as measured by the Neale Analysis of Reading Ability (Form A) given for the third time (given in t.o. to both i.t.a. and t.o. groups). 256

106. Showing a comparison between the mean scores of the i.t.a. and t.o. groups on Reading Comprehension as measured by the Neale Analysis of Reading Ability (Form A) given for the third time. 256

107. Showing a comparison of the correlations, calculated for the i.t.a. and t.o. groups separately, between the initial tests of reading readiness abilities and the Schonell Graded Word Reading Test given for the fourth time (given in t.o. to both i.t.a. and t.o. groups). 258

108. Showing a comparison of the correlations, calculated for the i.t.a. and t.o. groups separately, between the initial tests of reading readiness abilities and Reading Accuracy as measured by the Neale Analysis of Reading Ability (Form A) given for the third time (given in t.o. to both the i.t.a. and t.o. groups). 259

109. Showing a comparison of the mean scores attained on the Schonell Graded Word Reading Test by sub-groups of i.t.a. and t.o. children

who attained similar levels of performance on
the author's Visual Discrimination Test.   260

110. Showing a comparison of the mean scores
attained on the Schonell Graded Word Reading
Test by sub-groups of i.t.a. and t.o. children
who attained similar levels of performance on
the Harrison-Stroud Visual Discrimination
Test in i.t.a.   260

111. Showing a comparison of the mean scores
attained on the Schonell Graded Word Reading
Test by sub-groups of i.t.a. and t.o. children
who attained similar levels of performance on
the Harrison-Stroud Visual Discrimination
Test in t.o.   261

112. Showing a comparison of the mean scores
attained on the Schonell Graded Word
Reading Test by sub-groups of i.t.a. and t.o.
children who attained similar levels of
performance on the author's Auditory
Discrimination Test.   261

113. Showing a comparison of the mean scores
attained on the Schonell Graded Word
Reading Test by sub-groups of i.t.a. and t.o.
children who attained similar levels of
performance on the Harrison-Stroud Auditory
Discrimination Test.   262

114. Showing a comparison of the mean scores
attained on the Schonell Graded Word Reading
Test by sub-groups of i.t.a. and t.o. children
who attained similar levels of performance on
the Wechsler Scale of Intelligence for
Children.   262

115. Showing a comparison of the mean scores
attained on the Schonell Graded Word Reading
Test by sub-groups of i.t.a. and t.o. children
who attained similar levels of performance on
the Goodenough Draw-A-Man Test.   263

116. Showing a comparison of the mean scores
attained on the Schonell Graded Word Reading

Test by sub-groups of i.t.a. and t.o. children who attained similar levels of performance on the author's Vocabulary Profile. 263

117. Showing a comparison of the mean scores attained on Reading Accuracy measured by the Neale Analysis of Reading Ability, by sub-groups of i.t.a. and t.o. children who attained similar levels of performance on the author's Visual Discrimination Test. 264

118. Showing a comparison of the mean scores attained on Reading Accuracy measured by the Neale Analysis of Reading Ability, by sub-groups of i.t.a. and t.o. children who attained similar levels of performance on the Harrison-Stroud Visual Discrimination Test in i.t.a. 264

119. Showing a comparison of the mean scores attained on Reading Accuracy measured by the Neale Analysis of Reading Ability, by sub-groups of i.t.a. and t.o. children who attained similar levels of performance on the Harrison-Stroud Visual Discrimination Test in t.o. 265

120. Showing a comparison of the mean scores attained on Reading Accuracy measured by the Neale Analysis of Reading Ability, by sub-groups of i.t.a. and t.o. children who attained similar levels of performance on the author's Auditory Discrimination Test. 265

121. Showing a comparison of the mean scores attained on Reading Accuracy measured by the Neale Analysis of Reading Ability, by sub-groups of i.t.a. and t.o. children who attained similar levels of performance on the Harrison-Stroud Auditory Discrimination test. 266

122. Showing a comparison of the mean scores attained on Reading Accuracy measured by the Neale Analysis of Reading Ability, by sub-groups of i.t.a. and t.o. children who attained

similar levels of performance on the Wechsler
Scale of Intelligence for Children.   266

123. Showing a comparison of the mean scores
attained on Reading Accuracy measured by
the Neale Analysis of Reading Ability, by sub-
groups of i.t.a. and t.o. children who attained
similar levels of performance on the
Goodenough Draw-A-Man Test.   267

124. Showing a comparison of the mean scores
attained on Reading Accuracy measured by the
Neale Analysis of Reading Ability, by sub-
groups of i.t.a. and t.o. children who attained
similar levels of performance on the author's
Vocabulary Profile.   267

125. Showing a comparison between the mean
scores attained on the Schonell Graded Word
Reading Test given a fourth time, by sub-
groups of i.t.a. and t.o. children with similar
mental ages.   269

126. Showing a comparison between the mean
scores attained on Reading Accuracy
measured by the Neale Analysis of Reading
Ability given for the third time, by sub-groups
of i.t.a. and t.o. children with similar
mental ages.   269

127. Showing a comparison of the correlations,
calculated for the i.t.a. and t.o. groups
separately, between the initial tests of reading
readiness abilities, and the two measures of
reading achievement given in the children's
ninth term at school.   270

128. Showing a comparison between the mean
scores attained by the boys and girls on the
reading readiness measures (118 boys, 120
girls).   272

129. Showing a comparison between the mean
scores of the boys and girls in the i.t.a. group
on three reading achievement measures (given
in i.t.a.).   273

130. Showing a comparison between the mean scores of the boys and girls in the t.o. group on three reading achievement measures (given in t.o.).   273

131. Showing a comparison between the mean scores of the boys and girls from both i.t.a. and t.o. groups on four reading achievement measures (given in t.o. to both groups).   274

132. Showing a comparison of the mean scores attained by the children in sixteen schools on the four administrations of the Schonell Graded Word Reading Test (given in i.t.a. to i.t.a. schools for the first and second times; given in t.o. to the i.t.a. schools for the third and fourth times).   275

133. Showing a comparison of the mean scores attained by the children in sixteen schools on the three administrations of the Neale Analysis of Reading Ability (given in i.t.a. to i.t.a. schools for the first time; given in t.o. to the i.t.a. schools for the second and third times).   276

Figures

1. An example of the reformed spelling proposed by John Hart.   53
2. Showing the title page of 'The English Primrose' by Richard Hodges.   55
3. An example from an early phonetic reader by Benn Pitman.   56
4. An example of simplified spelling called the 'Nue Speling'.   58
5. An example of a printed passage using the Initial Teaching Alphabet.   60
6. Showing the 44 characters of the Initial Teaching Alphabet.   62

7. Showing an example of Cuneiform – the equivalent of the word 'rain'.   144

8. Showing the top line of Runic inscriptions in Anglo-Saxon on one face of a whale bone box (8th–9th century) in the British Museum.   145

9. Showing an example of Oghams which are of Celtic origin and date from about the 5th century.   145

10. Showing the 26 graphic characters used to devise the test items for the author's Visual Discrimination Test.   146

11. Histogram showing distribution of standardized scores on the author's Visual Discrimination Test.   180

12. Histogram showing distribution of standardized scores on the author's Auditory Discrimination Test.   182

13. Histogram showing distribution of standardized scores on the author's revised Vocabulary Profile.   188

14. Graph showing the reading progress of the children in the eight i.t.a. schools as measured by the Schonell Graded Word Reading Test.   275

15. Graph showing the reading progress of the children in the eight t.o. schools as measured by the Schonell Graded Word Reading Test.   276

16. Graph showing the reading progress of the children in the eight i.t.a. schools as measured by the Neale Analysis of Reading Ability.   277

17. Graph showing the reading progress of the children in the eight t.o. schools as measured by the Neale Analysis of Reading Ability.   277

PART I
REVIEW OF THE RESEARCH
RELEVANT TO THE INVESTIGATION

Introduction

The author has been both interested, and actively engaged in research, in the field of reading during the past nine years, particularly in the area of the reading readiness and early reading progress of children. A thesis was submitted to, and accepted by, the University of London in 1964 in fulfilment of the requirements for the degree of Master of Arts in Education; this thesis had as its title, 'A Study of the Relationship between Some Specific Evidence of Reading Readiness and Reading Progress in the Infant School'.*

The aims of the thesis were, firstly, to ascertain the level of competence of first year infants in certain specific aspects of reading readiness, and secondly, to correlate these reading readiness skills with later achievement and progress, in order to determine the relative importance of these skills in learning to read and making progress in reading.

In this first investigation a representative sample of 183 children was tested in a number of reading readiness skills when commencing their second term in school (average age 5 years 4 months); the sample was tested also for three other important factors in reading readiness, namely, general ability, home environment, and emotional and personal attitudes. The following measures were used:

1. The Harrison – Stroud Reading Readiness Profiles (anglicised by the writer) consisting of using symbols, making

*Summary of this research in *Brit. J. of Educ. Psychol.*, Vol. 35, June 1965, pp. 252–254.

visual discriminations, making auditory discriminations, using the context and using context and auditory clues.
2. The Kelvin Measurement of Ability Test for Infants, and teachers' ratings of general ability.
3. A multiple-choice picture Vocabulary Test, constructed by the writer, and teachers' ratings of language and speech.
4. Teachers' ratings of self-confidence, co-operation with adults, co-operation with other children, persistence, stability and prevailing attitude.

Later, when commencing their fourth (average age 6 years) and fifth (average age 6 years 4 months) terms, the children were given parallel forms of the Southgate Group Reading Test 1.

The raw scores obtained from all measures were standard-ized, and the earlier results were correlated with the later reading results by the product moment method.

The results indicated that, in the sample selected, the Reading Readiness Tests proved to be a valid measure of readiness for reading (.59), and of these, auditory and visual discrimination correlated the most highly with reading achievement (.53 and .50, respectively); general ability was found to be important (.47), but not as important as auditory and visual discrimination; home environment was found to be of lesser importance (.42) and emotional and personal attitudes relatively unimportant (.10 – .36). It was also found that a mental age of 5 years 6 months was adequate for a satisfactory beginning to the formal teaching of reading.

After studying the results of this experiment, the author came to the following conclusions:

1. The fact that children come to school at five years with vary-ing degrees of readiness from the viewpoint of specific readiness skills, mental age, and home environment, lends stress to the importance of the teacher treating each child as an individual when deciding at what stage he is ready to be introduced to his first reader.
2. As visual and auditory discriminative skills were found to be very important in reading readiness, it becomes important for the reception class teacher to gain some estimate of her children's abilities in these skills, so that

3

if weaknesses are detected, exercises to develop these skills may be used during the pre-reading activities. Simple tests of auditory and visual discrimination, given soon after school entry, would be a valuable aid in determining reading readiness.

As a result of this previous research into reading readiness the author tends to support those who in very recent years have questioned the necessity of a mental age of six for reading readiness, and who feel that a critical re-examination of the concept of reading readiness is required at this present time. This re-examination is carried out in Chapter 2.

The introduction of new methods of teaching reading is providing further evidence on the reading readiness of infants, and one of the more widely known of the new methods is the Initial Teaching Alphabet (usually abbreviated to i.t.a.). The author followed the i.t.a. experiment with great interest from its beginning in September 1961 to its completion in 1966, and it is from the writings of Dr Downing,* the research officer who designed and carried out the experiment, that the idea of this present investigation sprang.

All the descriptions of the differences between i.t.a. and the traditional orthography (usually abbreviated to t.o.) have stressed that the former is more simple, both in its visual and auditory characteristics; another claim for i.t.a. is that the problems to be solved in mastering it are of a simpler nature than those of t.o.

The protagonists of i.t.a. have suggested that because of the simpler approach to reading through the medium of i.t.a., children may be ready to read earlier than they would be if learning to read with the more complex t.o. The author, knowing the importance of visual and auditory discrimination and mental ability from his own research, felt this suggestion was a reasonable one, and decided to test the hypothesis experimentally. He was encouraged in his proposed research by statements made by Dr Downing that here was a valid and worthy research problem. For example, in Downing's Interim research report to the 27th Educational Con-

*Formerly Head of the Reading Research Unit of London University Institute of Education.

4

ference in the City of New York in November 1962, the problem is highlighted in the statement.

The majority of 4 years olds may not be 'ready' to learn *traditional orthography*, but this does not appear to be true of their ability to read i.t.a.

and again in the question, 'When are children "ready" to begin reading i.t.a.?'

In an article in *Educational Research* in November 1963,* Downing challenges the concept that a minimum mental age of six is required for successful reading. He points out that learning to read with i.t.a. presents the child with fewer and simpler problems to solve, and so a lower mental age level might be adequate for children to read with i.t.a. This again implies that the children might be ready to read earlier with i.t.a. than with t.o.

The main purpose of this study, then, is to test experimentally the hypothesis that children learning to read with the Initial Teaching Alphabet are ready to read earlier than children learning with the traditional orthography.

In the following Chapters of Part One the research literature relevant to this problem is reviewed. In Chapter 1 the research into the factors involved in reading readiness is summarised, and in Chapter 2 the concept of reading readiness is re-appraised. Chapter 3 describes the medium of i.t.a., and Chapters 4 to 6 discuss the design, results and conclusions of the main i.t.a. experiment.

*Downing, J. A., 'Is a "mental age of six" essential for "reading" readiness?', *Educational Research*, Vol. 6, 1963, pp. 16–28.

Chapter 1

A Summary of the Research into the Main Aspects of Reading Readiness*

Definition

The term 'readiness' for any kind of learning refers to the stage when the child can learn easily, effectually and without any emotional disturbance. Havighurst (1953), suggests that there is an optimum time for the learning of any particular task, when efforts at teaching, largely wasted had they come earlier, give gratifying results. He uses the expression 'teachable moment' to describe this optimum time for learning. This idea is obviously linked with readiness, for if the child is ready to learn, then the 'teachable moment' has arrived.

In relation to learning to read, the concept of reading readiness is generally understood to mean a developmental stage at which maturational and environmental factors have prepared the child for reading.

Most of the extensive literature on the subject of reading readiness is American, and nearly all the experimental investigations in this field have been carried out in the USA, where numerous reading readiness tests have been produced and are widely used. Comparatively little has been written about reading readiness by British educationalists, and there are no reading readiness tests constructed and standardized for

*As the research literature is so extensive, only the more important researches are mentioned in this summary.

British children, though in very recent years a growing interest has developed in this field of study and the validity of reading readiness has been questioned (see Chapter 2).

Development of the concept

Smith (1950), discussing the development of the concept of reading readiness, has suggested that the growth and application of this concept can be divided into three stages. These stages she describes as:

first, a long slow period of evolution in which the idea was formulated; second, a comparatively short period of intensive application and investigation in the area of beginning reading; third, a gradual awakening to the desirability and possibility of applying the readiness concept to all stages of growth in reading at all levels of maturation.

Although the specific term 'readiness' is relatively new in education, being first used, it is thought, in 1925,* the concept undoubtedly goes back at least two hundred years and possibly more, but it is very difficult to determine exactly when the concept originated, as one writer is influenced by the ideas of his predecessor. The crude, but nevertheless clear, beginnings of the readiness concept can be found in the writings of Rousseau (1762), Pestalozzi (1907), Froebel (1909), and a more vigorous crystallised form in the writings of Dewey (1898), and his disciple Patrick (1899).

The following two quotations, the first from Rousseau (1762), the second from Dewey (1898), illustrate the above point:

I would rather he [referring to Emile] would never know how to read than to buy this knowledge at the price of all that can make it useful. Of what use would reading be to him after he had been disgusted with it forever.

Present physiological knowledge points to the age of about eight years as early enough for anything more than an incidental attention to visual and written language form.

---

*Report of the National Committee on Reading, 24th Year-Book of the National Society for the Study of Education, 1925.

8

In 1925 the Twenty-fourth Year Book of the National Society for the Study of Education was published in the USA and marked the beginning of a short period of intensive application and investigation of reading readiness. This lasted until approximately 1938–1940, the peak period for investigation into the nature of reading readiness. Among the more important experiments which contributed to our understanding of the main factors involved were those made by Deputy (1930), Davidson (1931), Eames (1932), Frank (1935), Harrison (1939), Hildreth (1933), Morphett and Washburne (1931), and Gates (1937).

The fact that the number of investigations and articles concerned with reading readiness has declined in recent years does not indicate that all the important problems have been dealt with adequately; rather, it indicates a shift of emphasis, plus the recognition of the fact that the readiness concept can be applied at all levels. Factors contributing to readiness for beginning to read are found to be the same factors which contribute to reading success at any level. Reading readiness and all readiness is now being thought of in broader terms.

Factors involved in reading readiness

Reading readiness is a complex of many abilities, skills, influences and interests, each of which contributes in some measure to the process of learning to read. Some lists of specific traits and influences that determine a child's readiness for reading, number in the hundreds. For example, Sutton (1955), studied 150 children and compared reading readiness test scores with 246 other measures. Obviously many factors will be found to correlate with readiness to read, not because they are causes, but because they are symptoms of a causal factor; for example, in Sutton's experiment, two of the measures, father's occupation and possession of a record player, correlated positively with reading readiness. However, the important causal factor here may be the cultural level of the home, of which these correlates are only symptoms.

Studies in reading have indicated that the presence or absence of specific factors may not be as important as the general pattern of factors in affecting the development of

9

reading. The grouping of the specific correlations of readiness into meaningful determinants, or factors, is a somewhat arbitrary matter. Some investigators prefer to group important factors under a small number of broad headings; Harrison (1939), and Inglis (1949), use the three broad headings of physiological, intellectual and personal readiness; Schonell (1961), Hildreth (1958), Betts (1946) and Smith (1950) use physiological readiness and intellectual readiness but sub-divide personal readiness further, using such headings as social, emotional, experiential, linguistic and environmental readiness.

Another system of grouping* proposes two main categories, one comprising environmental factors, such as language spoken in the home, range of experience; and the other, educational factors associated with maturation, such as mental maturity and physical status. Other investigators prefer a rather larger number of areas of readiness; for example, Smith and Dechant (1961), have eleven areas, Gray (1937), has seven areas and Gates (1949), eight areas. Nevertheless, there are certain important factors involved in reading readiness which are generally recognised and discussed in the literature. For the purpose of this summary these will be dealt with under the following four headings:

(i) The Physiological Factor, comprising general maturity or growth philosophy; cerebral dominance and laterality; neurological considerations; vision; hearing; condition and functioning of speech organs.

(ii) The Intellectual Factor, comprising general mental ability and the perceptual abilities of visual and auditory discrimination.

(iii) The Environmental Factor, comprising linguistic background of the home and social experience of different kinds.

(iv) The Emotional and Personal Factor, comprising emotional stability and a desire to learn to read.

In order to find out the relative importance and the predictive value of various reading readiness measures, the

*Appraisal of Growth in Reading, Board of Education of the City of New York, Nov. 1941, p. 8.

10

American researchers usually give tests and make assessments when the children concerned are at the beginning of the First Grade (normal age is six years). A few months later and perhaps again a year later, reading achievement tests are given to the same children, and the later results correlated with the earlier results. The coefficients of correlation thus obtained are accepted as measures of the importance to the success in reading of the factors involved. Where children who can read are tested, the measures for correlation are usually given at the same time.

(i) *The Physiological Factor*

General Maturity

During the last two decades there has been a revival of interest in the relationship between reading and reading readiness and the total growth, or level of maturity, of the child. This revival of interest and investigation is partly due to the work of Olson and his associates in the University Elementary School at the University of Michigan, who have developed the idea that reading achievement is a function of general maturity, or total growth, and conversely, that reading failure stems from immaturity. Olson has used the term 'organismic age' to represent the average of a certain number of growth ages. The ages he averages for this concept are, mental age, dental age, reading age, weight age, height age, carpal age and grip age. (Carpal age refers to the ossification of hand and wrist bones).

With regard to the relationship between reading ability and general maturity, an analysis of the research findings of Olson (1940), Anderson and Hughes (1955), Abernethy (1936), Dearborn and Rothney (1941), Gates (1924), and Schonell (1961), indicates that slight positive correlations, rarely exceeding .2, have been found, but these have not been significant. Again, the addition of physical measures to mental age scores increases the coefficient by a negligible amount.

Neurological Considerations

A study of the relationship between neurological factors and reading belongs more to the field of reading disability

11

than to that of reading readiness, but it is dealt with here because a very small proportion of children find great difficulty in learning to read in the very early stages, and the difficulty is often attributed to neurological causes.

Before the turn of this century, medical hypotheses to explain reading difficulty were dominant and neurological explanations tended to be accepted. Early investigators of reading who were in the medical field usually assumed that if the child showed no observable deficiencies of general mental development or health, the reading difficulties were the result of brain defects, which made it difficult or impossible for a child to remember and identify printed words.

In a fairly recent conference on word blindness, or specific mental dyslexia, Gallagher* stated that 'the term "word blind" was used as early as 1878 to describe children who, despite adequate vision and intelligence, were unable to read and spell, but there is still disagreement as to its basic cause'.

Malmquist (1958) mentions that in an article in the British Medical Journal for 1896, Morgan used for the first time in medical literature the term 'congenital word blindness' to describe an adolescent case of reading disability; soon a distinction was made between congenital word blindness, or *dyslexia*, and acquired word blindness, or *alexia*, the latter resulting from disease of, or injury to, the brain.

During the two world wars psychologists and educators have minimised the neurological aspects of reading difficulties, but in recent years, with medical advances in every direction, interest in these aspects of reading problems has grown.

Regarding the relationship between neurological defects and reading and reading readiness, Hinshelwood (1896), Witty and Kopel (1939), Harris (1961), Vernon (1962), Gesell and Armatruda (1941), Jenson (1943), Delacato (1959), Smith and Carrington (1959), Benton (1959) and Morris (1966) have made valuable contributions, though no definite conclusions can be reached at this stage. As Reid (1968) points out, the controversy continues between those who

---

* Gallagher, J.R., of the Children's Hospital Medical Centre, Boston, Massachusetts. Reported in *The Times Educational Supplement*, 20th April 1962.

maintain that all reading delay is environmentally caused and those who believe that in some cases a 'more fundamental constitutional condition' is involved.

Cerebral Dominance and Laterality

Lateral dominance is a generic term meaning the preferred use, and usually superiority, of one of the externally paired parts of the body (hands, eyes, feet). We observe, both popularly and experimentally, that some people are right-handed, some are left-handed and some few are ambi-dextrous. A less commonly observed fact is that individuals also display preference for the right or left eye when occasion demands the use of only one eye, for example, looking through a microscope.

Burt (1937), Buswell (1937), MacMeeken (1939), Monroe (1946) and Schonell (1941), who have studied the distribution of dominance in handedness and eyedness and mixed domin-ance (when the dominant hand and eye are on opposite sides of the body), agree that in a large unselected group of people, approximately 5% are left-handed, 35% are left-eyed, and mixed dominance occurs in about one out of three people. The most plausible explanation as to why left-eyedness should occur so much more frequently than left-handed-ness, is that of social conditioning supported by Burt (1937), who postulates that great benefit accrues from right-handed-ness and as the heredity disposition to handedness is slight, early pressure is brought to bear on the child to use his right hand.

Theories of cerebral dominance have been used to explain laterality, the ones most quoted in the literature being those of Orton (1929) and Dearborn (1933). For example, Orton, a neurologist, contended that reversals in reading, found very frequently in backward readers and those just beginning to read, were the result of uncertainty of orientation. This, in turn, was due to lack of clearly established dominance in one hemisphere of the brain. This lack of brain dominance, he felt, was evidenced by mixed hand-eye dominance, though this is an unproved hypothesis and further investigation is required.

Most investigators in the field of reading have studied the relationship between aspects of lateral dominance, such as

13

handedness or eyedness or mixed dominance, on the one hand, and reading ability and reading errors, particularly reversals, on the other. Among the more important studies are those of Witty and Kopel (1936), Frank (1935), Teegarden (1932), Davidson (1934), Hildreth (1934), Kennedy (1954), Furness (1956), Schonell (1940), Monroe (1946) and Gates (1949). The evidence suggests that although handedness is not significantly related to reading ability, mixed hand-eye dominance is slightly related. A satisfactory summation of the research results would be that of Gates:

> The idea that confused brain dominance should be the cause of reading difficulties was considered too speculative to be serviceable.

Vision, Hearing and Speech

A comprehensive review of the research into the relationship between visual defects and reading difficulty shows that the evidence is conflicting. Dalton (1943), Witty and Kopel (1936), Swanson and Tiffen (1936), Monroe (1946), and Edson, Bond and Cook (1953) found little or no relationship, whereas Park and Burri (1943), Eames (1938) and Robinson (1946) obtained evidence of a relationship between visual defects and reading ability. All investigators are of the opinion that it is important to have an early routine check on children's vision, and to keep close watch on their progress in the early stages of reading.

Betts (1943), Bond (1935), Gates and Bond (1956), Witty and Kopel (1939), Kennedy (1942) and Robinson (1946) have studied the relationship between auditory acuity and reading ability. It would appear from their researches that, given a degree of hearing sufficient to enable the child to join in the normal activities of the classroom, then auditory acuity is not closely related to success in reading. From the point of view of reading readiness, the main conclusion for educational practice is that children should be examined expertly for defects in their auditory abilities when they enter school, or before they start to read. By far the most satisfactory way to measure hearing in the schools is to use an audiometer.

The evidence into the relationship between speech defects

14

and reading achievement provided by Gates (1949), Witty and Kopel (1939), Bond (1935), Bennett (1938), Gaines (1946), Monroe (1946) and Robinson (1946) indicates a positive relationship, but there is insufficient evidence to claim a causal relationship.

With regard to the broad factor of physiological readiness, the general conclusion to be drawn is that this area seems a relatively unimportant one for educational practices, provided that children are examined expertly for defects of vision, hearing and speech when they enter school.

(ii) *The Intellectual Factor*

General Mental Ability

General intelligence is a sampling of many different abilities, some of which are more important than others in the process of learning to read. Some abilities, such as memory and attention, are hard to distinguish from general intelligence in young children, but other abilities, such as the perceptual abilities of visual and auditory discrimination, do seem to be relatively specific.

Numerous writers have emphasised that intelligence is an extremely important determinant of reading readiness and general reading achievement. General intelligence, which is an average of many phases of mental growth, implies the ability to learn and apply what is learnt; as reading is a thinking process, and one which must be learnt, a clear relationship between intelligence and reading would be expected.

In order to study the importance of this factor in learning to read, and to try to establish the extent of the relationship between mental age and reading readiness, many investigators have obtained mental age scores of groups of children soon after entering school, and then at least six months later obtained reading achievement scores. The two sets of scores have then been correlated and, generally, high positive correlations have been found. For older children, able to read, correlations have been made between intelligence and reading tests given at the same time. Correlation coefficients in these studies of the relationship between general intelligence and reading achievement have been found to range from about .35 to .70, the average being about .6.

With regard to these correlations, Lennon (1950), Bond and Tinker (1957), and Manolakes and Sheldon (1955) emphasise the importance of taking into consideration the great differences in the correlations between reading ability and intelligence which occur at various grade levels, and Witty and Kopel (1939), Inglis (1949) and Durrell (1933), among others, point out that the common elements which exist in intelligence and reading tests must be borne in mind when interpreting results.

All the investigators studying the relationship between intelligence and reading at various age levels have emphasised the important causal relationship. McLaughlin (1928), Raybold (1929), Hayes (1933), Deputy (1930) and Tinker (1932) have claimed that mental ability is the most important single factor in determining reading progress, but Schonell (1942), Stroud (1956) and Monroe (1946) indicate that caution must be used when interpreting results.

Minimum Mental Age Concept

Because mental ability correlates more highly with progress in reading than with any other factor, studies have been made to see if a minimum mental age was necessary before children could learn to read successfully. According to Betts (1946), the most widely quoted and misquoted study on this particular question is that of Morphett and Washburne (1931), who concluded:

> Consequently it seems safe to state that by postponing the teaching of reading until children reach a mental level of six and a half years, teachers can generally decrease the chances of failure and discouragement and can correspondingly increase their efficiency.

In similar experiments and studies, Dean (1939), Bigelow (1934), Dolch and Bloomster (1939) and Witty and Kopel (1936), all claim to have found that a minimum mental age was required for successful reading, and mental ages of six, six and a half and seven were mentioned in these studies.

Since these experiments, writers too numerous to mention have stated categorically that there is a minimum mental age necessary for success in beginning reading, and Betts (1946) and Dolch (1950), provide evidence that many school systems in America have accepted these statements and put the underlying ideas into practice.

Other investigators, however, have criticised the concept of a minimum mental age for reading for all children in all circumstances. Evidence has been provided that some children can learn to read successfully with a mental age of below six years six months. The obvious example of this is in our own country, where children start compulsory schooling at five years and are fairly quickly introduced to formal reading; most of our children learn to read before they attain a mental age of six years six months. Winch (1925) pointed out this fact to American investigators as early as 1925.

Hollingsworth (1942), Terman and Oden (1947), Davidson (1931), Lynn (1963) and Thackray (1964) provide evidence of pre-school children learning to read between three and five years and Doman (1965) and Morris (1963) below three years. Roslow (1940), Gates (1937), Thackray (1964) and Downing (1963) show in their studies, carried out in normal classroom situations, that children below a mental age of six can learn to read successfully if the instruction and materials are of an appropriate standard.

Betts (1946), Gray (1956), Harris (1961), and other modern writers on this question of a minimum mental age, agree that the different methods and materials used in the teaching of reading, and the differing skills of teachers, make it impossible to state firmly that a certain minimum mental age is required for success.

Perceptual Abilities of Visual and Auditory Discrimination

As the skill of reading consists, firstly, of discriminating visual patterns of words and secondly, of associating sound units with the correct visual patterns, the abilities of visual and auditory perception and discrimination were soon investigated, and were found to be closely related to reading readiness and to reading progress. Durrell (1956) states that the minimum requirement in visual discrimination appears to be the ability to match letters, and for auditory discrimination, the ability to notice the separate sounds in spoken words.

17

Earlier experiments carried out by Gates, Bond and Russell (1939), (1956) and (1939), Sister Mary of the Visitation (1929) and Fendrick (1935) provided evidence of high correlation (usually between .5 and .6) between word perception tests, which involve visual and auditory discrimination, and reading success. Where non-verbal visual perception tests were used, lower correlations were found.

More recent investigations carried out by Sister Mary Nila (1940), Durrell, Murphy and Junkins (1941), Harrington and Durrell (1955), Nicholson (1958) and Thackray (1964) have shown that visual and auditory discrimination are more important than mental age in reading success, and that auditory discrimination ranks first. Nicholson (1958), Olson (1958) and Gavel (1958) claim that of all readiness measures, the one which measures knowledge of letter names provides the best prediction of success in reading. As knowledge of letter names involves both visual and auditory discrimination, this claim is a reasonable one. Lineham (1958) and Durell and Murphy (1953) show by their experiments that training in these important skills improves reading achievement.

(iii) *The Environmental Factor*

This broad factor, often referred to as home background, includes a number of environmental aspects such as economic conditions, opportunities for social experience, language and speech patterns in the home, attitudes towards, and provision for, reading and writing in the home. Research shows that some of these aspects are more important than others, but that all affect the total experience the child brings to the reading situation, and that experience is a basic prerequisite for reading.

Reading includes much more than the ability to recognise and pronounce words printed on a page; it includes the gaining of meaning from the printed symbol. However, in order simply to pronounce a word, the child should, at some time, have heard the word spoken by others; so in this way, the nature and amount of speech and language patterns are important in the reading situation. But even if a child can pronounce a word, the meaning is not invested in the symbols themselves; the meaning comes from the mind of the reader, who gives meaningful ideas to the symbols in terms of his own experience. Experience clothes words with meaning, and the extent and quality of the experience depends upon the environmental factors mentioned.

Where research workers have confined themselves mainly to investigations of the home background from the economic level, rather than the cultural level, and considered such things as family income, size of house and father's occupation, only a slight relationship, sometimes even a negligible one, has been found. Evidence of this can be found in the studies of Anderson and Kelly (1931), Ladd (1933), Bennett (1938) and Fleming (1943).

Gray (1937) believed that the nature of the home and the intelligence and education of the parents exert a strong influence on the development of a child's reading ability. He felt that a child who had grown up in an environment where there were plenty of books and much reading was done, had a better chance of becoming a good reader than a child brought up in a home where the parents were not interested in books and the cultural level was low.

Gray's views on the important influence of the cultural level of the home are confirmed by the studies of Hilliard and Troxell (1937), Hildreth (1933), Almy (1949), Witty and Kopel (1939), Sheldon and Carrilo (1952) in America, and by those of Burt (1937), McLelland (1942), Schonell (1942), Fleming (1943), McClaren (1950) and Morris (1966) in this country. It can be said that, in most of the studies investigating the relationship between home background and reading readiness and reading progress, there has been found a positive relationship, but one which has been obscured by probable differences in intelligence of the children concerned, for since social status correlates quite significantly with intelligence, one would expect to find also a positive relationship between reading achievement and socio-economic status.

(iv) *The Emotional and Personal Factor*

It is always difficult to determine what part emotional and personality difficulties may have played in causing reading difficulties. Some authorities believe that emotional disturbances precede and cause reading difficulties, and that those reading difficulties are one of the symptoms of inadequate personal adjustment. Other authorities believe that emotional disturbances affecting reading ability arise from the reading difficulties themselves, or from unpleasant experiences associated with learning to read. Again, other authorities feel that it is extremely difficult to decide whether emotional disturbances are causes, concomitants or results of reading difficulties.

However, nearly all investigators of this problem agree that emotional disturbances do appear frequently where there is difficulty in learning to read, and on this point the studies of Witty and Kopel (1939), Gates (1941), Harris (1961) and Schonell (1961) provide typical evidence.

In the investigations of Bird (1927), Blanchard (1928), Monroe (1935), Robinson (1946), Young and Gaier (1951), among others, evidence is provided which indicates that difficulties in learning to read may be a result of emotional and personal difficulties. On the other hand, Ladd (1933), Gann (1945), Preston (1940), Orton (1937), Monroe (1946) and Schonell (1961) maintain that personality difficulties and emotional problems are more frequently the results, rather than the causes, of reading disabilities.

It becomes apparent then, that although the majority of the investigators who have studied the relationship between emotional and personality factors and reading progress agree that emotional difficulties and symptoms of personality maladjustment are frequently found in association with reading difficulties, they disagree as to whether emotional problems are causes or effects of reading difficulties.

Another important personal factor, and one on which greater stress has been laid in recent years, is that of motivation, or the child's interest in schoolwork and his desire to learn. Some children come to school eager to learn to read, filled with enthusiasm and expectancy. Other children are passive to learning to read, and have no apparent incentive for learning. Still other children are opposed to learning to read, sensing fear or dread of the process. The studies of Brumbach (1940), Gates (1949), Stroud (1956) and Burton (1956) point out the importance of motivation to reading success, though there is insufficient research in this area to draw any definite conclusions.

Sex Differences in Reading Readiness and Early Reading

Most of the American investigations of the relationship between boys and girls, regarding reading readiness and reading achievement, report that girls show a certain superiority over boys in the normal school situation. The records of reading clinics and special classes for children with reading disabilities, both in Britain and America, show that practically without exception the majority of cases are boys.

Monroe (1946), Anderson and Kelly (1931), Fendrick (1935), Fernald (1943), Betts (1948) and Durrell (1940) all provide evidence to show that the majority of cases in clinics and special classes are boys. The figures given are very impressive (usually between 80–90%) but Gates and Bennett (1933) point out that the ratio of boys to girls among reading failures is not as great when the entire school population is investigated, as when only clinic cases are considered. They feel that reading problems are thought to be more important for boys than for girls, or that boys who are backward readers may become more troublesome in school than girls who are backward readers, and so are more readily referred to clinics.

Even so, boys still outnumber girls among reading problems, even when school groups are studied as a whole, as is shown by the investigations of Durrell (1940), Schonell (1942), MacMeekan (1939), Gates (1933) and Morris (1966).

Some studies have examined the difference in readiness to read between boys and girls entering school, and also the difference between their respective achievements during the first year in school. Most American investigations, among the more important being those of Samuels (1943), Carroll (1948), Anderson, Hughes and Dixon (1957) and Prescott (1955) show significant differences between boys and girls on reading readiness measures in favour of the girls, though one or two investigators, for example Konski (1955) and Potter (1949), found no significant differences.

In the author's first experiment with British children, the scores of the girls were significantly superior to those of the boys on two of the five reading readiness measures, namely,

21

those of auditory discrimination and using context and auditory clues.

There is, then, a considerable measure of agreement among research workers that there are significant differences between boys and girls, both in reading readiness and in reading difficulties, in favour of the girls. However, there is not the same measure of agreement as to the reason for these differences.

One of the main explanations is that girls tend to mature earlier than boys physically, intellectually and emotionally, and so may be ready to read earlier than boys, and generally maintain their advantage during the ensuing years. This view is supported by Anderson and Dearborn (1951), Harris (1961) and McCarthy (1935).

The other main explanation is the difference in the cultural pattern which exists between the sexes. Boys tend, even in pre-school years, to spend more time and energy on the larger muscular activities, while girls spend more of their time in sedentary activities, and it is suggested that the activities of girls are far more likely to foster reading readiness and reading than those of boys. This explanation is supported by Betts (1946) and Gates (1961).

The evidence from research workers in this country concerning the relative performance of boys and girls on reading tests is rather conflicting. Some reading surveys, such as those carried out in Brighton, Middlesborough and Swansea, found girls superior to boys in reading ability. However, the Ministry of Education Reading Surveys of 1948, 1952 and 1956 found, if anything, that boys were superior to girls.

The author, in his first experiment, found the girls' scores significantly superior to those of the boys, yet Morris's (1966) latest survey resulted in a mean score favourable to the boys, but not significantly so. Morris seems to think that the 'suggestion made by the Ministery that the content of tests largely determines any sex differences observed in the average reading attainment of children in the final year of their primary school course' is a reasonable one.

The Appraisal of Reading Readiness

There can be no decisive answer to the question, 'When is a

child ready for reading?' because there is no single criterion that applies to all children or to all school situations. Children grow towards readiness for reading at different rates, and vary widely in the various abilities, skills and understandings which make for reading readiness. Again, reading methods and materials differ from classroom to classroom, affecting the threshold requirements of readiness. Perhaps the question should be, 'When is *this* particular child ready for reading *this* particular reading programme?'

The three main methods by which teachers in American schools may gather information concerning the readiness of their children are as follows:

(i) the use of a reading readiness test.
(ii) the use of a general ability or intelligence test.
(iii) directed observation of pupils' behaviour.

Investigations by Dean (1939), Robinson and Hall (1942), Henig (1949), Kottmeyer (1947) and Fendrick and McGlade (1938) have been made to find out which of the above methods is the most predictive, if only one is used, or whether a combination of two of the methods or of all three methods, lessens the chance of making erroneous judgements about the readiness of an individual child. The research findings are not clear, but indicate that, when methods are combined, the correlation figures are altered only very slightly, if at all. As to which method is the most predictive, the findings of Robinson and Hall (1942), who analysed the data of over twenty investigations carried out between 1930 and 1940, are still valid, as shown by the more recent investigations of Spaulding (1956), Bremer (1959) and Thackray (1964)., Robinson and Hall found from their survey that the median correlation between reading readiness tests and measures of reading success was .58, the median correlation for intelligence and measures of reading success was .51, and the median correlation of teachers' ratings using rating scales and measures of reading success was .62. In the author's first experiment with British children, it is interesting to note that the corresponding figures for the reading readiness and intelligence tests used were .59 and .47 respectively.

23

(i) Reading Readiness Tests as a method of Evaluation

Reading readiness tests in America are numerous and quite widely used. The tests are usually group tests, consisting of a number of sub-tests. These tests are similar to intelligence tests, and there is often overlapping, but they differ in that they are directed specifically at skills which the research literature shows are connected with reading. Most of the tests have sub-tests of visual discrimination and vocabulary, and among other sub-tests commonly found are those of auditory discrimination, articulation, rhyming of words, motor control, memory, and handedness and eyedness.

The most widely used reading readiness tests* in America are Gates Reading Readiness Tests, the Harrison-Stroud Reading Readiness Profiles, the Metropolitan Readiness Tests and the Monroe Reading Aptitude Test. In addition to general reading readiness tests, a number of tests are used in America which are connected with a basic reading series. These tests are composed of sub-tests, and some items relate to the material to be found in the basic readers.

More recent American reading readiness tests, such as the Harrison-Stroud Reading Readiness Profiles, aim to be diagnostic rather than predictive. In these tests, rather than giving a total readiness score, a profile of the child's strengths and weaknesses in readiness measures is provided by the information obtained. The authors of the tests claim that validity has been built into the tests through the selection of test items. As reading readiness tests gain in accuracy and precision, they can be useful tools to the teacher in diagnostic use, to enable her to discover or, perhaps more important, to create the moment of readiness for each child. Again, reading readiness tests enable the teacher to gain an immediate impression of a child's needs and abilities, rather than having to wait and acquire this by the slower process of personal observation.

Reading readiness tests are not used in this country, and Morris (1959), who investigated reading in sixty Kent primary schools, found that although the Kent teachers interviewed had considerable experience in measuring ability and attain-

*See Appendix for details of tests mentioned.

24

ment by means of standardized tests, they were unfamiliar with reading readiness tests. This is understandable, as there are no British readiness tests and it is generally felt by psychologists that children of five years are too young to be subjected to widespread testing.

(ii) Intelligence, or General Ability, Tests as a Method of Evaluation

Since it is claimed by many that general intelligence is the most important single factor in readiness for reading, and since many authorities have indicated that a certain minimum mental age is necessary for success in reading, group or individual intelligence tests are often used in American schools for appraising certain phases of readiness for reading. Most American schools rely on group intelligence tests, and those most widely used are the Pintner-Cunningham Primary Test, the Detroit Beginning First Grade Intelligence Test, the California Test of Mental Maturity and the Kuhlmann-Anderson Intelligence Test. Individual tests commonly used are the Stanford-Binet and the Wechsler Intelligence Scale for Children.

Schonell (1961) feels that, for the appraisal of reading readiness among British children, mental age is useful. He recommends the same two individual tests of intelligence mentioned above, and the Moray House Picture Intelligence Test as a group test. Schonell's recommendations are not realistic ones, in the view of the author, as British teachers are not generally allowed to use the Stanford-Binet and the Wechsler Intelligence Scale for Children, and in his own experiments the author found that the Moray House Picture Intelligence Test was too difficult for children below the age of six years.

(iii) Directed Observation of Pupils' Behaviour as a Method of Evaluation

Teachers' judgments as regards a child's readiness for reading have been shown by research experiments to be very sound. Most American writers of books on basal reading schemes have suggested the form a teacher's record sheet for each child should take, and the ways in which notes on all the important abilities and skills involved in reading readiness could be recorded. Some useful forms have been suggested by Betts (1946), Russell (1949), Gray (1956), Harris (1961) and Lamoreaux and Lee (1943), and typical of the areas of observation suggested are social adjustment, mental maturity, home background, language adjustment and physical and motor development.

Schonell (1961) has produced a check list in the form of a printed card for use in British schools, which he calls a Reading Readiness Chart, and which covers similar areas of readiness to those mentioned above. To the best of the author's knowledge this card is not very widely used, but most infant teachers do make notes of their day-to-day observations of the children in their classes, and these records prove very helpful.

Of the three methods of appraising reading readiness discussed in this Chapter, it would appear that no one method shows clear superiority over the others in the prediction of future achievement. However, the results of a diagnostic reading readiness test would enable the teacher to know immediately the weaknesses of individual children and, with this knowledge, to plan a suitable reading readiness programme.

In very recent years, the validity of the concept of reading readiness has been questioned, and it has been suggested that a re-examination of the concept is necessary. In the next Chapter, the validity of this concept will be reappraised in the light of the most recent research evidence and current discussion.

Chapter 2

A Re-Examination of the Concept of Reading Readiness

In very recent years, both in America and in this country, the validity of the concept of reading readiness has been questioned. Educationalists are becoming uncertain, and teachers are becoming confused. For example, Lynn (1963), writes: '... it seems doubtful whether the concept of reading readiness has sufficient substance to be worth retaining', and from a primary teacher* comes a plea for advice:

> The concept of reading readiness used to be discussed as something important and which teachers ought always to take into account. Are we now being asked to ignore it completely?

There is certainly a need for a new approach to reading readiness, but there is also a danger of putting back the educational clock if a balanced view of recent findings on this subject is not presented.

The validity of the concept has been questioned as a result of:

(i) growing evidence of children learning to read with mental ages of well below six years, the fairly widely accepted minimum mental age limit for successful reading;

Teachers World, 17 Jan. 1964, p. 33.

(ii) a closer scrutiny of the perceptual abilities required by children for successful reading;

(iii) the introduction of newer methods of teaching reading, which are providing new evidence on the reading readiness of infants.

(i) *The Minimum Mental Age Controversy*

Three recent articles on reading readiness written by Sanderson (1963), Lynn (1963) and Downing (1963), attacked the theory that a minimum mental age of six or six and a half is necessary for beginning to read. The authors of these articles make the somewhat exaggerated claims that this theory is very widely held by psychologists and educationalists in the USA and in Britain, and imply that the majority of teachers put this criterion of a mental age of six to six and a half into practice. The following quotations illustrate this point:

Many educationalists have, however, made no objections; and there is no doubt that the idea of a minimum mental age of six and a half years has been widely accepted as a *sine qua non* of reading readiness; as a pre-requisite which must always exist, without which reading cannot begin.

The notion of reading readiness at the mental age of six to eight years is almost universally accepted in the United States and very widely in Britain – by 75% of head teachers, according to Morris (1959).

The consensus of results from educational research indicates that for normal pupils the more formal approach to to reading should not begin before a mental age of six is reached.*

A summary of the American research made in the first Chapter indicates that although the minimum mental age concept has been fairly widely held there until recently, and is still stated unequivocally in some text books on reading, for example, Hester (1955) and Smith and Dechant (1961), many modern writers agree with Gates, who pointed out as early as 1937 that:

*A quote from Schonell's *Psychology and Teaching of Reading* (1945).

statements concerning the necessary mental age at which a pupil can be instructed to learn to read are essentially meaningless. The age for learning to read under one program or with the methods employed by one teacher may be entirely different from that required under other circumstances.

Gray (1956) sums up, more fairly, modern American thought on the minimum mental age question as follows:

(i) A mental age of six and a half years is accompanied by rapid progress in learning to read if pupils are well prepared for reading in other respects.

(ii) A mental age of six is usually accompanied by satisfactory progress if pupils have developed normally in other readiness factors.

(iii) Many pupils who have not acquired a mental age of six can learn to read provided the reading materials are very simple and based on interesting familiar experiences and the methods used are adapted to the specific needs of the learners.

The above conclusions of Gates and Gray throw light on the obvious discrepancy between the British and American school systems as regards the teaching of reading. Most American children enter school at the age of six; they are then usually given a short reading readiness programme, after which they are given reading readiness tests and mental tests; the results of these tests are compared with the teachers' check list of observations. The children are then usually divided into three groups, a fast reading group, a slower reading group, and a group where reading is postponed in favour of a further period of reading readiness activities, though in very recent years experiments in individual instruction are also being assessed. By the time these decisions are made the children have reached the age of six years and six months.

At this same age the children in British schools who started school at five have made considerable progress in learning to read. This discrepancy is explained partly by the fact that standards, materials and methods are simpler in this country— more appropriate for younger learners. For example, in some American school systems, children are required to have a large sight-word vocabulary before a first reader is begun, whereas in our schools little emphasis is put on the knowledge of a certain number of sight words. If the child can recognise sufficient words to enable him to 'read' the first few pages of the introductory reader, he is usually allowed to begin to read. Again, the child in this country is allowed to proceed at his own pace, without undue pressure as no set standard is in view; whereas in American schools a certain standard is set for the end of the year, which tends to make the teachers push the children along.

With regard to British thought on this question, it is certainly not true to suggest that a minimum mental age of six to six and a half is accepted 'very widely' in Britain.

In an article on the teaching of reading from the researcher's point of view, Yates (1954) stated:

> There is considerable opposition in this country to the idea that positive steps should be taken to ascertain that children have reached the stage in their development at which formal instruction in reading should begin.

Again, Morris (1959) found from her survey of 60 Kent schools that it was only the exceptional child who would not have started a reader by the end of the third term in school, and the author found that, in the schools he used in his experiments, most of the children had started formal reading by the end of the second term. This means, of course, that most children would start formal reading before a chronological age of six, and so have mental ages below six also.

Lytton (1964) is correct in pointing out that Lynn's (1963) statement quoted earlier, implying that 75% of British head teachers accept a minimum mental age of six to eight years, is misleading. Lytton points out that in Morris's (1959) survey 75% of 60 head teachers expressed a vague belief in the concept of reading readiness, but did not indicate any minimum mental age. In the practical classroom situation it seems that teachers are being guided more by 'instinct' than by mental age. Morris (1959) has shown that the teacher's instinct usually means the observation of each child's desire to learn to read by his showing an interest in books, coupled with an interest in words. The author found that these methods were mentioned by a number of infant teachers in his discussions with them regarding methods of assessing readiness for reading. In addition, a method mentioned by a number of teachers was that of noting the ability to recognise and remember the words shown on 'flash' cards – words from the introductory reader to be used.

Even though the writers of the three articles mentioned above have made somewhat exaggerated claims regarding the widespread acceptance of a minimum mental age of six for reading readiness, Lynn (1963) is just in suggesting that the teacher trying to appraise the reading readiness of her children is only given this one definite clue from the research literature – an association of reading readiness with mental age. This being so, it is understandable that in America, where children start school at six and can be tested fairly successfully in groups, this statement has been widely accepted and put into practice.

In critical appraisals of the minimum mental age concept, evidence is usually cited of children learning to read with mental ages of below and well below six years of age, but before considering this evidence a definition of reading must be established.

Most authorities agree that reading is much more than just word recognition, and that it is the ability to gain meaning from the words read. Gray (1943), discussing the reading act, suggests that its dimensions include even more than gaining the meaning from the word. He says it includes perception, understanding, reaction and integration. By reaction and integration he means that, once the reader has been stimulated by the author's words, he in turn vests the author's printed words with his own meaning by thinking about, judging, and critically evaluating the ideas he has read. So, reading is a complex process. A child reads not only with his eyes and voice, but with his experience and cultural heritage.

The studies of Dolbear (1912), Terman (1918), Fowler (1962), Terman and Oden (1947), Diack (1960) and Lynn (1963) provide evidence of very young children under the age of three learning to read. However, a careful study of the cases described suggests that, in the main, the children concerned were above average children; instruction was individual and enjoyable; and perhaps more important, by 'reading' was really meant the recognition of letters or of words. Both of the author's daughters, when three, could read the introductory reader in the 'Janet and John' series. In each case during the two months prior to their third birthday they were encouraged to play games with, match, and then say the words they would later meet in the introductory reader; they were both above average ability for their age, the materials used were simple, and the 'reading' activity was stimulating and enjoyable. However, the 'reading' was mechanical, and they soon seemed to lose interest in the activity. A similar loss of interest was reported by Fowler (1962) and Lynn (1963) when they were teaching their daughters to read.

This later resistance to reading, although perhaps temporary, most likely indicates that the effort has been unrewarding and that the activity has not been very meaningful. This kind of reading is with the eyes and voice but not with understanding, which comes with experience and the development of concepts.

Lytton (1964) points out that, in the normal classroom situation, children who are not really ready for reading learn a few words at sight, perhaps also a sentence or two. Then comes a halt to their progress and little further reading is accomplished.

Durkin (1959, 1961, 1963, 1964) has made four studies of children learning to read at home with mental ages of three, four and five; but, again, the evidence suggests that the children were precocious, instruction was individual from parents or older siblings, and, by 'reading', word recognition only was implied.

A truer assessment of the evidence of early reading should include only those studies which relate to children of average ability and normal or near normal classroom situations, as such studies have most relevance in a critical re-examination of the minimum mental age concept. Holmes (1962) has pointed out:

> Other things being equal, the earliest age at which a child can be taught to read is a function of the amount of time or help the teacher can give the pupil.

Nearer the classroom situation is Davidson's experiment, using groups of *five* children, which is often quoted to support the claim that children with mental ages of four can learn to read. She conducted her experiment with three groups of pre-school children – a bright three year old, a normal four year old, and a dull five year old group – all having Stanford-Binet mental ages of approximately four years. Each group received ten-minute reading lessons daily for four months, and reading tests were given at the end of that period. She comments that at the end of the experiment the bright three year old children recognised on average 129.4 words out of context, the average four year olds 55.3 words, and the dull five year olds 40.0 words. This shows that, with a small group of children, even dull five year olds can be taught to recognise words. But Lytton (1964) points out that when the children's retention was tested four months after the close of the experiment, the dull children recognised on average 9 words, and the bright children, somewhat earlier, recognised on average 105 words. He comments:

> This must raise a doubt whether four months reading instruction had yielded a worth while economic return for these five year old children with a mental age of approximately four years.

On this question as to whether a minimum mental age is necessary for reading or not, Gates (1937) has made a valuable contribution, often quoted to show that children can learn to read with mental ages below six years of age. In this important study he examined studies made of four groups of children. In the first of the four groups, where modern and effective instruction, well adjusted to individual differences, was provided, a mental age of five years appeared to be sufficient for learning to read. In a second group, a minimum mental age was found to be half a year higher. A third group required a mental age of six years to make satisfactory progress. In a fourth group, representing the opposite extreme from the first group, children with a mental age of six and a half fared none too well, and some of them with mental ages of seven or over had difficulty. From this study Gates pointed out that a child's progress is not entirely dependent upon his ability, as the difficulty of reading materials used, the speed with which the pupils were required to learn, and the skill of the teacher are important. However, he did note in his study that practically all near-failures fell in the group with mental ages of less than five years, and states:

Although the data seems to imply that it is possible to organise materials and methods to teach children to learn to read at a mental age of 5.0 or higher, they do not in any way imply that it is *desirable* to do so. Decision on the optimum time of introducing reading to pupils must be based upon investigations of the value of this activity at different stages of development.

In the author's first investigation, the 179 children tested on Kelvin Measurement of Ability Test* soon after they entered school and who also completed the two reading achievement tests given later, were grouped according to their mental ages, with group intervals of six months. For each mental age group, the raw scores of the children on the two reading achievement tests were averaged, and Table 1 was compiled.

The figures in Table 1 illustrate the marked relationship between mental age and reading achievement and progress, in that an increase in mental age is paralleled, in general, by an increase in the average reading achievement score.

The group of children having mental ages below five years made relatively low reading achievement scores – 5.9 on Southgate A and 6.6 on Southgate B, and progress after a term's reading practice was only very slight,.7. (A term's progress is indicated by the difference between the figures for the 1st and 2nd Reading Achievement Tests found in the bottom row of Table 1.)

However, the average reading achievement scores for the children having mental ages between five years and five years six months show a relatively large increase for Tests A and B – to 10.45 and 11.5, respectively. But further increases in mental age bring only very gradual increases in the average reading achievement scores. Again, the children's progress in reading is rather slow where mental ages below five years six months are in evidence. But where the children have mental ages above five years six months, their progress is very satisfactory.

It could be argued that, for the children in the author's first experiment, a minimum mental age of five years six

*See Appendix for details of tests.

34

TABLE 1 Showing the comparison between the mental ages of 179 children and their reading achievement and progress

Mental age in years & months	Below 5 yrs	5.0 5.6	5.6 5.11	6.0 6.5	6.6 6.11	7.0 7.5	7.6 7.11	8.0 8.5
No. children in mental age group	10	20	27	27	21	33	29	12
Average raw score of chn. on 1st. Rdg. Achievement Test (Southgate) A.	5.9	10.45	10.1	11.78	11.86	15.88	16.31	18.75
Average raw score of chn. on 2nd. Rdg. Achievement Test (Southgate) B.	6.6	11.5	12.89	14.00	12.76	18.45	17.76	21.08
Difference between 1st. & 2nd. Rdg. Achievement Tests	.7	1.05	2.79	2.22	.9	2.57	1.45	2.33

months was necessary for the beginning of formal reading, and for making satisfactory progress in reading.

Lytton (1964) quotes the following typical cases from psychologists' files of children who on entry to school would have mental ages of three and a half to four years:

Girl A. CA 6–4, MA 5–2, IQ 82. Reading after being 'exposed' to the activity for over a year: nil.

Boy B. CA 6–4, MA 4–10, IQ 77. After one year's systematic reading instruction he could read the first page of 'Vanguard', Book 1, but not later pages.

Boy C. CA 6–11, MA 5–6, IQ 80. After two years' systematic reading instruction he had been given 'Vanguard' Book 2, where he could barely manage material that he had previously practised. Unpractised new material was impossible. On the Burt-Vernon Word Recognition Test he read 9 words. RA: 4–9 Discrimination of visual shapes, including letters, poor.

The evidence from the experiments described so far in this Chapter indicates that children have been taught to read – though with what degree of understanding it is difficult to assess – with mental ages of four or less, but the children were nearly all above average intelligence, and they were taught individually or in very small groups. In the normal classroom situation, the mental age requirement will vary with the methods and materials used, but it would seem that a mental age of at least five or five and a half years is necessary for reasonable success, as there is ample evidence to show that worthwhile progress in reading is not made where mental ages fall below five years.

However, this does not answer the question as to whether it is desirable to teach children with mental ages of five to read in the normal classroom situation, granted that it is possible. One must consider if the time and effort expended in teaching an average five year old to read is justified by the progress he makes, bearing in mind our definition that reading readiness is the stage when the child can learn to read easily, effectually and without any emotional disturbance. In the next section this problem will be considered.

Discussion of the evidence concerning delaying formal reading

The recommendation that reading instruction should be preceded by pre-reading activities was made in the 24th Yearbook of the National Society for the Study of Education, published in 1925, mentioned earlier. Since that time, many authorities on reading, and research workers in the field of reading readiness, caution against starting formal reading too early, before the child is ready, and point out forcibly the harm that can be done if such a thing happens.

The 1933 Infant and Nursery Schools Report* recommends that the child should begin to learn the three R's when

*HMSO, *Infant and Nursery School*, London, 1933, p. 133.

he wants to do so, whether he be three or six years of age.

The Australian Council for Educational Research* recommends that:

> to ensure that children will not fail in reading when they come to school, there has been a growing recognition that we should not press them and that for many, normal teaching of reading must be postponed until they are mentally and experientially ready for it.

Stroud (1956) has cautioned American teachers not to rush the child into reading. He has pointed out that it is difficult to find any benefit from spending a year making little, or no progress, and it is easy to see that much harm may result. He feels that the too early introduction to reading may create a situation in which the child actually learns *not* to read, and this is quite different and more serious than not learning to read.

King (1941), studying the relationship between age at entering school and subsequent achievements, used two groups of children entering First Grade. The first group consisted of 54 children whose ages were between four years eight months and four years eleven months. The second group consisted of 50 children between six years five months and six years eight months. She found that the majority of children who entered Grade 1 before the age of six years did not realise their optimum academic achievement at the end of six years in school.

Bear (1958) compared two groups of 73 children, matched on IQ and sex. One group entered First Grade at an average age of 10 months older than that of the other group. After 11 years in school the older group was found to have received significantly higher grades and achievement test scores over the entire period.

Downing (1963), in his main i.t.a. experiment, found that in the t.o. classes the 'very young' (four year olds) had made significantly less progress than the 'young' (five year olds). However, in the i.t.a. classes this difference did not exist, as the 'very young' appeared to have made as good progress as

---

*Australian Council for Educational Research, *The approach to reading,* Victoria, Melbourne University Press, 1952, p.6.

the 'young'. (This experiment will be discussed in greater detail in a later Chapter.)

Other writers list the early introduction to reading as one of the prime causes of reading disability. Bond and Tinker (1957) explain clearly how this can happen:

> Reading disability is frequently caused by starting a child in a standard reading program before he has acquired the readiness which will assure success in classroom reading activities. Due to his lack of experience, verbal facility, intellectual or emotional maturity, or a combination of these, he is unable to achieve enough of the learning, day by day, to handle satisfactorily what is coming next. He gets farther and farther behind as time goes on. Inability to cope with the assignments produces frustration, which leads to feelings of inadequacy, inferiority, insecurity and perhaps even rebellion. Such a child is likely to develop an attitude of indifference to reading. He may even come to hate reading and all persons and activities connected with reading activities.

Witty (1949) points out that the child's lifelong attitude towards reading may be coloured by his first experience with it. Strang and Bracken (1957) suggest that it is extremely difficult to teach reading to a child who has failed in reading. A Ministry of Education pamphlet on Reading Ability* suggests that faulty training is one of the main causes of backwardness in reading. It also mentions the danger of beginning formal reading too early, and states: 'What is of prime importance is that as far as teaching conditions permit, the individual child should proceed at his own uninterrupted pace'.

Stroud (1956) writes that 'a pretty good defense could be made for the thesis that our reading clinics and remedial reading programs are testimony to the unwisdom of our haste'.

Whipple (1944), studying 83 backward readers from Detroit schools, concluded that in 59 cases the early introduction to reading had led to the reading difficulties experienced later.

Jensen (1943), studying 22 cases of reading disability,

---

*HMSO, *Reading ability; some suggestions for helping the backward*, Pamphlet No 18, 1950.

concluded that nine were driven to neuroses because of the unrelenting pressure to force the child to read when he was not capable of reading.

Gates (1949) states that the point of view he wishes to represent in his book on improved reading ability is:

> That most difficulties, ranging from the least to the most serious, are due, primarily, to failure of the pupil to acquire techniques that might have been acquired had the right guidance and instruction been given at the right time.

Doll (1953) goes so far as to say that the *principal* cause of poor reading is premature instruction. He recommends that formal pressure to learn the three R's should be postponed until the Third Grade.

All writers who advocate delaying the start of formal reading, where necessary, emphasise the fact that the time before reading commences should be used to prepare the child for reading by a broad reading readiness programme.

Most reading specialists feel that this preparatory, or reading readiness, period should be broad in its objectives, and must cater for the very wide range of abilities and backgrounds found among new school entrants. Witty (1949) lists the following items which help to prepare American children for efficient reading:

1. Various forms of language activity associated with children's experiences and interests.
2. Opportunities for children to hear and to tell stories.
3. Activities which enable boys and girls to enjoy rhymes, jingles and poems.
4. Experiences which lead children to become interested in books.
5. Activities in which pupils enjoy and interpret pictures.
6. Experience in dictating stories, and in examining records or charts.
7. Exercises in auditory and visual discrimination and in other simple habits related to reading skill, such as the tendency to make left to right movement of the eyes.

Schonell (1961) has a similar list of points for use with British children in a reading readiness programme:

1. Varied use of language for increasing concepts, vocabulary, and knowledge of sentence patterns; stories and discussions centring round classroom activities.
2. Listening to stories to improve attention.
3. Asking questions to develop the desire for understanding.
4. Free activities with self-chosen play material to develop that sense of purpose, concentration and persistence so necessary in learning to read.
5. Rhymes and songs to develop a sense of sound.
6. Drawing and tracing to aid in the understanding of ideas and recognition of word patterns.
7. Projects to develop a train of ideas, expand vocabulary and increase knowledge.
8. Participation in group work to develop co-operation and initiative.
9. Participation in group activities which involve following teacher instructions.
10. Becoming acquainted with books through opportunities to handle picture books connected with everyday activities, or centring round a project.

Investigations, mainly carried out in America, into the value of a reading readiness programme are generally favourable, and have shown that the delay of systematic instruction in reading for a few weeks, or even for several months, does not retard progress by the end of the primary grade.

Scott (1947) found that membership in the readiness class was more effective in preparing for reading than either kindergarten attendance, or reading without preparatory work. Peterson (1937) used the results of reading readiness tests, and other types of information, in classifying First Grade pupils into 'ready to read', and 'transition' groups. The latter group was given special training to prepare them for reading, and the rapid progress made in reading with this group, when they did begin, led Peterson to conclude that the programme had been successful.

More valuable are studies involving matched groups of children, which compare the results of an immediate start in reading with those of a readiness period before starting. Sister Nila (1953) matched two groups of First Grade entrants who were low in readiness scores. To the experi-

40

mental group she gave three months' readiness training and five months' reading, while the control group started reading immediately and had the full eight months' reading. At the end of the year the experimental group scored 2.1, the control group 1.9.

In a similar experiment Bradley (1955–6), matched two groups of First Grade children, each group consisting of 31 children and matched on the basis of sex, chronological age, intelligence quotient and the father's socio-economic status. The experimental group participated in a programme which was built on the concept of readiness, and designed to stimulate growth in all aspects of development. Formal systematic instruction was not given to any child until he was considered ready. In the control group, formal systematic instruction was provided immediately upon entrance to Grade 1. Each group was studied for a two year period, and a comprehension test was administered at the end of the third year for additional study. Test results clearly indicated that the children who participated in the readiness programme attained a degree of achievement in reading equal to that of the control group, by the end of the second year. By the end of the third year the experimental group was up to grade standard in reading, and equalled the progress of the control group. Also, by the end of the same year the experimental group was above grade standard in other skills, such as work-study skills and basic language skills, and showed light gains, some statistically significant, over the control group.

Washburne (1941) reported the effects of postponing reading for an experimental group until the middle of the second year, substituting an activity programme for this group. During the ensuing three years the reading attainments of the pupils were below normal, but after five years had elapsed from the time of commencement, they were a year ahead in reading achievement and in other measures of school attainment.

Gray (1956) reports an interesting experiment of a similar nature carried out in Brazil by Dr Lourenço-Filho. Filho prepared tests designed to measure certain abilities essential to success in learning to read; these tests were given to the pupils on entering school. On the basis of the results, they were divided into three groups – superior, medium and poor –

41

and the teaching of reading was adapted to the needs and rates of learning of the three groups. When objective tests were given at the end of the school year, 80% of the pupils obtained the score necessary for passing, as compared with 50% the year before. The next year no adjustments were made to provide for differences in learning ability; the percentage of passes dropped to 50% again. Two years later the experiment was repeated. The percentage rose again to 80.

In this country the main experiment which bears on the problem of delayed reading instruction is that of Gardner (1948). She showed that children in some English schools, taught by informal methods from the time they entered school, seemed to gain in later powers of persistence, intelligent application and understanding, over children in classes where formal methods were used. As regards reading, the results indicated that if the teaching of reading is postponed, although ground is lost initially compared with children taught to read at once, the disadvantage disappears within the next two years and children who made the delayed start scored slightly higher than comparable children who made an immediate start in reading.

All these experiments indicate the value of finding out the individual differences and needs of the children when they enter school, and of substituting reading readiness programmes where children are not found ready to commence formal reading. Most of these experiments have been carried out in the USA, where compulsory schooling begins at six years. As pointed out earlier, every reading situation is different from every other because of the materials and methods used, the skill of the teacher and the standards looked for, and so the results of these experiments must be approached with caution.

However, compulsory schooling in this country is at five and, as Schonell (1961) points out that some entrants to infant school classes are nearer four plus and a few three plus years in intellectual, experiential, verbal and/or emotional equipment, it would seem that a consideration of individual differences is even more important for the British teacher than for the American, when children start school.

If in a class of five year olds, IQ's range from 80–120 which is quite usual, there is a mental age range from four to six years. If we made the reasonable assumption that with the methodology usual in our infant schools a mental age of five years was adequate for successful reading, then some of the children would not be ready to start, and some of the children could well have started earlier.

In social development there are wide differences in readiness for participation in group life. Some children are timid, shy and retiring; others are troublesome, interfering, or are distracted by the group. Again, children differ enormously in language development. The speaking vocabularies of some are greater than they really need, while those of others are meagre and inadequate. Some children speak in complex sentences; others are almost unintelligible. Regarding the broad factor of experience, children's experiences are as varied as the homes from which they come.

Schonell, after pointing out that some children come to school unready to tackle formal reading, writes:

> What calamitous maladjustment must ensue from a too early start in formal reading with these children; with such a picture in mind it is impossible that anyone should doubt the wisdom of a preparatory readiness programme in learning to read.

Discussion of the perceptual abilities required by children for successful reading

Lynn (1963) and Downing (1963) have recently suggested that the perceptual abilities required by children for successful reading have been over-estimated, and that the theory of maturation which Benda (1954) describes as 'a biological process which cannot be accelerated by artificial means' is no longer tenable. They show that perceptual powers can be improved with training.

Benda, after reviewing a number of studies of children's abilities in copying letters or figures, feels that children with mental ages below six cannot perceive words or letters. For example, it has been found that a mental age of seven is required before a child can copy a diamond accurately in the Stanford-Binet test. Lynn's (1963) comment on this finding is that:

43

All this evidence shows is that children do not *draw* accurately until this mental age ... However ... when naming or pointing is used instead of drawing as an index of perceptual ability, it is evident that children can make perceptual differentiations at considerably lower mental ages.

Lynn also quotes Vernon as subscribing to Benda's view, but her conclusions are more guarded than Lynn suggests. When summarising the evidence on the ability of children to perceive details of word shapes, Vernon (1958) writes:

However, in the normal child this ability seems to develop and mature rapidly at the age of five to six years, or at an earlier age in highly intelligent children.

It would seem clear, from the evidence provided by the studies of Dolbear (1912), Terman (1918), Fowler (1962), Diack (1960) and Lynn (1963), that children with mental ages of less than five can perceive enough detail in words to help them to recognise them.

With regard to whether one must await maturation, or whether special training to cultivate readiness is useful, the evidence is conflicting. Olson (1959), Hymes (1958) and Benda (1954), among others, feel that parents and teachers cannot accelerate the child's development of readiness. On the other hand Scott (1947), Peterson (1937), Sister Nila (1953) and Bradley (1955–6), among others, have shown that readiness programmes have enabled children who were not considered ready to read, to achieve the same standards, in later years, as those who were considered ready earlier.

Taylor (1950) designed an experiment to determine whether the factors involved in reading readiness depend solely on maturation, or whether they are affected by training. She compared the scores on reading readiness measures of Scottish children at six with those of American children at six, and found the Scottish scores higher. She concluded that since the age was the same, and the only substantial difference was the fact that Scottish children generally start school at five and American children at six, reading readiness could be affected by training and is not dependent solely on maturation.

Again, specific training carried out in auditory and visual

44

discrimination by Durrell and Murphy (1953) and Lineham (1958), and also in the ability to discriminate reversals of letters and words by Hildreth (1934) and Teegarden (1932) indicate that children, with training, can improve in these abilities.

The weight of the evidence favours the view that we have perhaps underestimated the perceptual abilities of children when beginning school, and not taken into full consideration the extent to which we can develop these various abilities through training. However, it must be borne in mind that reading as a meaningful task requires more than competency in the perceptual abilities.

Discussion of new methods of teaching reading

Success with new methods of teaching reading to young children has led to a further questioning of the reading readiness concept.

Although most reading specialists in the USA favour the postponement of systematic reading instruction until the child shows signs of real readiness, there is a minority view that favours incorporating readiness in actual reading lessons, starting all children in reading from the beginning of the First Grade. This approach has been termed 'forcing' by Olson and Hughes (1944), as against 'pacing' and delaying methods.

One 'forcing' method of recent years is the project carried out in New Castle, Pennsylvania, and so called the New Castle method. This method has been publicised by Mc-Cracken (1952, 1953, 1954, 1959) in a series of articles and a book. According to McCracken, the concept of readiness is of little value; he feels that all children who are not mentally defective can be taught to read with good methodology. Harris (1961) feels that the New Castle method is distinctive in the following aspects:

   (i) the whole class is taught together, although some supplementary group work occurs in the afternoon;

  (ii) the concept of readiness is ignored and reading instruction is started for all at the beginning of the First Grade;

(iii) all new material is first taught by the use of coloured, illustrated slides projected from film strips;

(iv) after intensive study of the projected slides, including identification and analysis of words, and orally reading the sentences many times, the children read the corresponding page or two in the correlated reader;

(v) an intensive phonics programme, not originally part of the method, seems to have been added after McCracken read Flesch's* book.

McCracken's published results indicate highly successful First Grade reading, and Lichtenstein (1960), who more recently used the method, also reports outstanding success.

Another fairly recent experiment, carried out in Denver, Colorado, by Brzeinski (1964), attempted to involve parents in the pre-reading activities of their children, by means of a specially prepared guide book of pre-reading activities linked with sixteen programmes on television. The report on the findings suggests that parental help does enable children to be ready for reading at an earlier age. This result is to be expected when the school starting age is six years.

Another major issue on which current practice is being challenged is the place and extent of phonics in the beginning of reading. Some authorities, for example Flesch (1955) and Durrell (1956) in the USA and Daniels and Diack (1956), Gattegno (1962), and Stott (1964), want intensive phonic instruction to play an important part in the very early stages of reading.

Flesch's book was very forceful in attributing poor reading to lack of systematic phonic instruction. One of the ideas which Flesch criticised strongly was that of readiness. He states that the idea that a six year old cannot learn to read is a new invention, tracing the idea back to Dolch and Bloomster in 1937. The author's summary of the research on reading readiness indicates this statement is not strictly true, though Flesch was no doubt thinking of phonic readiness. However, Flesch condemns readiness programmes as a waste of time.

When describing his scheme 'Royal Road Readers', Diack

*Flesch, R., *Why Johnny can't read*, Harper Bros, 1955.

46

(1965) suggests that, although the approach is phonic (phonic word method), his scheme should be wedded to all kinds of creative activities.

However, the tendency of the methods using fairly intensive phonic instruction is to ignore the readiness period and begin formal reading very soon after the children enter school at five. For example, Gattegno (1962), who has designed the 'Words in Colour' scheme, believes that we underestimate children, and that they are capable of much more intellectually at five than we normally assume. The approach, as he plans it, makes no concessions to a readiness period of creative activities. Again, Stott (1964), who designed the 'Programmed Reading Kit', feels the distinctive advantage of the Kit is that the learning sequence can be adjusted to the learner's needs, and that all can progress through the programme together, though naturally the bright child will progress more rapidly than the slow child.

An interesting new experiment is the teaching of reading with the initial teaching alphabet (i.t.a.), which will be discussed more fully later. Certain results, however, have indicated that a number of four year old children appeared to be ready to learn to read earlier with the new medium of i.t.a. In discussing the minimum mental age concept in relation to i.t.a., Downing (1963) points out that i.t.a., by removing the complexities and ambiguities of the traditional orthography of English, may enable children to learn to read with a lower average mental age level. He writes:

> Thus these results from the i.t.a. experiment seem to confirm that the necessary mental age for reading readiness is relative to yet another arbitrary factor in the child's learning situation – the difficulty of the conventional English alphabet and spelling for beginners.

The author has tested this hypothesis experimentally in his present investigation.

Another interesting new development in the teaching of reading has been Doman's book 'Teach your Baby to Read', published in 1963 in the USA and in 1965 in this country, in which he claims that a baby can learn to read at two years, at three years, even at fourteen months – at any pre-school age

47

when it is decided to teach him. Doman (1965) insists he will learn faster and more easily earlier than when he is older; he will love it, and his later adjustment to school will not suffer.

The 'babies' begin by learning to recognise the words 'mummy' and 'daddy' as whole words, the words being printed in large red lower case letters (4" high) on white cards (5" high). The first lessons last only a minute or two. When they have learned to recognise those two words, the 'babies' then go on to learn to recognise a number of words in various groupings called the 'self' words, for example toes, elbow, hand; the family words, for example brother, sister (cards now 3" high, red letters 2" high); objects, possessions, doing words and sentences. They then go on to a book and later learn the alphabet.

Apart from the larger print used and the younger age of the child taught, there is nothing revolutionary about the method— which is a straightforward individual 'look and say' method. Again, much evidence has already been cited of 'babies' learning to 'read' in similar ways. The following comment of Diack's (1965) is very sound:

> It would be as well too, for parents who try to teach their babies to read to be aware that the word recognition stage is a very easy one. The trial of the teacher's patience comes when she is trying to get the child to understand what the letters are there for. Children will appear to be able to read long before they are actually able to do so in the full sense of the word.

The kind of reading 'babies' can accomplish is obviously simply word recognition. The development and understanding of concepts comes through experience, which takes time to acquire, so although an earlier start to reading may be made with Doman's system, the true reading process cannot be hurried to this great extent, as the reading of words must go hand in hand with the understanding of them.

This latest development is the extreme position of that of Patrick, who wrote an article in 1899 entitled 'Should children under ten learn to read and write?' and argued that they should not.

Success in varying degrees is claimed for all these new methods of teaching reading, but it is always difficult to know whether the success is due to the method or to the enthusiasm of the innovator and his disciples. In the research literature, when new methods are described, they are often claimed to be more successful than previous ones. However, the success claimed by these new approaches once again brings into focus the question of whether or not, with good methodology, all children could start formal reading on entering school, or even in pre-school years.

In summing up this chapter, the question 'Is the reading readiness concept still a valid one?' must be answered.

Lynn (1963), after reviewing the evidence on the perceptual abilities of children, writes:

> With the disposal of the spurious concept of delayed perceptual maturation, it seems doubtful whether the concept of reading readiness has sufficient substance to be worth retaining.

Neale (1967), in her appraisal of the results of the i.t.a. experiment writes:

> These findings represent a revolutionary breakthrough in current psychological thinking, toppling one of the long established corner-stones in educational practice – that of 'readiness' for reading.

McCracken (1959) and Flesch (1955) feel the idea of reading readiness should be abandoned, but Downing (1966), states that:

> The concept of reading readiness does have value and should be retained, provided that the role of learning in development towards readiness is given greater recognition.

This view of Downing is the one to which the author would subscribe, as it is a realistic approach to the recent research findings. Children are not born able to read, so readiness for this task must come at some stage or another, varying from individual to individual, and from one reading situation to another.

If the concept of reading readiness were abandoned or minimised, the tendency would be to start all children on formal reading very soon after they entered school. In the normal classroom situation in this country, where children start school at five and reception classes are large, many children will be below average in ability. The evidence is clear that where five year old children are nearer four mentally, experientially and emotionally, they do not learn to read easily and effectually, and are not ready to read. Hence, if individual differences were ignored, many of our children would become failures from the start, and this would be a putting back of the educational clock.

In the USA, where children start school at six, it may well be that the concept could be abandoned or minimised. Most American children will have mental ages of at least five when entering First Grade, and with the probable spread of individual rather than group teaching, and of less demanding approaches to reading, all children could start formal reading on entering school without undue harmful effects. In future the concept may be minimised or ignored in the USA, and the danger is that we may be tempted to follow suit; this would be a retrograde step, and very unsound psychologically and educationally.

It is true that a re-thinking of the concept is necessary, and research findings should now be taken into consideration. There is no one minimum mental age for reading, and intellectual powers can and should be developed in the classroom. For example, Dockrell (1959) recommends that the primary school curriculum should:

> be planned with more attention to ultimate future achievement and less stress on immediate attainment, so getting the multiple dividend of providing the child not with learning but with the intelligence on which future learning will depend.

Perceptual abilities of visual and auditory discrimination are as important, or, perhaps more important than general mental ability, and these skills can be developed.

The approach to readiness which seems to offer the most realism is to study the learning situation which involves motivation, individual differences and the way reading is taught.

More and more we are realising that the main task of the reception class teacher is, firstly, to provide a stimulating programme of pre-reading activities which actively develop reading readiness for those who are not ready, but secondly, to be aware of those children who are ready, so for them an early start can be made to formal reading.

Chapter 3

A Brief Description of the Initial Teaching Alphabet (Formerly Called Augmented Roman) and a Discussion of the Relationship Between i.t.a. and Reading Readiness

i.t.a. in historical perspective

The orthography of the English language was very diverse in the past; the characters themselves changed over the years, and with them the spelling.

Pitman (1966) summarises early development in these words:

> The early Anglo-Saxon and Latin characters vied with each other during a long period of gestation while our alphabetic system was becoming established as a mixture of upper-case and lower-case Latin characters, the correct mixture being based on context. The spellings with these characters also changed considerably and it was not until the sixteenth century that the introduction of printing became finally decisive, and established the general conformity to an orthography in both characters and spelling which is virtually that of the present.

In the middle ages Latin, both written and spoken, was the normal and expected means of scholarly communication, and also a mark of distinction. It was this fashion which determined that English should be written, not with its own characters, but with Latin characters, which while alphabetically adequate and perfectly suited to Latin sounds, were considerably deficient and very unsuited to the representation of many of the English sounds. Printing started wholly in Latin, and once type was established for printing Latin, it became inevitable that printers should use the type they had at hand for all other languages, and should meet deficiencies by improvising with the characters they had. In this way the upper-case and lower-case Roman Alphabet became conventional for printed English, and with very few changes has remained so until today. Hence, it was in medieval times that the great part of the two thousand different spellings for the mere forty sounds of English were created.

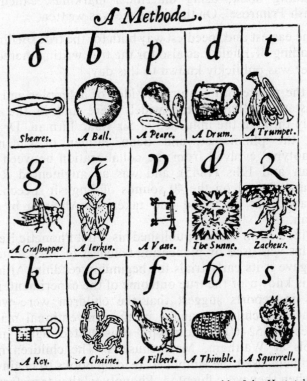

Figure 1 An example of the reformed spelling proposed by John Hart, taken from the Special Report on i.t.a. in the 1965 Britannica Book of the Year.

Many teachers of reading and educationalists from the sixteenth century onwards have recognised that the inconsistencies and ambiguities of our English spelling may be a cause of difficulty for children in learning to read. For some, radical reform of the entire spelling system was considered to be the only solution, but others have advocated that children learning to read should use a simpler and more consistent alphabet in the early stages.

In 1551 Hart wrote of the 'vices and faults of our writing; which cause it to be tedious, and long in learning: and learned hard and evil to read'. In 1570 he designed 'A Methode or Comfortable Beginning for all Unlearned, Whereby They May Bee Taught to Read English, in a Very Short Time, With Pleasure'.

In 1644, Hodges, a schoolmaster of Southwark, published a reading book, using diacritical markings, called 'The English Primrose'. On the title page was written:

> The easiest and speediest way both for the true spelling and reading of English as also for the true writing thereof that ever was publickly known to this day.

In the nineteenth century the idea of a simpler and more consistent spelling spread widely here and in the USA, mainly through the influence of Sir Isaac Pitman, Dr. A. J. Ellis, the philologist, and Benn Pitman of Cincinnati. 'Phonotypy' evolved from the collaboration between Isaac Pitman and Ellis (1845), and was an augmented Roman Alphabet based on the 40 sounds of English speech. This Alphabet was perfected and taken to America by Benn Pitman.

In 1855 Benn Pitman published his 'First Phonetic Reader' and this was used by pioneering teachers of Massachusetts, who gave it its early trials for beginning reading. Although little is known of the true outcome of the experiment, references in reports suggest that the children were well in advance of children taught in the conventional manner. Between 1852–60, 'Phonotypy' was tested again in ten schools at Waltham, Massachusetts. The children in the experiment used the simplified reading books to begin with, and when they were fluent in 'Phonotypy' they transferred to the conventional orthography. In the description of the ex-

THE ENGLISH PRIMRÔSE:

Far furpaffing âl others of this kinde, that ever
grêw in any English garden : by the ful
fight whêreof, thêre wil ma-
nifeftly appêar,

The Eafieft and Speedieft-way, bôth for the
trûe fpelling and rëading of English, as
âlfô for the Trûe-writing thereof :
that ever was publickly
knôwn tô this day.

Planted (with nô fmâl pains) by Richard
Hodges, a School-mafter, dwelling in Southwark, at the midle-gate within Moun-
tague-clôfe : for the exceeding grêat
benefit, bôth of his ôwn Coun-
trêy-men and Strängers.

Approved âlfô by the Learned, and publifht
by Âuthority.

If the trumpet give an uncertain found, whô
fhâl prepäre himfelf tô the battel? 1 Cor. 14. 8

LONDON
Printed for Richard Côtes. 1644

Figure 2 Showing the title page of 'The English Primrose' by Richard Hodges,
taken from *The i.t.a. Reading Experiment* by J.A. Downing, 1964a.

periment in the American Philosophical Society's Report
of 1899, success was reported for the venture.

This two-stage method set the pattern for all subsequent
research, and during the next hundred years several other
experiments with simplified orthographies for the beginning

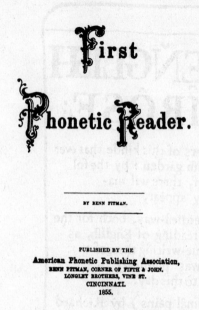

Figure 3 An example from an early phonetic reader (1855) by Benn Pitman taken from *The i.t.a. Reading Experiment* by J. A. Downing, 1964a.

stages were tried out. Among the most notable were those at St. Louis and Boston in America, using Leigh's alphabet; in Scotland, using Miss McCullum's own alphabet; and the experiments carried out between 1915–24 in fifteen British Schools, using the 'Nue Speling'.

When describing Dr Edwin Leigh's alphabet to the Social Congress at Brighton in 1875, Sir Charles Reed* called it a 'Pronouncing Orthography'. He explained this term by saying:

It shows the exact pronunciation of every word and a special form of letter is used for each sound of it. Letters which have no sound are printed in a hairline, or light-faced type. It thus shows the pronunciation without changing the

---

* Reported address of Sir Charles Reed, Chairman of the London School Board, to the Society of Arts in London, 29th May, 1877. Details of report printed in *A Plea for Phonetic Reform*, ed. Isaac Pitman, 1878.

spelling, and even preserves the familiar form or face of the words, as we are accustomed to see them.

In 1914 Miss McCullum,* an infants' teacher in Scotland, used her own simplified alphabet for the children's reading and writing lessons during their first year at school. With her alphabet she found she could choose words for reading and writing lessons drawn from the children's own vocabulary. After a year on this phonetic scheme the children transferred to the conventional alphabet.

Between 1915 and 1924 fifteen British schools experimented with the 'Nue Speling' devised by the Simplified Spelling Society.† This alphabet was an interesting one in that its appearance was more carefully related to the traditional alphabet, to ensure an easy transition from the one to the other.

Great improvements in reading attainment were reported from all these experiments, but as the experiments were not scientifically controlled and the reports were subjective, the evidence could not be accepted as proving that the inconsistencies of English spelling were a major cause of reading difficulty.

In 1960 the University of London Institute of Education established a Reading Research Unit to conduct a scientific investigation into the effectiveness of Pitman's Augmented Roman Alphabet (later called the Initial Teaching Alphabet) as a medium for beginning to read. The Unit's main task was to find the answer to two main questions:

(i) Does the use of a simpler and more consistent orthography in the early stages of learning to read make learning easier?
(ii) Can the children readily transfer their reading skills to the more complicated system of conventional English spelling?

For the first time, a controlled scientific experiment was initiated, to find out if the inconsistencies of English spelling were a major cause of reading difficulty.

---

*Reported by M. R. Jackson, Lecturer in Phonetics, Dundee Training College.

†Simplified Spelling Society, Pamphlet No. 7, Pitman, 1924.

Gon Out.

A man went too hiz naiborz hous and rang the bel. The maidservant oepnd the dor. "I wish too speek too eur maaster," hee sed. "Hee'z gon out," shee aanserd. "Then I wil speek too eur mis-tris," hee sed. "Shee'z gon out, too." "That's a piti; but per-haps thai'l soon kum bak. I wil kum in and sit by the fyer and wait for them." "I m sori, ser," the maid sed, "but the fyer'z gon out too."

7. A page from Book I of *A Reeder in Simplifyd Spelling*

Figure 4 An example of simplified spelling called the 'Nue Speling', published in 1918; taken from *Instant Reading* by M. Harrison, 1964.

Brief Description of the Initial
Teaching Alphabet (i.t.a.)

Sir James Pitman's alphabet evolved from the 'Phonotypy' of Isaac Pitman (his grandfather), and from the 'Nue Speling of the Simplified Spelling Society of Great Britain. It was designed by Pitman in association with the Monotype Corporation Limited.

Pitman (1959, 1961) has claimed that the inconsistencies of English spelling are a major cause of difficulty for children learning to read. These inconsistencies occur because our traditional alphabet has insufficient symbols to represent all the sounds used in speech. As a result, our 26 letters have to be combined in over 300 ways to spell the 40 or so sounds of our spoken language.

Pitman describes the purpose of his alphabet as follows:

> . . . . the purpose of which (the alphabet) is not, as might be supposed, to reform our spelling, but to improve the learning of reading. It is intended that, when the beginner has achieved the initial success of fluency in this specially easy form, his future progress should be confined to reading in the present alphabets and spellings only.

He stressed the fact that the alphabet was not an attempt at spelling reform, but was designed to help children to learn to read more easily, and once they were fluent in the easier medium it was to be discarded in favour of the traditional orthography (t.o.). Pitman's aim of providing a simple systematic medium for reading without permanent spelling reform called for a compromise in his design of i.t.a. between the need for simplification and consistency for the initial reading code, and the need to make i.t.a. compatible with t.o., so that the transition from i.t.a. to standard print should be less dramatic for children when they reached the transfer stage. For example, 'c' and 'k' were both kept to represent the single phoneme, in order to reduce the number of words whose spellings, and hence visual clues, had to be changed at this transfer stage; for example, 'back', 'kick'. Similarly double letters were retained to help preserve the over-all pattern of words, for example, 'rabbit', 'letter'. In order to present a consistent visual pattern for each whole word, only lower-case characters were used, and capitalisation was achieved by using a larger version (a majuscule) of the same lower case shape.

A passage in i.t.a. can be seen in Figure 5 on the following page, and illustrates these points.

wee ʃhall fiet

bie Sir Winston ᴄhurᴄhill

ɛɛven thœ larj tracts ov uɛrop, and meny œld and
fæmus Stæts hav fɑullen or mæ fɑull intœ the grip ov the
gestapœ and ɑull the œdius apparætus ov nazi rœl, wee
ʃhall not flag or fæl. wee ʃhall gœ on tœ the end, wee ʃhall
fiet in frans, wee ʃhall fiet on the sees and œʃhans, wee
ʃhall fiet with grœiŋ confidens and grœiŋ streŋth in the
ær, wee ʃhall defend our ieland, whotever the cost mæ
bee, wee ʃhall fiet on the beeᴄhes, wee ʃhall fiet on the
landiŋ grounds, wee ʃhall fiet in the feelds and in the
streets, wee ʃhall fiet in the hills; wee ʃhall never surrender,
and ɛɛven if, whiᴄh ie dœ not for a mœment beleev, this
ieland or a larj part ov it wer subjœgæted and starviŋ,
then our empier beyond the sees, armd and garded bie
the britiʃh fleet, wœd carry on the struggl, until, in
god's gœd tiem, the nue wurld, with ɑul its pouer and
miet, steps forth tœ the rescue and the liberæʃhion ov the
œld.

Figure 1.6. *From Sir Winston Churchill's War Memoirs as reproduced in*
"The Initial Teaching Alphabet"
by J. A. Downing, Cassell.

Figure 5 An example of a printed passage using the Initial Teaching Alphabet,
taken from *The i.t.a. Reading Experiment* by J. A. Downing, 1964a.

It is generally agreed that when we read fluently and
quickly, we look only at the upper part of a line of print
Pitman's aim, both in letter designing and spelling, was to
leave the 'top coast line' of the printed words and sentence:
undisturbed as far as possible, so that the main cues used by
the fluent reader would remain the same. To illustrate thi:
point the author has prepared a short passage* by masking
the top and bottom halves of each line of print in both the
t.o. and i.t.a. versions.

*Neale, M. D., *Neale analysis of reading ability*, Macmillan, 1963. Form B, p. 21.

The Swiss puppet watched the children
arranging the puppet theatre. He felt useless.
He was not often chosen to act because he
wore unusual clothes

Jhe swiss puppet woçht jhe çhildren
arranging jhe puppet jheater. hee felt useless.
hee wos not often choozen too act becauz hee
wor unuezueal clothz

(The Swiss puppet watched the children arranging the puppet
theatre. He felt useless. He was not often chosen to act
because he wore unusual clothes.)

As there are approximately forty phonemes (sound units)
used in the spoken English language, and there are only 26
letters of the alphabet, Pitman augmented the Roman alphabet with the additional characters needed to supply one for
each of those English phonemes which conventionally have
no letter of their own. These additional characters were carefully designed to achieve a close resemblance to the common
conventional English spelling of those phonemes. The addition of these new i.t.a. characters to the 24 lower-case letters
of the standard alphabet which are retained in i.t.a. (N.B. 'q'
and 'x' are not used) brings the total number of letters to be
learned to 44.

Each symbol effectively stands for its own phoneme. For
example, the letter 'o' represents the one phoneme common
to 'on', 'off', 'orange', 'ox', and is not used ambiguously to
represent a variety of different phonemes as it is in the conventional spellings of 'odd', 'other', 'only', 'move'. Individual
characters replace the complex combinations of letters so
often used to spell phonemes in standard spelling. By providing a new character for phonemes which traditionally have no
letter of their own in English, Pitman sought to remove a
complexity which he felt represented a barrier to progress
in the early stages of phonic learning. For example, 'ch', a

Figure 6 Showing the 44 characters of the Initial Teaching Alphabet (i.t.a.), taken

a	apple
a	arm
æ	angel
au	author
b	bed
c	cat
ꜭh	chair
d	doll
ee	eel
e	egg
f	finger
g	girl
h	hat
ie	tie
i	ink
j	jam
k	kitten
l	lion
m	man
n	nest
ng	king
œ	toe
o	on
ω	book
ω	food
ou	out
oi	oil
p	pig
r	red
ꞧ	bird
s	soap
ʒ	treasure
ſh	ship
ʒh	three
t	tree
th	mother
ue	due
u	up
v	van
w	window
wh	wheel
y	yellow
z	zoo
ʒ	is

most common digraph for a phoneme which lacks its own symbol in the conventional alphabet, is represented by 'ʧ' in i.t.a.

Another strength claimed for Pitman's alphabet is that the left to right sequence is maintained consistently. The beginner at word building does not have to make a move back from right to left in order to decipher a word as in 'line' and 'dine', as these words become 'lien' and 'dien' in i.t.a., giving three successive phonemes from left to right.

Pitman (1959, 1961) and Downing (1964a) have written frequently that the simplicity and regularity of i.t.a. makes the task of the child learning to read easier in three important ways. They claim that i.t.a. is more simple, both in its visual and auditory characteristics and in the nature of the problem-solving involved in deciphering the print-code. As visual discrimination, auditory discrimination and mental age (which is linked with problem-solving ability) have been shown to be very important factors in reading readiness, these three claims will now be carefully considered.

Visual Discrimination and i.t.a.

The majority of infant teachers use one or other of the global methods of teaching reading in the very early stages; for example, 'look and say', 'whole word' or 'sentence' methods. In these methods the main aim is that of helping the child to form associations between the meaning of the word presented and its visual pattern in print. The child's attention is not at this stage directed towards the individual letters in the word, but towards the total pattern. It is claimed that i.t.a. helps to make 'look and say' teaching more effective, as for each word there is only one visual pattern presented to the child, whereas in the conventional orthography, as many as five different whole word patterns might be presented to the child for the one word.

The following example compiled by Downing (1964), shows the various ways in which the word 'dog' is often presented traditionally to young children.

Dog   dog   DOG   dog   Dog

For the word 'dog', i.t.a. has only one form which varies only in size, as we have seen already that capitalisation is achieved by using a larger version of the same lower-case shape, for example, 'dog'.

Downing (1964a) feels that this simplification should make it easier for the beginner to develop clear visual images of words, firstly because there is no disturbance of the visual image through the presentation of alternative patterns, and secondly because every possibility for repetition of the word is utilised, there being no alternatives.

Auditory Discrimination and i.t.a.

i.t.a. has been designed to provide a more systematic relationship between its characters and the phonemes of the spoken language which they are meant to represent. This is in contrast to traditional orthography, in which 26 letters have to represent 40 or so sounds, resulting in the inconsistencies of English Spelling.

Downing divides these inconsistencies into two kinds:

(i) one letter or group of letters can represent several different sounds, for example, the letter 'o' in 'gone', 'go', 'do', 'women', whereas in i.t.a. different phonemes would be represented by different characters, for example, 'gon', 'gœ', 'dω', 'wimen'.

(ii) one sound can be spelt in several different ways, for example, the sound represented by 'eye' can be spelt as; 'I', 'lie', 'sigh', 'buy', whereas in i.t.a. as they have a common phoneme they would have a common character: 'ie', 'lie', 'sie', 'bie'.

Problem solving in learning to read with i.t.a.

In an article discussing the minimum mental age concept, Downing (1963) has claimed that the problems for the child to solve when learning to read with i.t.a. are of a simpler nature than those needed to be solved with t.o., because of the simplified and regular nature of the medium. Because the mental tasks are easier, he feels children may be able to read i.t.a. with a lower average mental age than they would need to learn to read with t.o. As already mentioned, the author has tested this hypothesis experimentally.

Downing (1963) feels there are five important ways in which i.t.a. represents a much easier set of problems, and it will be convenient, in discussing the visual discrimination, auditory discrimination and problem solving involved in learning to read with i.t.a., to use his five headings.

1. *i.t.a. contains fewer ambiguities.*

t.o.	*i.t.a.*
no	nœ
do	dω
on	on
one	wun
women	wimen

Downing comments that in t.o. the character 'o' signals a different phoneme in each of the five words above, whereas in i.t.a. these five different phonemes are signalled each by a different printed symbol. He says elsewhere on this point of ambiguity that 'Each symbol effectively stands for its own and only its own phoneme'. But Stott (1964), in an appraisal of i.t.a., points out that there is also ambiguity in the use of the i.t.a. symbols, and mentions among others the following:

(a) 'y' stands for two distinct phonemes in 'yellow' and 'happy'.
(b) 'a' stands for two distinct phonemes in 'apple' and 'a dog'.
(c) the ignoring of the devaluation of our unstressed vowels, for example, 'even', 'open', 'wanted', 'ribbon', 'motor', means that practically every word of two or more syllables when written in i.t.a. contains at least one major ambiguity.

Also recently a teacher,* who has returned to teaching backward readers with the traditional alphabet after having used i.t.a., writes:

* Reported in a letter to the *Times Educational Supplement*, Friday, 21 April 1967.

In spite of the claim that the values of the letters in i.t.a. are completely regular, I found it necessary to refer to a spelling list even after four terms. Is it not significant that the publication of a spelling list was necessary?

Downing's evidence to support the view that spelling irregularity is a cause of difficulty in learning to read is drawn from the successes of the earlier experiments with simplified alphabets, described at the beginning of this chapter. However, one recent investigation into the relationship between the unsystematic spelling of English and reading difficulty is that of Lee (1966), who drew up lists of regular and irregular words for the 275 children in his sample to read. Commenting on his results he says:

> As far as the words [in his lists] are concerned there is no correlation between the irregularity of their spelling and the extent to which they are successfully or unsuccessfully read.

Lee concluded from his experiments that irregular spellings were by no means a major cause of reading difficulty for the children who took part in them.

Downing (1962), however, questions the validity of Lee's conclusions, pointing out (and rightly so) that, as the children in the experiment were between six and ten and could read, the effects of the irregularity of the spelling may have been obscured by the frequency of occurrence of the words in the children's reading – a variable Lee had not taken into consideration. The evidence on this question provided by the main i.t.a. experiment will be discussed in a later chapter.

On the other hand, even though there may be ambiguities in the English spelling, it must be realised that there is quite a strong relationship between the spoken and written codes of our language. Hanna and Moore (1953) analysed a 3,000 basic word vocabulary list, and found that approximately four out of five of the phonemes contained in the words were spelled consistently with the same one or two letters. They also found that ten of the consonant phonemes were spelled regularly 90% of the times they occur. They write:

We must not be so discouraged with the 20% irregularity that we fail to profit from the 80% regularity.

It has been pointed out many times that Pitman's aim of providing a systematic medium for early reading without permanent spelling reform did mean a compromise. For example, Diack (1965) writes:

The Pitman alphabet is an easy target for those who advocate a simplification of English spelling on purely phonetic principles ... What i.t.a. does is to provide in print a guide to the sounds of the spoken word *without confusion*.

However, Stott's comments on the ambiguities of i.t.a. are helpful, as there is a common tendency to think and write in terms of a one sound – one symbol relationship when discussing i.t.a.

2. *i.t.a. is much less complex*

t.o.	*i.t.a.*
chat	ͨhat
hash	haʃh
when	ωhen
then	ҭhen
thin	ҭhin

In i.t.a. the pupil is provided with an individual printed symbol for each of the phonemes which have no character of their own in our standard Roman alphabet. The child learns these new characters, for example, 'ͨh' and 'ʃh', as single letters in their own right, each representing a particular phoneme. This process is felt to be much less complex than the conventional medium, where the child must learn that multiple character spellings such as 'ch' and 'sh' do not signal the sounds which initially they learned to associate with the individual letters 'c', 'h', 's' and 'h'.

Stott feels that as far as the consonants are concerned, the claim to greater consistency rests upon a perceptual fallacy. He writes:

It is hard to believe that children fail to recognise the two separate letters of which the 'single' symbols are composed. Any unknown shape is grasped in terms of its simpler, more familiar components ... Consequently, the claim that the joined double letters of the i.t.a. are perceptually single symbols is psychologically unplausible and would need much substantiation.

Downing (1967b) admits that Stott may be right in thinking that children see 'ch' as 'c' and 'h' joined, but feels the point is not relevant, as this fact does not affect the aim of using these joined characters to represent a single sound, and so avoid confusion in the young reader's mind.

Stott also feels that, regarding the voiced and unvoiced 'th', ('th' and 'th'), children already know which form to use in native speech, and so this extra character is of no help to the child. This point has also been voiced by teachers using i.t.a.

Neale (1967), in her appraisal of the i.t.a. experiment, points out that careful discrimination and memory are required to learn the new characters, and writes that 'an impartial look at the characters indicates that confusing stimuli remain'.

3. *i.t.a. is consistent in the left to right sequence of spelling English phonemes*

t.o.	i.t.a.
bone	bœn
wine	wien
brave	bræv
tune	tuen

In the traditional spellings, before a child can pronounce the vowel correctly he must be aware of the final silent 'e' which modifies the vowel. Downing (1963) feels this probably causes uncertainty about the left to right reading habit, and may be responsible for reversals of the 'saw' and 'was'

68

variety. In i.t.a. this type of spelling is eliminated and the left to right sequence maintained.

Stott feels that, in any course planned on phonic lines, it is easy to defer the general introduction of the unpronounced 'e' which modifies any preceding vowel, until children have mastered the regular phonic conventions. He points out that the effect of i.t.a. is to defer this convention, but children have to learn it later if they are to become fluent readers in t.o. Regarding the question of confused eye movements, Stott feels that adults visually run a word or two ahead of the vocal reading, and children probably run a letter or two ahead and so would visually have reached the end of a word before it is pronounced. He comments:

It is therefore extremely doubtful if, as Downing asserts, the use of the modifying 'e' requires any reversal of the forward movements of the eye.

Again, Gibson (1963) does not believe that young beginners process individual characters from left to right, and quotes evidence to support her contention from Newman (1966), and Kolers (1963). She comments: 'However graphemes are processed perceptually in reading, it is not a letter-by-letter sequence of acts.' This view is based on the results of experiments carried out at Cornell University, but the evidence presented is not clear-cut. However the available evidence does not seem to support Downing on this point.

4. *There are far fewer items to be learned*
   in i.t.a. code for phonemes.

	t.o.			i.t.a.
1.	u	ruby	1.	⍵ rⵡby
2.	u..e	rule	1.	⍵ rⵡl
3.	U..E	RULE	1.	⍵ rⵡl
4.	o	do	1.	⍵ dⵡ
5.	o..e	move	1.	⍵ mⵡv
6.	O..E	MOVE	1.	⍵ mⵡv

7.	ui	fruit	1.	ω frœt
8.	ui..e	bruise	1.	ω brœz
9.	UI..E	BRUISE	1.	<u>ω brœz</u>
10.	ou	group	1.	ω grœp
11.	ou..e	troupe	1.	ω trœp
12.	OU..E	TROUPE	1.	<u>ω trœp</u>
13.	ough	through	1.	ω thrω
14.	OUGH	THROUGH	1.	<u>ω thrω</u>
15.	oo	moon	1.	ω mωn
16.	ooe	wooed	1.	ω wωd
17.	OOE	WOOED	1.	<u>ω wωd</u>
18.	oo..e	ooze	1.	ω ωz
19.	OO..E	OOZE	1.	<u>ω ωz</u>
20.	hue	rheumatism	1.	ω rωmatism
21.	HEU	RHEUMATISM	1.	<u>ω rωmatism</u>
22.	ue	flue	1.	ω flω
23.	UE	FLUE	1.	ω flω
24.	oeu	manoeuvre	1.	ω manωver
25.	OEU	MANOEUVRE	1.	<u>ω manωver</u>
26.	ew	grew	1.	ω grω
27.	EW	GREW	1.	ω grω
28.	oe	canoe	1.	ω canω
29.	OE	CANOE	1.	<u>ω canω</u>
30.	wo	two	1.	ω tω

In i.t.a. there is only *one* printed symbol for the phoneme common to the words on the previous page, whereas this single phoneme is spelt differently in each of these 30 words in the conventional code of English. This situation exists for many other phonemes, and Downing mentions frequently that it has been estimated that if upper case, lower case, and script characters are counted separately, there are over 2,000 different ways of spelling the 40 basic phonemes of English. In i.t.a. it has been estimated that the beginner has only 88 visual symbols to learn for these same basic phonemes.

Stott (1964) makes two relevant points concerning Downing's claim above. Firstly, he points out that Downing's examples of traditional spellings are all of vowels, whereas it is the more consistent and distinctive consonants which help children to recognise words. Secondly, his analysis of Downing's list of 30 ways of writing the 'oo' sound, shows that twelve of these are upper case versions, and seven of them are exceptional irregularities, 'bruise', 'troupe', 'wooed', 'ooze', 'rheumatism', 'flue', 'manoeuvre' – which would hardly be met by a child prior to transfer to t.o. He feels there are seven genuine alternative ways of writing the 'oo' sound – 'oo', 'ou', 'ue', 'ow', 'u', 'ough', and 'o', but points out that in i.t.a. there are at least seven alternative ways of writing the 'er' sound: 'e'(the), 'er'(her, river), 'ir'(girl), 'or'(motor), 'ur'(hurt), 'a'(indefinite article), 'o'(revision).

In making his case there is no doubt that Downing has been somewhat unrealistic in his examples, but the regularity of the print code does inevitably lead to a reduction in the learning load.

5. *There are also fewer items to be learned*
   in i.t.a. for whole words

	t.o.	i.t.a.
1.	bag	bag
2.	Bag	bag
3.	BAG	bag
4.	bag	bag
5.	bag	bag
6.	Bag	bag
7.	Bag	bag

In the conventional print it is claimed that there are at least three different visual patterns for each word of English, whereas in i.t.a. there is only one single visual pattern for each word the child must learn.

Stott (1964) points out that much of the argument concerning the variety of visual patterns presented for the same word in t.o. is not very relevant. He makes the point that we do not teach children to read words entirely in capitals, and that only eight of our capitals are quite different from the lower-case forms (A, B, D, G, H, L, Q, R.). He also gives evidence to show that mentally handicapped children can learn capital letters if they are introduced systematically. The author feels that the number of Stott's different capitals is somewhat underestimated and would suggest the addition of E, F, I, J, M, N and T, as being significantly different also.

Downing (1964a), himself realises that the good infants' teacher attempts to reduce, in her own printing, the number of different ways of presenting the one word, and again, as both child and teacher print in the early stages of reading, the different written forms often instanced can be discounted.

The author's investigation provides experimental evidence concerning the extent to which i.t.a. is more simple than t.o. in its visual and auditory characteristics, and in the problems to be solved in learning to read.

Stott, in his appraisal of i.t.a., stresses the fact that it is not the number of new associations that a child has to make which is the limiting factor to learning, but the ability to structure them; that is, to recognise them as variants of something he has met before and which fit into a familiar pattern. This ability to recognise the essential character of an object is now well known by psychologists.

Bearing in mind the points which Stott has made, it would seem that some of the criticisms made of the traditional orthography can be made of i.t.a., which is possibly presented as something much more simple and consistent than it really is. Downing (1967a), after observing the use of i.t.a. for a number of years, has himself suggested ways in which it could be improved.

The extent to which the problems to be solved in learning to read in i.t.a. are simpler than those to be solved in learning with t.o. is difficult to assess. It is probably true that i.t.a. does contain fewer ambiguities than t.o., and each symbol does stand effectively for its own phoneme, and in this way the learning task is easier. With regard to visual simplicity for the 'look and say' approach, and to the consistency of left to right sequence of spelling, these two considerations may not add greatly to the ease of learning to read with i.t.a.

Chapter 4

A Critical Appraisal of the Design
of the Main i.t.a. Experiment

The fundamental question to be investigated by the Reading Research Unit set up by the London Institute of Education, and headed by John Downing, was that of learning to read in the early stages 'when the matter to be read is printed in a special form alleged to be easy to learn, and leading easily to a full reading skill'.* The main hypothesis to be tested was that the complexity and irregularity of the traditional orthography of English is an important cause of difficulty in learning to read.

It must be stressed that the investigation was into the effects of *a* system of simplified spelling, not any one particular system. Pitman's i.t.a. was chosen, in effect, as a representative system of simplified spelling, and this has an important bearing on final conclusions and recommendations discussed in Chapter 6.

In considering how to design the experiment, Downing (1967a), felt that although the aim was to conduct a rigorous investigation into the value of Pitman's i.t.a. as a medium of teaching reading, the results 'should be immediately meaningful to teachers and administrators'. This lead him to the

---

*This quotation is from the front page of the pamphlet issued in June, 1960 seeking moral and financial support for the i.t.a. experiment.

adoption of what is known as a 'field experiment',* which is one conducted under normal classroom conditions rather than under laboratory conditions. Burt (1967) agreed that the field experiment approach was the correct one to follow, but did point out that an approach of this kind 'entails sacrificing some of the more rigorous requirements of an ideal experimental and statistical research'.

Discussion of the variables

In a large scale field experiment, such as the one set up in 1961, there will be a large number of variables other than the one being studied, which may affect the final results. Downing (1967a), refers to these variables as 'incidental variables', and he tried as far as possible to control their influences in his design. He grouped these variables as follows:

(1) Pupil Variables:
   a) Individual, e.g. age, sex, intelligence.
(2) School Variables:
   a) Tangible,   e.g. size of school, pupil-teacher ratio.
   b) Intangible, e.g. direction of policy by headteacher, 'tone' of school.
(3) Teacher Variables:
   e.g. experience, personality.
(4) Teacher-School Interaction Variables:
   e.g. curriculum, method.

But he also points out that apart from the above variables, which can be found in any educational situation, there are certain variables which may arise as a consequence of an experiment, from circumstances incidental to its setting up or its administration. One such variable is the often referred to 'Hawthorne Effect', which results in the improved motivation of those taking part in an experiment, and which will be discussed more fully later in the chapter. Of these variables Downing writes:

*A term used by French, J. R. P. (Jr), 1954, Experiments in field settings. In Festinger, L., and Katz, D. (Eds.), *Research Methods in the Behavioural Sciences*, London, Staples Press.

One cannot claim that complete control was established over all these variables ... but by initial matching ... and later statistical analysis a determined effort was made to limit bias arising from such variables.

There were three groups of children in the first experiment, an experimental group, a control group, and a rather unusual *special* control group. The children in the experimental group of classes began reading with the basic readers and other supplementary books printed in i.t.a., whereas the children in the control group of classes began reading with the same basic readers printed in t.o. The children in the *special* control group consisted of children who had entered the control group schools one year before the experiment started. In this *special* control group no attempt had been made to induce the 'Hawthorne Effect' artificially, whereas in the control group a deliberate attempt had been made to induce the kind of motivation which seemed likely to occur in the experimental group. A comparison between the control group and the *special* control group provided a check on the success of the attempt to simulate an artificial 'Hawthorne Effect' on the control group.

The experimental and control groups were matched, as well as was possible in the circumstances, on intelligence, age, sex, social class, size of school, pupil-teacher ratio, urban/rural location, type of school organisation and certain school amenities. The vital questions posed, which will be discussed more fully in the next chapter, were answered by comparing the attainments of the experimental and control groups.

Soon after the children joined the experimental or control classes they were tested individually on Raven's Coloured Progressive Matrices, and the Crichton Vocabulary scale. Other information required for matching was obtained by questionnaire, and by visits to the schools during the first year after the school joined the research project.

The testing of the reading achievement of the children in the experiment was by standardized tests, and by the assessment of progress made through the series of basic readers. When the children in the experimental classes were learning to read with i.t.a., the standardized t.o. tests used –

the Schonell Graded Word Reading Test, and the Neale Analysis of Reading Ability, – were transliterated into i.t.a., and so were identical in every way with the t.o. tests, apart from the use of the i.t.a. writing system. In the later stages of the experiment, when the i.t.a. children had transferred to t.o., both groups of children were tested with the t.o. versions.

Downing (1967a) points out that he did not succeed in his original aim of recruiting, in the first instance, sufficiently large numbers in experimental and control groups to facilitate later matching. In September 1961 only twenty schools were found willing and able to introduce i.t.a. for beginning reading, and thirty-three schools agreed to act as controls. During the next two years schools were recruited to the experimental and control groups, but it was not until September 1963 that numbers in each group were large enough for satisfactory matching.

This modification of the original design meant that interim results, which were published in November 1962, May 1963 and December 1963,* were compiled by comparing small sections of the proposed total sample, and sections which were not completely matched. Although these interim reports urged caution until more definitive reports became available, they led on the one hand to premature controversy and criticism, and on the other to premature enthusiasm and the spread of the use of i.t.a.

One of the variables controlled was that of the reading materials used by the experimental and control groups. As the 'Janet and John' series† was the most popular series of basic readers at the time, it was decided that both groups should use it; but the experimental classes had their readers printed in i.t.a., while the control group continued to use 'Janet and John' books in t.o. To match the book corners in the t.o. classrooms, books in i.t.a. were produced for the i.t.a. classrooms, though in the early stages there were few i.t.a. books available for the book corners, and many of them had to be improvised.

---

*The three reports in Downing, J. A., *The i.t.a. Reading Experiment*, London, Evans, 1964.

†O'Donnell, M., and Munro, R., *Janet and John*, Welwyn, Nisbet.

To maintain the normal classroom conditions as far as possible, it was decided not to attempt to isolate children learning i.t.a. from their normal t.o. environment, so reference books in t.o. were still to be found in i.t.a. classes, and, of course, children from i.t.a. classes still lived in a t.o. environment at home and in the streets. However, i.t.a. books were made available in public libraries, and parents were encouraged to buy books in i.t.a. for their children for birthdays and for Christmas.

Regarding this matching of materials, Southgate (1965) points out that the favourable results of the experiment may not have been due to the new alphabet, but have been the results of what she calls a 'reading drive' which could, among other things, be initiated by a new reading scheme. She describes this drive for reading as follows:

> A reading drive is basically a new surge of inspiration through the teaching of a subject. It ferments in the teacher and bubbles over on to the children who are thrust forward on its waves of enthusiasm. The drive is accompanied by an increase in interest, motivation and application which is inevitably followed by an improvement in attainments.

She mentions some of the changes in the classroom environment which could cause a reading drive, for example, a new teacher, a new scheme or method, testing and recording. Southgate feels that.

> of all the means available to an adviser or head teacher who wishes to initiate a reading drive the introduction of brand new books must be rated most highly.

For this reason she claims that in the i.t.a. experiment the provision of reading materials favoured the i.t.a. classes, as they were provided with complete new 'Janet and John' schemes and 'they have also received stocks of new books for the book corners', whereas the control classes, in the main, just carried on with the books they had.

Downing (1967a) points out that in the initial stages there were few i.t.a. books for the book corners, and improvised 'paste-in' books had to suffice, so the i.t.a. classes were at a disadvantage in this respect. He comments:

It must be recognised that the matching of the conditions in respect of materials fell short of the ideal in the first experiment. The i.t.a. classes had new and fresh readers but suffered from a restricted choice of book corner materials, many of which were of the improvised 'paste-in' variety. The t.o. classes often had 'tired' copies of the readers, but had a much wider selection of materials for the book corner. Possibly these differences may have balanced each other out to some extent, but this must remain a matter of conjecture.

This would seem to be a fair summation of the true position with regard to the reading materials used in the experiment.

Methods of Teaching Reading

Daniels (1966) criticised the use of the 'Janet and John' scheme, as it is a series using the whole-word method, with limitations of vocabulary control and repetition; he feels that as i.t.a. is regular phonically there was no need for rigid vocabulary control in the i.t.a. primers.

Diack (1965) also criticised the choice of 'Janet and John' as the common reading scheme, and believes that the choice of 'look and say' books biased the results of the experiment from the start in favour of i.t.a. He feels that i.t.a. is a phonic approach, as against a 'look and say' approach, and feels 'it would have been rather more difficult to show that i.t.a. pupils were superior in reading ability to pupils taught by a letter-based method'.

However, both Pitman (1961) and Downing (1967a) have stressed the fact that i.t.a. is a medium, not a method, and that it lends itself to a 'look and say' or a phonic approach. Pitman writes:

It is important to appreciate that 'teaching method' is not involved . . . The mere fact that A R (i.t.a.) lends itself much better than t.o. to a 'phonic' method is immaterial to the question whether the teacher should use a 'phonic' rather than a 'look-and-say' emphasis. Equally, the fact that A R (i.t.a.) also lends itself better to 'look-and-say' than t.o. is no reason for discarding a belief in the importance of a phonic approach.

In the i.t.a. experiment methods of teaching were not prescribed for either group, and teachers were asked to carry on with their normal methods. Downing (1967a) states that the majority of teachers in i.t.a. and t.o. classes used an eclectic approach to the teaching of reading, starting with a 'look and say' approach and introducing phonics at a later stage.

Daniels (1966) feels that giving teachers a choice of method with i.t.a. debases method, and with it the skill of the teacher. He writes:

> i.t.a. only makes sense in the context of its regularity of spelling as a mechanism whereby children discover the phonic basis of reading skill.

However, from various sources comes the information that although teachers were asked to continue with their usual eclectic approach, the regularity of the i.t.a. medium encouraged both the children and the teachers in the i.t.a. classes to be aware of, and to take advantage of, the more phonic approach of i.t.a.

Downing (1964a) mentions an observer's comments that the children had been doing 'Look-Say the Phonic Way'. Similarly, Harrison (1964) writes:

> In one school the headmistress very conscientiously decided that the look and say methods used in the earlier years would be strictly maintained ... Before the end of the first term the headmistress told me the children had beaten her. The brighter ones had detected the sound values of letters and were happily word building. In the class teacher's words, 'the children had extracted the phonics through the visual consistency without any definite lead. We did not want to use phonics but by Christmas, 1961, we had to have a reappraisal of method and to follow a phonic programme side by side with "look and say".'

In describing his second i.t.a. experiment which began in 1963, and was an attempt to control more carefully the variables of the classroom situation, Downing (1966), mentions that, although the teachers were frequently reminded to use the same methods with both i.t.a. and t.o. classes:

five out of twelve teachers said that they did phonic work earlier with the i.t.a. class than with the t.o. class, but this was not seen as a change of method, because it was said to be response to the children's interest and development.

Similarly, in another context, Downing (1965) has written that 'with i.t.a., phonics is still postponed until after an initial look-say period, but now with i.t.a. it comes a good deal earlier – but still *not at the start*'.

Again Reid (1967), in her appraisal of the i.t.a. experiment, questions whether 'method' is an uncontrolled variable. She mentions that clues such as 'a few children seemed to develop phonic analysis and synthesis skills spontaneously', and i.t.a. pupils 'appeared to show readiness for phonics earlier than is usual when t.o. is used,' suggest the answer. She writes:

> It is hardly reasonable to doubt that many teachers, no longer faced with exposing children to these frustrations, would take advantage of the opportunity to give them one of the keys to the door of 'Janet and John.'

Southgate (1965), after mentioning that the training the i.t.a. teachers received in the use of i.t.a. would help towards the creation of a reading drive noted earlier, writes:

> Further, it is difficult to imagine that teachers who have undergone such training would not in some measure change their usual methods of teaching. It is unrealistic to take for granted that, because they were asked not to change their methods, they will still be proceeding as formerly.

Sceats (1967) feels that the method used is important, and points out that since the i.t.a. experiment was launched in 1961, when method was held to be of little importance, a body of opinion has emerged which holds that the chief value of i.t.a. lies in its phonic regularity. He writes:

> It is quite possible that i.t.a. may have great value when used in one way, and very little when used in another. It is even possible that the development of new methods will make the use or non-use of i.t.a. with them a matter of comparative unconcern.

Similarly, Stott (1964) points out that the main justification for i.t.a. is that it makes learning easier, by introducing greater phonetic consistency, and so if the method of teaching were not phonic this justification would be meaningless. He feels the transliteration of the 'Janet and John' books makes them phonic readers, and comments:

> It cannot therefore be maintained that use of the i.t.a. versions of these readers involved no changes in method, and the injunction to the teachers of the experimental classes to continue using their own method must have been difficult to follow.

Tudor-Hart* also maintains that there should have been some control of the teaching methods used in the main i.t.a. experiment, and in January 1965 she designed and began an experiment involving 400 children and 18 schools, all using i.t.a. However, one group of 200 children from nine schools was taught to read, using i.t.a. with an initial 'look and say' approach. The second group of 200 children from nine schools was taught, using i.t.a., but with an initial phonic approach. The full report of this interesting experiment has not yet been published, but a very recent newspaper article in The Sunday Times, 19 January 1969, commenting on this research, suggests that children learning to read using a phonic approach with i.t.a. were more advanced after four years than the children learning to read using a 'look and say' approach with i.t.a. The supporting fact was given that after four years a comprehension test showed that 38.8% of the phonic group read fluently, as against only 20% of the 'look and say' group. Although full details are not available, this experiment seems to indicate that the methods used in the main i.t.a. experiment may have been an important variable.

From the above observations of teachers and educationalists alike, it would seem that, in practice, there is some substance in Diack's (1965) criticism that in the i.t.a. experiment a comparison was made between a phonic and a 'look and say' approach (a comparison biased in favour of i.t.a.), even though the criticism is not completely valid. Diack (1965)

---

* Report by Beatrix Tudor-Hart to the Second International Reading Symposium at London in 1965.

points out that Downing himself has suggested that i.t.a. should be compared with a phonically graded scheme in orthodox print, and both Southgate (1965), and Burt (1967), suggest an experiment with a second experimental group.

It is interesting to note that in the American experiments with i.t.a., started in 1963, methodology has been more rigorously controlled. For example, Fry (1967) had three groups of children in his experiment, one group learning to read with i.t.a., one group learning to read by a Diacritical Marking System (DMS – a system of marking letters to help pupils learn their sounds), and a normal t.o. group, using a basal series of readers. The results of the American experiments will be discussed in the next chapter.

Downing (1967a), when discussing this problem in his final analysis, agrees that the matching of teaching methods was only in the general sense of leaving the teacher free to use the approach she felt was appropriate for her class, and comments:

> The weakness of this aspect of the initial experiment is that a number of variables known to be of importance in reading are not under deliberate and direct control. On the other hand, this matching of the liberal approach to teaching methods in both groups is a strength in terms of its fulfilment of the 'Field Experiment' aim to reproduce, as far as possible, the real life situation of this country, for it is probable that variations in emphasis in teaching methods may be balanced out in the quite large samples used.

The 'Hawthorne Effect'

Another aspect of the design of the experiment which caused much comment and criticism concerned the extent to which the 'Hawthorne Effect' had been controlled, in the two groups of children and their teachers.

The 'Hawthorne Effect' is the motivation which is produced in human beings by the knowledge that their behaviour is being studied in a particular experiment. This effect, well known is social psychology, derived its name from the Hawthorne works of the Western Electric Company, where a study was carried out on the effects of better illumination on production. It was found that better illumination produced an increase in output in the experimental group, which was expected, but production also increased in the control group, without improved lighting. In further experiments various changes were initiated, such as provision of rest pauses, piece-work rates, shorter working hours; and all the changes brought an increase in output in both groups. Even when all these incentives were removed, output continued to increase. The conclusion was that the workers felt that as they were being observed and were part of an experiment, it was up to them to do their best, and this was the main reason for their increased efforts, rather than the other changes mentioned above.

Downing was aware of the 'Hawthorne Effect' and took certain measures to control it in his experiment, by trying to stimulate the degree of this motivating effect in the control group, which might be expected to have been created in the experimental group, by the novelty of i.t.a.

Downing (1967a) planned that contact between the research team and the experimental and control groups should be approximately equal, but admits that, with regard to school visiting, his aim was not effective in several of the schools. Because of initial difficulties in the provision of i.t.a. materials, advice was needed on the improvisation of materials, and this led to extra visits to the experimental schools. He points out that if the early problems had not been dealt with satisfactorily some experimental schools might have withdrawn from the research project.

With regard to other visitors to the classes taking part in the experiment, Downing did not make any definite plans as he could not foresee the great public interest that would be aroused by i.t.a. He writes:

> One may generalise with some certainty that some of the experimental schools had considerably more visitors than any of the control schools.

He points out that there are likely to be both positive and negative effects arising out of such visits, but these effects are difficult to assess.

Downing (1967a) also discusses in his report the unusual publicity in the press and on television and radio for the teaching of reading with i.t.a. He comments that 'this may have been positively motivating to teachers, parents and perhaps children in the experimental group', and includes in this publicity the interim reports issued in the second year, which were very favourable to i.t.a.

In the original planning, Downing wanted to arrange meetings of teachers from both the experimental and control groups, in order to try and control the 'Hawthorne Effect' generated by the necessary meetings of i.t.a. teachers. However, as there was much more incentive for the i.t.a. teachers to meet, particularly in the initial stages, and meetings of i.t.a. teachers were greater in number, and of more vital interest than the meetings of the teachers in the control groups, Downing (1967a) comments:

> It seems probable that these meetings of control group teachers have not been truly matched in quality with those of the teachers using i.t.a.

In order to test the effectiveness of his procedures for stimulating the 'Hawthorne Effect' in the control classes to match that of the experimental classes, Downing (1967a) compared the reading standards of the control group with those of the *special* control group, who had started a year earlier and whose teachers had not participated in the experimental procedures. He states:

> In the large majority of cases there was no significant difference between the results for the pre-research pupils and the results for the pupils whose teachers participated in the research project with the special attempts to enhance factors believed to cause Hawthorne Effect... These results indicated... that there is no evidence of Hawthorne Effect in the control group.

Opinions are divided regarding the extent to which the 'Hawthorne Effect', if developed in the experimental group, affected the outcome of the experiment.

Stott (1964), feels that Downing's attempt to balance the 'Hawthorne Effect' in the experimental and control groups, by arranging meetings for both groups of teachers, failed for two reasons. Firstly, because the teachers in both groups were not performing the same functions; by this he means that the introduction of i.t.a., by causing a radical change both in the methods of the teachers and in the learning of the children, changed the functions of the experimental group. Secondly, only the experimental group teachers felt the success of the method depended upon them, and this feeling could not permeate the control group of teachers, as the harder they worked, the more their efforts would count against the success of i.t.a.

Stott (1964) also points out that headteachers took an interest in i.t.a. classes, visitors were numerous, and teachers were brought into the experiment by receiving a brochure and being invited to talks about the experiment. None of these events took place with the control classes. Stott feels that the 'Hawthorne Effect' was present in the experimental groups, and probably affected the outcome of the experiment.

Southgate (1965) feels that perhaps more important than the 'Hawthorne Effect' on the reading performances of the children in the experimental group was the effect of the 'reading drive' described earlier. She writes:

> The teacher in the experimental class trying a new way of teaching reading is certainly conscious of a drive towards better performance. Any unconscious motivation in the children attributed to the Hawthorne Effect would be increased in the experimental classes as a result of a reading drive. The more than usual pleasure and approval of the teacher when good progress is made may well raise the children's motivation to a conscious level.

Southgate (1965), in this same article, quotes examples of reading drives which have resulted in greater reading achievement, but makes the point that 'there has never been in the country, a drive in the teaching of reading in any way approaching the magnitude of the current drive'. To illustrate her point, she mentions lectures to i.t.a. teachers, workshop courses, the i.t.a. journal and pamphlets about i.t.a., visitors, the featuring of i.t.a. on radio, television and in the press, the production of a film, and the announcement of successful results from 1962 onwards.

Gardner (1965), Sceats (1967), Marshall (1965) and Daniels (1966) stress the importance of motivation in teachers and in children, and feel it a reasonable supposition that the i.t.a. groups were more highly motivated. For example, Daniels writes:

The effect of the unusual circumstances in which children and teachers using i.t.a. found themselves clearly provided a trememdous boost to motivation. I don't think the 'lectures' given to the control groups could compensate for this.

In a second, smaller experiment, Downing (1966) tried to control some of the incidental variables, including the 'Hawthorne Effect', more rigorously than the earlier study had done. In this experiment, begun in 1963, each participating school contributed one experimental and one control class, running parallel. Pupils were allocated in a random manner to these two classes, ensuring that age and sex distributions were kept constant. In any one school the two class teachers involved were asked to share their time between the classes evenly, but one of the teachers was asked to take the main responsibility for the teaching of reading with both classes, one in i.t.a., the other in t.o. The teacher concerned was asked to use the same methods, and give the same amount of time to the teaching of reading with both classes. The 'Janet and John' scheme was used in both classes, but printed in i.t.a. for the i.t.a. class, and as far as possible class library facilities were the same for both classes.

To control the differential operation of sources of motivation, meetings of parents of i.t.a. children were paralleled by similar meetings of parents of t.o. children. Visitors were excluded as far as possible, and where allowed, visited both classes. Outside publicity was prevented as far as possible.

Hence, in this experiment, school and pupil variables were controlled; some important teacher variables were controlled, such as the ability of the teacher; and an attempt was made to control the 'Hawthorne Effect'. Downing (1966) reports that the experiment was not conducted entirely as planned, but the results provided an interesting comparison with the results of the main experiment, and will be discussed fully in the next chapter.

However, certain findings in this second experiment bear on the question of motivation under discussion. Downing points out that as the same teacher took both the experimental i.t.a. and the control t.o. classes, she was able to make continuous comparisons between the two classes, and so her attitude could be affected by the differing progress the classes were making. For example, if the i.t.a. class made quicker progress than the t.o. class she might develop a more positive attitude towards teaching with i.t.a., becoming more enthusiastic about teaching in the experimental class. On the other hand, a more negative attitude might be developed towards teaching with t.o., and if progress was slower her enthusiasm for this medium might decrease.

In order to gain evidence on this particular motivational aspect, Downing asked the teachers concerned to fill in a questionnaire at the end of the first year, and he gives this information:

> Nine out of twelve reading teachers said *in retrospect* that, at the beginning of the experiment, they were of the opinion that i.t.a. would be better than t.o. . . . seven out of twelve teachers said that they had preferred teaching with i.t.a. . . . Ten out of the twelve teachers said that, quite apart from their preference for the writing system, they preferred teaching the experimental i.t.a. class.

It is interesting to note that although the possible motivational effects were controlled, differential motivational effects arose out of the teaching situation as the experiment progressed, and may have affected the results of the experiment.

On the other hand, other writers feel that the 'Hawthorne Effect' has been exaggerated. Neale (1967) feels that even if Downing's attempts to produce stimulating effects in the control group were unsuccessful, other conditions may have had a compensatory effect. In this context she mentions the 'professional pride' of the control group of teachers who would want to prove the value of t.o., and the reinforcing quality of the printed word in advertisements and books and on television, which would favour the control group.

Hemming (1967) states that he is not very impressed by the critics who say the i.t.a. results are caused by the 'Hawthorne Effect', and writes:

If Hawthorne Effect is indeed as great as some critics suggest, then we should have to write off here and now all research into methods based on matched groups hitherto attempted, including much of the research on which the methods supported by the critics are based.

After considering the evidence from both experiments on the effects of motivation, Downing (1967a) suggests that the 'Hawthorne Effect' has been exaggerated. He comments:

Indeed its absence in the Control Group of the first experiment, despite deliberate efforts to stimulate Hawthorne Effect in it, raises doubts as to whether this concept can validly be taken over from industrial experiments to educational ones – at least when such young children are the subjects.

It must be pointed out here that, from the point of view of motivation, the teachers are the subjects in the experiment, rather than the children, although it is the children's progress which is being measured. Unless the teachers are motivated and enthusiastic the children cannot be.

On Downing's final conclusion above, Reid (1967) comments:

I do not think the case for its [Hawthorne Effect] non-existence in this experiment has been proved. All that has been shown is that the efforts made to simulate it were not successful.

Warburton (1969), in his report on i.t.a. for the Schools Council, made a detailed appraisal of seventeen pieces of research on i.t.a. carried out in the UK and the USA. He comments:

There is only a small amount of contradictory and rather obscure evidence concerning the Hawthorne Effect, which seems to have had little influence in the t.o. classes, but may account for nearly half the initial superiority shown by the i.t.a. classes.

Both Hemming (1967) and Downing (1966) feel that a better way of controlling the 'Hawthorne Effect' would have been to organise a longitudinal study with groups entering the experiment in successive years, as it can be assumed that any initial enthusiasm aroused by newness and public interest would diminish to vanishing point over the years.

In summing up, the weight of opinion regarding the degree of motivation engendered in the experimental and control groups, either by the 'Hawthorne Effect', or a reading drive, or both, seems to favour the contention that the experimental group using i.t.a. was strongly motivated, and that the final results of the experiment may well have been influenced by the motivating influence of the teachers on their children.

The quality and the amount of teaching given

Other criticisms of the design of the experiment are concerned with the selection of the teachers involved in it, and with the amount of time devoted to reading in the experimental classes as compared with the control classes.

Downing (1967a) points out that a random sampling procedure was impracticable because most schools would not have co-operated, and hence, after outlining the design of the experiment at head teachers' meetings, he had to rely on volunteers both for i.t.a. classes and for the t.o. classes.

This meant, of course, that teachers could not be matched for the quality of their teaching, nor the strength of their commitment to, and enthusiasm for, a particular approach to reading. Holmes (1967) and Fry (1967) feel that Downing's inability to use a random assignment of teachers to treatments was a weakness in the design of the experiment, although unavoidable.

It has been suggested by Stott (1964), Sceats (1967) and Burt (1967) that on the whole the i.t.a. teachers were likely to be more reliable, experienced and enthusiastic than their t.o. counterparts, as they were being entrusted with a new and novel method, whereas the t.o. teachers were simply being asked to carry on as usual.

For example, Burt (1967) writes about the teachers and the 'Hawthorne Effect':

> The teachers who volunteer to try the new method are often persons with a fervid belief in its merits, and keen to demonstrate its superiority. The children's interest is excited by the change from the ordinary humdrum routine.

90

With the present inquiry the visits from the educationalists, journalists, radio and television producers threw a good deal of extra limelight on the experimental groups, and so introduced a further exciting factor.

Again, with regard to the time spent on reading in the classes taking part in the experiment, Stott (1964) and Sceats (1967) felt that it was likely that, as there was no control on this variable, more time would be given to reading in the i.t.a. classes than in the t.o. classes.

Stott writes:

If a teacher knows that her results will be carefully measured she is likely to give greater emphasis to the subject in question than if left to teach according to her own judgment. The timetable in Infants' classes is not a rigid one, so that without realising it she may give a much greater proportion of the time to reading.

And in similar vein, Sceats reports a headmaster's comment:

But one headmaster reported a common belief among his colleagues that those schools which had adopted i.t.a. had been determined to make it work to justify their decision, no matter what other things might have been dropped. Results of testing show that arithmetic did not suffer in these schools, but it might well not be arithmetic which was considered expendable.

Hence, with regard to the design of the main experiment, it would seem that the matching of the two groups was not satisfactory from the point of view of methods of teaching reading used, the 'Hawthorne Effect' involved and generated, and the quality and quantity of the teaching. In fairness to Downing it must be stressed that, because of the unusual nature of the experiment, it was impossible to control some of these variables. On the other hand, the inadequacies of the matching must be taken into consideration when the final results and conclusions drawn from those results are studied.

Chapter 5

A Discussion of the Results of the Main i.t.a. Experiment

In appraising the final results of the main i.t.a. experiment, which were released in 1967, each key finding will be presented in turn, followed by a relevant discussion of it. A convenient order of presenting the results is that adopted by Downing (1967a) in his final report, and so the questions he posed and the hypotheses he states have been used as headings throughout this chapter.

Question 1:   *Can children learn to read more easily with i.t.a. than they can with t.o.?*

Hypothesis 1:   Children in i.t.a. classes should make significantly more rapid progress through their basic reader series.

In order to provide the information to test this hypothesis, the teachers of the children in both the experimental classes and the control classes recorded their children's progress through the 'Janet and John' series, using individual record cards for each child. The most relevant part of the table Downing presents refers to the progress of the children after $2\frac{1}{3}$ years, and this is reproduced opposite. It can be seen that the experimental group using the i.t.a. edition made significantly more rapid progress through the readers. These figures are used to support the first hypothesis.

TABLE 2 Adapted from Downing (1967a), showing progress in reading basic reader series and percentage frequency distribution of reading primer reached.

	After 2⅓ years	
Reading Primer Reached	Exp. (i.t.a.) %	Cont. (t.o.) %
Non-Starters	0.7	0
At Books. Intro. I or II	9.4	25.9
At Book III	5.0	19.1
At Book IV	4.3	11.2
At Book V	2.5	6.1
Beyond Book V	78.1	37.8
N	278	278
Median Primer Position	Beyond V	IV
% Level of Significance		.1

Downing (1967a) points out that teachers were asked to note on the record cards when their children had *successfully* completed each book, but that the chief limitation of this method was the lack of a common standard of measurement among the teachers. The author, using the same criterion of progress in his experiment, found this same difficulty. Some teachers would not allow a child to move on to the next book until the current book could be read fluently and accurately. Other teachers moved a child on to the next book the moment he had struggled through the current one.

Stott (1964) accused Downing of over-generalising from these results, in claiming that children can learn to read more easily with i.t.a. than with traditional orthography. He points out:

The most that Downing's experiments would have shown (if they were valid in other respects) is that children can learn to read the Janet and John books in i.t.a. faster, etc., than the same books in traditional spelling. The danger of over-generalising from experimental conditions is well recognised in scientific method. Yet the extension of the results to reading of all kinds in t.o. is made without excuse, or even apparent awareness.

Diack (1967) is of the same opinion, and feels that the most that can be claimed from the results is that children learning to read with i.t.a. version of 'Janet and John' made better progress than children learning to read with the t.o. version of the same readers. He writes:

> If we accept the superiority of i.t.a. as proved in this context, can we go further and say therefore that any children taught by means of i.t.a. books will be superior to comparable children taught by means of books in traditional orthography? To do so would, I think, be stretching logic too far.

Diack points out that if Downing had designed phonically graded material to be used in the experiments with i.t.a., the two sets of material would have been identical in the early stages. Wall (1967) suggests that by using this argument Diack is 'begging the question', but does not proceed to elaborate.

This criticism made by Stott and Diack seems relevant and fair, as results of experiments carried out in America by Hayes and Nemeth (1965), and Tanyzer, Alpert and Sandel (1965), in which phonic approaches were compared with i.t.a., show no superiority of the i.t.a. approach over the phonic approaches in traditional orthography.

Burt (1967) gives the clearest picture of what the results in Table 2 mean to the teacher, when he writes: 'Roughly speaking, it would seem that those taught by the new method were more than one book ahead.'

Hypothesis 2: Pupils learning to read with i.t.a. should achieve significantly higher scores on reading tests in which lower-order decoding skills have an especially important role to play.

To test this second hypothesis, two tests* were used: the Schonell Graded Word Reading Test (a word recognition test) and the Neale Analysis of Reading Ability comprising three sub-tests of accuracy, speed and comprehension. The

*See Appendix.

children in the i.t.a. classes were tested on i.t.a. versions of the tests, all other conditions being held constant.

The relevant findings are presented in Tables 3 and 4, and indicate that the i.t.a. experimental group achieved significantly superior scores on all four of the measures.

TABLE 3 Adapted from Downing (1967a), showing results for Schonell Graded Word Reading Test after $1\frac{1}{3}$ years (given in i.t.a. to i.t.a. groups and in t.o. to t.o. groups).

Group	After $1\frac{1}{3}$ years	
	N	Mean
Experimental (i.t.a.)	585	33.93
Control (t.o.)	585	14.74
% Level of Significance		.1

TABLE 4 Adapted from Downing (1967a), showing results for Neale Analysis of Reading Ability measuring Accuracy, Speed and Comprehension in fifth term (given in i.t.a. to i.t.a. groups and in t.o. to t.o. groups).

Group	N	Accuracy (Mean Score)	Speed (Mean Score)	Comp. (Mean Score)
Experimental	459	24.79	26.41	6.99
Control	459	13.68	24.77	4.86
% Level of Significance		.1	5	.1

A number of writers have questioned the use of transliterated tests as a valid procedure when wishing to compare early reading ability and progress between the experimental and the control groups.

Hemming (1967) feels that when comparing reading performances it is not permissible to use, for research purposes, tests which were standardized in their t.o. forms and have been transliterated into i.t.a. Discussing Schonell's Word Test, he writes:

The list of words in this test gradually becomes more difficult to read, partly because of spelling difficulties, partly
because of increasing length, and partly because of increasing unfamiliarity. Once translated into i.t.a., the first of
these three variables is eliminated. Thus, in i.t.a. the word
'ceiling' (the 33rd in the list) becomes no more difficult to
read than 'little' (the 2nd word in the list).

Similarly, Southgate (1963–64) feels that the use of transliterated copies of well-known standardized reading tests is of
little real value. She comments·

Once a child can recognise and sound the 44 characters of
AR (i.t.a.), and has learned to blend these sounds together
to make words, it is theoretically possible for him to read
any word in AR (i.t.a.) regardless of how difficult the word
may be considered in normal print.

Again, Diack (1965), commenting on the results obtained
by both groups on the Schonell test, writes:

The i.t.a. group were shown to be significantly superior in
these tests – not unexpectedly I think. Why should not
regularly spelt words be easier to read than irregularly
spelt ones? In the i.t.a. version of the Schonell test which
was given to the experimental group all the words were, by
definition, regularly spelt.

Stott (1964) claims that the control classes were placed at
a disadvantage by the choice of the Schonell test. He shows
that in the first three books of 'Janet and John', covering 172
words in all, only four of the words appear in the first twenty
words on the test. He comments:

This means that a child taught by a sight method such as
these books are designed for, and who has used them and
no other, cannot get above a reading age of five years five
months.

Stott's point is relevant, as the author found when using
the Schonell test in his experiment that most of the words
read successfully by the children from the t.o. classes were
those which appeared in the reading scheme they were using
Schonell's own reading scheme naturally contains many o

the words which are in the test, but the 'Janet and John' series does not.

The criticisms levelled at the transliterated Schonell test apply equally to the accuracy test in the Neale Analysis of Reading Ability. With regard to Neale's sub-test of comprehension, the validity of these results can be questioned on another score. Downing (1967a) points out that in the Neale test the accuracy score sets an upper limit on the comprehension score, and because of the nature of the transliterated test, discussed above, the accuracy scores of the i.t.a. children are greater than those of the t.o. children. For example, if a child makes sixteen errors in the first of the six passages comprising the whole test, he is asked to read and answer questions about the next passage; if he makes more than sixteen errors, the test is terminated, both for reading and comprehension.

The author used this test in his investigation, and the termination of the test at this arbitrary point made him suspect the validity of the comprehension scores. Again, the tester is permitted to supply words which the child has failed to read, but many of these words are the answers to the questions asked a few moments later. Many children remembered and repeated these words when questioned; although verbally correct, the comprehension involved was questionable. Morris (1963) has also pointed out that, just by word recognition, a sentence could be read and a question answered correctly, but without true understanding.

With the foregoing points in mind, the conclusion from the results on this first question, 'Can children learn to read more easily with i.t.a. than they can with t.o.?', must be drawn with caution. A reasonable conclusion would be that young children provided with the simplified and more regular orthography of i.t.a., do master certain aspects of reading more speedily than they appear to do with the usual eclectic approach in the traditional orthography. One cannot generalise and say, as Downing does, that children learn to read more easily with i.t.a. than they can with t.o., because a comparison of i.t.a. and phonic t.o. approaches, in the American experiments, do not show i.t.a. to be superior.

Downing's conclusion that the irregularity of the traditional orthography is a cause of difficulty in learning to read

97

in the early stages is a reasonable one, but, of course, it must be pointed out that i.t.a. is only one of many ways of simplifying and regularising the spelling of English in the early stages.

Question 2: Can pupils transfer their training in reading in i.t.a. to reading in t.o.?

Hypothesis 3: In i.t.a. classes, reading achievements in t.o. should not be inferior to previous achievements in i.t.a., once fluency in i.t.a. has been established.

In order to test this hypothesis a comparison was made between the scores of the i.t.a. children on the Neale and Schonell tests printed in i.t.a., and the scores made by the same i.t.a. children when the tests were in their normal t.o. forms. The different tests were given within a month or so of one another. The relevant results are presented in the following tables:

TABLE 5 Adapted from Downing (1967a), showing the transfer of learning from i.t.a. to t.o. in Accuracy, Speed and Comprehension as measured by Neale Analysis of Reading Ability in experimental (i.t.a.) groups only, i.t.a. and t.o. test results of same subjects; fifth term.

Test	N	Accuracy (Mean score)	Speed (Mean score)	Comprehension (Mean score)
i.t.a. (Form C)	433	25.36	27.04	6.92
t.o. (Form A)	433	18.88	32.00	6.15
% Level of Significance		.1	.1	.1

Hypothesis 3 is supported in respect of only one of the three measures, that of speed of reading. But Downing (1967a) points out that approximately two-thirds of the 433 children had not been transferred to reading t.o. books when the Neale Analysis in t.o. was given. The wording of the hypothesis included 'once fluency in i.t.a. has been established', so a further comparison was made, using only the results of children who had been transferred from i.t.a. to t.o. reading at least six-weeks before the Neale Analysis test in t.o. was given. These results are given in Table 6.

98

TABLE 6 Adapted from Downing (1967a), showing the transfer of learning from i.t.a. to t.o. in Accuracy, Speed and Comprehension as measured by Neale Analysis of Reading Ability. Only the scores of experimental (i.t.a.) group subjects 'transferred' to t.o. books at least 6 weeks prior to testing are included.

Test	N	Accuracy (Mean score)	Speed (Mean score)	Comprehension (Mean score)
i.t.a. (Form C)	152	42.2	40.6	10.8
t.o. (Form A)	152	33.4	53.5	9.9
% Level of Significance		.1	.1	1

The figures in Table 6 show that even when the i.t.a. children had all transferred to t.o. there was a significant falling off in performance when they were tested in t.o.

The results given in Tables 7 and 8 provide evidence on the same hypothesis, but present the results on the Schonell test. Out of the 257 children whose results are given in Table 7 only 48% had transferred to t.o. reading, and so Table 8 gives results of 135 children who had been transferred by their teachers to t.o. reading at least four months prior to the t.o. test.

TABLE 7 Adapted from Downing (1967a), showing the transfer of learning from i.t.a. to t.o. as measured by Schonell Graded Word Reading Test given in i.t.a. in fifth term, and in t.o. in seventh term. i.t.a. and t.o. test results of same subjects.

Test	N	Mean Score
Schonell i.t.a.	257	36.49
Schonell t.o.	257	31.54
% Level of Significance		.1

The results on the Schonell Test are similar to those obtained on the Neale Test, as again there was a significant falling off when the i.t.a. group was tested in t.o. instead of i.t.a. These results indicate that Hypothesis 3 was not supported, as reading achievements in t.o. were found to be in-

TABLE 8 Adapted from Downing (1967a), showing the transfer of learning from i.t.a. to t.o. as measured by Schonell Graded Word Reading Test. Only the scores of the experimental (i.t.a.) group subjects transferred to t.o. books at least four months prior to Schonell Test in t.o. are included.

Test	N	Mean Score
Schonell i.t.a.	135	51.63
Schonell t.o.	135	44.82
% Level of Significance		.1

ferior to previous achievements in i.t.a. even though fluency in i.t.a. had been established.

Until the time the above results were published, the impressions of the transition stage by teachers and educationalists have suggested that it was a smooth process with no obvious signs of difficulty or setback, and so these results have been questioned by teachers and administrators. For example, Bartlett (1967) writes:

The results which indicate regression at the transfer stage will cause comment, particularly from teachers using i.t.a. Many have not found this at all to the degree indicated and notice little setback except for hesitancy on the part of the child for a few days.

Warburton and Southgate (1969), after examining the verbal and research evidence regarding i.t.a., came to the following conclusion:

The verbal evidence, especially from teachers experienced in helping children to transfer from i.t.a. to t.o., almost invariably indicated that children found no difficulty in transferring from one medium to the other, as far as reading was concerned. On the other hand, evidence from research was not so uniform; some, but not all researchers noted a setback in reading attainment immediately after transition.

Harrison (1967) strongly rejects this setback at transfer, and writes in a letter to the *Times Educational Supplement*:

100

I can assure your readers that when any i.t.a. children are ready for the transition, that is, when they have become fluent readers in i.t.a. and fully comprehend what they read, then they are also effective readers in t.o. at that same level.

In the same letter he criticises the design of the experiment regarding transfer, and feels a false conclusion has been reached. Harrison claims that transition was tested much too soon, as many of the i.t.a. children had not been transferred to t.o. Downing (1967a) replies that similar results were obtained when i.t.a. children who had transferred were tested, and this, the author feels, is a fair comment.

The Schonell and Neale tests are criticised by Harrison as unsuitable measures for testing for transfer. He feels that the Schonell test was inappropriate, and writes:

The removal from the child of all contextual clues meant that the child was tested under artificial conditions, and was moreover denied all the help which reading in a natural situation may be counted on to furnish.

This point is a relevant one, as all concerned with the i.t.a. experiment agree that, before being transferred, the child should be reading i.t.a. fluently, glancing at the 'top coast-lines' of words.

The Neale test, which is a reading test using narrative passages, is obviously a more suitable test to use for transfer, but Harrison criticises the use of the Neale Test on the grounds that the speed, which is measured at the same time as the accuracy and comprehension, denied to the child the time to read on and benefit by the context. He comments:

The examiner sat with a stop watch, and the child knew well he was being asked to 'beat the clock'. Accuracy measured under these conditions cannot be reliable for measuring the ability to transfer.

This point is not quite so relevant as the previous one, as the test procedures were the same for both groups, and visual and contextual clues can be taken advantage of in this particular test.

If the simplification and regularity of i.t.a. make it easier for children to read in the early stages, then it seems reasonable to suppose that, if the words become more difficult and less regular after the transfer, the children will be slowed up in their reading. Burt (1967) feels that an inferior performance would be expected after transfer, and comments:

> The difficulties seem to arise chiefly over words in which the visible word-pattern is markedly different with the two methods of spelling.

However, Downing's (1967a) analysis of the errors made in reading the words in the Schonell and Neale tests suggests that the explanation given by Burt above does not account for all the mistakes made; it would seem that some features of i.t.a. are possible sources of pro-active interference. Reid (1967) comments on this point:

> What may well happen is that children, depending on how they have learned to read initially, bring to the reading of t.o. varying combinations of recognition of similarity (whole or partial), use of context and learning of *new* phoneme-grapheme relationships like 'igh', 'ough', and so on, and that no one of these 'bridges' is enough on its own.

Daniels (1966) carried out a small but interesting experiment on transfer with twelve children between the ages of two and four and a half years. He printed the three symbols 'ʧ', 'ch' and 'th' on the tops of three pill-boxes. One symbol was pointed out to a child and also the chocolate drop underneath the top. Now the three pill-boxes were slowly shuffled and the child was encouraged to find the symbol which had been pointed out. If successful he was able to eat the chocolate drop, if not, the correct symbol was pointed out again and he had another try. The trials were continued until the child had chosen correctly ten times, then the chocolate drop was put under a second letter and so on.

Daniels carried out his experiment with the following four groups of symbols.

1.	ʧ	ch	th
2.	sh	ʃh	th
3.	oo	ee	ω
4.	sh	ʃh	ʧ

He wanted to see if Pitman's assumption that i.t.a. symbols were so like their t.o. counterparts that transfer would present no problems. For example, he wanted to see if ω is seen to be so like oo that transfer will take place easily. Below are Daniel's (1966) conclusions. Where there is a cross, Pitman's assumption seems correct, but where there is an asterisk the children did not see the letter as Pitman thought they would:

1. (a) ꞔh is seen like ch more times than like th   +
   (b) ch is seen like ꞔh more times than like th   +
   (c) th is seen like ꞔh many more times than like ch   ?

2. (a) sh is seen like ʃh and th about an equal
       number of times   +
   (b) ʃh is seen like th many more times than like sh   **
   (c) th is seen like ʃh many more times than like sh   **

3. (a) oo is seen like ee and ω about an equal
       number of times   *
   (b) ee is seen like ω many more times than like oo   **
   (c) ω is seen like ee more times than like oo   **

4. (a) sh is seen like ʃh and ꞔh about an equal
       number of times   *
   (b) ʃh is seen like ꞔh many more times than like sh   **
   (c) ꞔh is seen like ʃh many more times than like sh   **

This experiment helps us to understand the difficulties children might have at the transfer stage, and points out the need for further research; firstly, into the ways in which present i.t.a. symbols may be modified to help the transfer, and, secondly, into the most effective way of carrying out the transfer.

Question 3: *After the whole process of beginning with i.t.a. and transferring to t.o., are reading attainments in t.o. superior to what they would have been without the intervention of i.t.a.?*

Hypothesis 4: Pupils who have first learned to read with i.t.a. and then made the transition to t.o. should read the latter with significantly greater accuracy, speed and comprehension than pupils who have not used i.t.a. in the beginning.

To test this hypothesis a number of measures were administered in t.o. to both the experimental (i.t.a.) group and to the control group during the second and third years of their schooling. The first test, the Neale Test A in t.o. was given to sub-samples of the experimental and control groups in the second half of the fifth term. The results are shown in Table 9.

TABLE 9   Adapted from Downing (1967a), showing reading in t.o. at mid-second year in Accuracy, Speed and Comprehension as measured by Neale Analysis of Reading Ability Form A. Experimental and control groups both tested in t.o.

Group	N	Accuracy (Mean score)	Speed (Mean score)	Comprehension (Mean score)
Experimental	457	18.61	31.33	6.24
Control	457	16.90	29.99	5.87
% Level of Significance		Not significant	Not significant	Not significant

It can be seen from the figures in Table 9 that although the experimental group had superior scores on all three measures, the differences were not statistically significant at the 5% level. This indicates that half-way through the second year, Hypothesis 4 was not supported, but at this stage about two thirds of the i.t.a. pupils had not been transferred to t.o.

Three other measures to test this hypothesis were given during the third year as follows:

Schonell Graded Word Reading Test	– Beginning of 3rd Year
Neale Analysis of Reading Ability, B (sub-samples)	– End of 3rd Year.
Standish NS 45 Test*	– End of 3rd Year.

The results of these three tests can be seen in Tables 10, 11 and 12.

The results on the Schonell and Neale tests seem to support Hypothesis 4, that pupils who first learned to read with i.t.a. and then made the transition to t.o. should read the latter

*Reading Test: Form N.S. 45, by E. J. Standish, BSc (NFER unpublished).

104

with significantly greater accuracy, speed and comprehension than pupils who have not used i.t.a. in the beginning. However, in the Standish test although the i.t.a. pupils were slightly superior to the t.o. pupils, the difference was not significant at the 5% level and so the Standish results do not support Hypothesis 4.

TABLE 10   Adapted from Downing (1967a), showing word recognition in t.o. at beginning of third year as measured by Schonell Graded Word Reading Test. Experimental and control groups tested in t.o.

Group	N	Mean Score
Experimental	291	29.70
Control	291	24.39
% Level of Significance		5

TABLE 11   Adapted from Downing (1967a), showing reading in t.o. at end of three school years in Accuracy, Speed and Comprehension as measured by Neale Analysis of Reading Ability. Experimental and control groups tested in t.o.

Group	N	Accuracy (Mean score)	Speed (Mean score)	Comprehension (Mean score)
Experimental	194	38.97	59.07	14.77
Control	194	31.66	51.59	12.60
% Level of Significance		1	1	1

TABLE 12   Adapted from Downing (1967a), showing silent reading comprehension in t.o. at end of third year as measured by the Standish NS 45 Test. Experimental and control groups tested in t.o.

Group	N	Mean score
Experimental	175	15.70
Control	175	15.03
% Level of Significance		Not Significant

The results presented by means of which Hypothesis 4 must be supported or rejected are not at all clear cut. From the second year results we learn, as Burt (1967) points out:

> ... that although the experimental group achieved superior scores on all three measures when tested in the middle of the second school year, the improvement was too small to be statistically significant. In the second experiment we learn that 'the overall comparison is slightly, though not significantly, in favour of pupils taught throughout with traditional orthography'.

Similarly, Swales (1966) did not find any differences between his i.t.a. and t.o. groups at the end of two years.

However, many children in the Downing experiment, when tested in the second year, had not transferred to t.o., so the third year results when all the children had transferred are more important. The results on the Schonell and Neale tests are significantly in favour of the experimental groups, though the levels of significance given for the rather reduced numbers contributing to these results are not too impressive; on the other hand, the results on the Standish test do not show a significant superiority in favour of the experimental group. As Reid, (1967) points out, the result of the Standish test is a surprising one after all the earlier superiority, and is difficult to explain. She comments:

> It cannot be ignored that all the previous tests of reading have been oral – the child has heard himself reading, and has been able to solve new words by 'sounding', even though this process may have come to be complex and rapid. Is it possible that when reading has to be silent those children will be at some disadvantage who, brought up on irregularities, have not had to replace sounding habits by scanning habits to the same extent?

In this context Artley (1967) points out that the Standish test would be more nearly similar to those used to measure reading achievement in the USA, since it is a silent reading test. It is therefore interesting to note that the results obtained in American experiments, and given in Table 13, compiled by Fry (1967), show that in all the studies except one, there was no significant difference between the i.t.a. and t.o.

results at the end of the first grade on a similar test – the Stanford Achievement Test Paragraph Meaning.

TABLE 13 Showing Stanford Achievement Test Paragraph Meaning raw scores of six studies comparing i.t.a. and t.o. taught populations after one year of instruction.

Study	i.t.a.	t.o.	N
Hahn – Oakland Michigan	21.5	20.9	885
Mazurkiewicz – Lehigh	20.6	21.1	730
Hayes – Pennsylvania	21.0	19.8	365
Fry – Rutgers	17.6	20.4	393
Tanyzer – USOE Study	23.1	16.4	656
Tanyzer – NY State Study	21.4	21.4	102

It must be pointed out that when the foregoing figures were compiled some i.t.a. children had not transferred to t.o. and only the t.o. test was used. However, the above studies have been continued for another year to the point where the children have all transferred, and Fry comments that:

Now the second year studies are beginning to come in, and the main test results still show no difference favouring i.t.a.

Warburton (1969) after studying seventeen research reports on i.t.a., writes:

In these investigations, the indications are that i.t.a. is the superior medium in learning to read, but that after transition to t.o. this advantage is lost.

Downing (1967a) feels that his Hypothesis 4 is supported by his results, and states that the use of i.t.a. generally produces superior results to t.o. reading by the end of the third year. A fuller discussion of the main conclusions of the main i.t.a. experiment will be carried out in Chapter 6.

Question 4: Will children's written composition be more fluent with the simpler i.t.a. code for speech? (i.e. will the gap between their spoken and written vocabularies be narrowed?)

Hypothesis 5: The written composition of i.t.a. pupils should be longer than those of children who began reading in t.o.

Hypothesis 6: The written vocabulary of i.t.a pupils should be more extensive than that of their t.o. counterparts.

In order to assemble evidence to test Hypotheses 5 and 6, one week's written work was collected from an experimental group of 54 children who had started with i.t.a., and from a control group of 54 children who started with t.o.; the work was collected during the children's seventh term in school. The criterion for testing Hypothesis 5 was a simple count of the total number of words used in one week by each of the 108 pupils; in order to test Hypothesis 6, the total was broken down to yield a 'net' vocabulary size, consisting of the total number of different words used, and a net 'more advanced' vocabulary. The results were presented for each of nine schools and Table 14 gives examples of one i.t.a. school and one t.o. school, to show how the information was presented.

TABLE 14   Adapted from Downing (1967a), showing part of the Staffordshire study of written composition results of word analysis.

t.o. School			
School 1	Vocabulary		
Type of Word	Net	Repetitions	Total
'Basic'	57.9	98.9	156.8
More advanced	32.3	7.8	40.1
TOTAL	90.2	106.7	196.9

i.t.a School			
School 6	Vocabulary		
Type of Word	Net	Repetitions	Total
'Basic'	67.4	139.3	206.7
More advanced	29.9	10.3	40.2
TOTAL	97.3	149.6	246.9

After carrying out a study of heterogeneity of individual results by statistical methods, Downing writes:

The overall impression is that the i.t.a. children were genuinely superior in their written composition work.

He points out that the differences found may have been due to uncontrolled factors; for example, certain themes such as 'the Zoo', and 'the seaside', often associated with visits, recurred frequently, and some themes may lend themselves more than others to higher word counts and a greater proportion of advanced words.

Vernon (1967) feels that the method by which the written compositions were assessed was not very satisfactory.

Hence these findings must be accepted with caution in view of the small numbers involved, the less rigorous matching of the two groups, and the possibility of uncontrolled factors affecting the results.

Question 5: *How will children's later attainments in t.o. spelling be influenced by their earlier experiences of reading and writing the different spellings of i.t.a.?*

Hypothesis 7: Spelling attainment in t.o. after the transition stage should be superior in classes where i.t.a. was used for the beginning stage.

To test Hypothesis 7, Schonell's Graded Word Spelling Test was administered as an individual test in the middle of the third school year (Form A), and as a group test in the middle of the fourth school year (Form B). The results for these two tests are presented in Table 15.

TABLE 15   Adapted from Downing (1967a), showing t.o. spelling in experimental (i.t.a) and control (t.o.) groups as measured by Schonell Graded Word Spelling Test.

Group	Mid-Third Year Form A Mean Score	Mid-Fourth Year Form B Mean Score
Experimental	28.44	39.11
Control	25.34	32.25
% Level of Significance	Not Significant	5

The results from both the tests indicate that the pupils who originally learned to read and write with i.t.a. have t.o. spelling attainments which are superior, after the transfer, to those pupils who learned to read and write in t.o. from the beginning. However, only on the test given in the fourth year is the difference statistically significant at the 5% level. Downing (1967a) claims that Hypothesis 7 is supported by the evidence from these tests, and it does seem possible that learning to read with i.t.a. developed in the children concerned an awareness of the relationship between sound and symbol, and that each awareness could help to develop better spelling in t.o. It must be noted, however, that the superiority after the transfer of the i.t.a. group over the t.o. group is slight, and is significant only in the fourth year.

Another group of important results presented by Downing in his report is that concerned with the differences between the i.t.a. and t.o. groups' results for varying levels of achievement. These results were worked out to decide to what extent i.t.a. helped the brighter children, the average children and the slower children, as many writers have commented that i.t.a.'s real value might be in helping the slower learners to read more quickly, so reducing the number of backward readers.

Downing (1967a) presented his findings in the form of graphs, and expresses his findings as follows:

(a) the High Achievers (scores falling in the three highest Achievement Categories) in the i.t.a. group were superior to the High Achievers in the t.o. group on most tests. Gererally, among the High Achievers, the i.t.a. group demonstrated a greater degree of superiority over the t.o. pupils than was found among the Middle and Low Achievers.

(b) the Middle Achievers taught by i.t.a., though not as markedly superior to t.o. pupils as among High Achievers, nevertheless showed an important degree of superiority over the t.o. pupils in the Control Group.

(c) Among the Low Achievers (scores falling in the three lowest Achievement Categories) on the earliest tests, little or no measurable differences existed between the scores of the i.t.a. and t.o. groups. However, later tests indicate that the i.t.a. Low Achievers became superior to their t.o. counterparts, but that this was not true of the poorest students of all, represented by the lowest ten per cent of the samples.

The above findings are inferences only, drawn by Downing from a study of the graphs. Burt (1967) in his appraisal, pointing out the danger of generalising about children as a whole from mean scores, writes:

Something of this sort seems discernible in Downing's graphs for successive 'categories' or grades. Here the inferences I should draw from 'inspection of the graphs' would, I think, differ from those that he suggests. Consequently, we must wait for the more detailed discussion which he is publishing elsewhere, and which will presumably supply tests of significance.

It is obvious from the foregoing discussion of the results of the main i.t.a. experiment, that any conclusions must be drawn with caution. A full discussion of both the immediate conclusions, and the wider implications of the i.t.a. experiment, will be carried out in the next chapter.

Chapter 6

An Appraisal of the i.t.a. Experiment

*Discussion of the statistical techniques
employed in the i.t.a. experiment*

Before discussing the main conclusions of the i.t.a. experiment, a consideration will be made of the statistical treatment of the results from which the conclusions were reached, in order to ascertain the degree to which the results and conclusions may have been affected by the statistical techniques used.

In Downing's (1967a) analysis of the data, equal numbers of children from matched control and experimental schools were selected by a random procedure. This approach reduced the number of subjects involved in the analysis, but led to a better match between experimental and control populations. However, certain criticisms have been made of this statistical approach. Holmes (1967) writes:

> As expected, the rigorous attempt to adhere to broad-scale matching materially reduced the size of his sample, and therefore all his data could not be utilised. Such a loss is of grave concern, first, because ordinarily the consequence is ruinous to a longitudinal study, and second, because a certain bias may be introduced by discarding groups for which a match cannot be found.

112

Similarly, Reid (1967) comments that:

> ... it detracts greatly from the value of the results that so many different sub-samples have been taken from the initial ones. Under these conditions, statistical inference is of doubtful validity.

Holmes (1967) points out that sometimes schools were matched, sometimes classes were matched and sometimes individuals were matched; he comments that some authorities would say that the class is the only true teaching unit, and Reid (1967), Burt (1967) and Vernon (1967) made the same point in different ways. For example, Vernon writes:

> Moreover, the children were matched individually and not the school classes. This procedure inevitably introduced the factor of inter-school variability.

Another criticism of Downing's statistical approach was concerning the levels of significance which he gave with his results, and, of course, on which his conclusions must have been based. Burt (1967) points out the limitations in comparing the mean scores of experimental and control groups, though he agrees that the significance of the various differences between the means must be assessed. He writes of the term 'significance':

> By this term is meant the *statistical* significance: but the ordinary reader is apt to interpret it as implying *practical* significance. By comparing very large samples, quite small and unimportant differences can be shown to be 'significant' in the statistical sense.

Reid (1967) echoes this same warning when she writes:

> Even those who are accustomed to the techniques and the language of statistics have sometimes to remind themselves that the term, as applied to (say) an observed difference between two measures, means only that this observed amount occurs in the sampling distribution less frequently than some predetermined – and arbitrary – proportion of times, and is therefore being regarded as indicating a 'real' difference in the populations from which the samples were drawn. What the term does not mean is that the results are important: a difference could

be hugely 'significant' in statistical terms and at the same time be educationally trivial.

Reid (1967) points out that in some of the hypotheses set up, the word 'significantly' is used, but without any specification of the level of statistical significance which will be accepted; because of this she feels the expression becomes meaningless and misleading. Holmes (1967) makes the same point when he comments:

> However, Downing's greatest technical oversight in reporting the results was in *not* setting the alpha level at 0.05 or 0.01 *before* the experiment began, and then sticking to it. This practice of switching back and forth from 0.05 to 0.01 in confidence levels as suited his purpose, was not only technically inadvisable but reflected a variable decision rule.

To test for the significance of the differences between the means of the two groups, Downing chose the Kolmogorov-Smirnov* technique as his test statistic, instead of the usual method of calculating the standard error for each difference. Both Burt (1967) and Holmes (1967) feel that this choice was not a wise one, and may have influenced the results: Burt writes:

> . . . as actual calculation quickly shows, the method is apt to ascribe significance to a relatively small difference which would be rejected as non-significant by the customary procedure.

Downing (1967a) himself states that the Kolmogorov-Smirnov test is 'not a particularly satisfactory procedure'.

The foregoing points concerning the statistical techniques used by Downing seem to the author very relevant and important, as any conclusions drawn from an experiment are based on the results and on the statistical significance of those results. If the results and the statistical significance of the results can be questioned, then so, too, can the conclusions based on them.

---

*Kolmogorov-Smirnov two sample test. In Siegel, S., *Nonparametric statistics for the behavioral sciences*, New York and London, McGraw-Hill, 1956.

Burt's (1967) final comments must be heeded. He concludes:

> ... the methods of comparison here adopted are far too crude and naive to carry conviction with a critical reader, particularly since many of the crucial differences prove to be so small that their statistical significance seems highly questionable.

In contrast to the cautious approach of the research worker, it is interesting to note the impressions of Bartlett (1967) and Harrison (1967) of the published results of the i.t.a. experiment, as their views are fairly representative of teachers and administrators who have had experience of i.t.a.; Bartlett belittles much of the criticism of the experiments as follows:

> ... some of the criticisms of other evaluers suggest a love of research for its own sake, and they do not see the real 'wood for the trees'.

He accepts the final results without question and writes: 'These results are remarkable by any standards and show to the enquirer that i.t.a. is worth its place in schools.'

Again, Harrison (1967), criticising one of the less acceptable results obtained by Downing, writes:

> It is perhaps not strange that different conclusions can be reached by those who teach and see all day, and by some who come to the classroom only occasionally to measure.

These contrasting approaches to the results show how subjective as well as objective appraisal influences the extent to which a new method is adopted.

A further point concerning research experiments in general, which might have a bearing on this particular i.t.a. experiment, is that the experimental group using a new method is nearly always shown by statistical investigation to be superior to the control group. This point is made in slightly different ways by Diack (1967), Burt (1967) and Southgate (1965). Southgate comments that this is understandable, as the drive and enthusiasm of the innovator has usually been so marked in the first stages that the children's progress has been far above average. She also makes the point that ordinary teachers in ordinary classrooms are unlikely to obtain the same superior results for the following reasons:

First, it is unlikely that the teachers will be able to put into the effort the same spurt of driving force as the initiator. Second, it is probable that the teacher will not have all the desirable equipment, or books. Third, it is rare to find a new approach being used exactly as the author planned, and deviations from the author's plan are more often a detriment than an asset to the scheme.

On Southgate's third point above, evidence has been produced by Daffon (1966) that i.t.a. is not being used as it was planned to be used in certain cases. He instances the following examples:

(i) The children are being taught to read i.t.a. but are only allowed to write in t.o.; in a few extreme cases, the children are actually being forbidden to write.
(ii) The teachers are purchasing only the first third to a half of a given reading series in the new medium, and as a result, because they lack sufficient material, the transfer to t.o. is made early.
(iii) The children are expected right from the beginning to read the same book of a series in both the i.t.a. and t.o. versions.

It would seem that Southgate's view, that ordinary teachers in ordinary classrooms using i.t.a. are unlikely to obtain results as superior as the first results, is a reasonable one and suggests caution in generalising from a particular experiment to the general school situation. Again, when other first experiments such as those of Swales (1966), Jones (1968) and Fry (1967) do not show superior results for i.t.a., and when Downing and Jones' (1966) second experiment, in which they tried to control the variables more rigorously, show less superior results for the i.t.a. group in the initial stages, and in the later stages show results generally favourable to t.o., it is questionable whether one is justified in generalising the results from the main i.t.a. experiment.

Discussion of the main conclusions from the i.t.a. experiment

Downing (1967a) draws three main conclusions from the results obtained, and it will be convenient to state his conclusions and then to discuss them.

Conclusion 1: i.t.a. as an example of a transitional writing system for beginning reading and writing in English, generally produces superior results in t.o. reading, and in t.o. spelling by the end of the third year of school.

Downing (1967a) comments that the better results were most marked on tests of word recognition and accuracy in reading t.o., but that in comprehension the results were less clear; the t.o. Neale test showed positive transfer from i.t.a., but the t.o. Standish NS 45 test did not. Gulliford (1967) points out that a regularised spelling does not naturally result in better comprehension. He feels that more accurate and fluent reading could help comprehension by enabling a child to read stories and information books at an earlier point in time, but writes:

> But good reading with comprehension depends on much more beside 'lower order decoding skills' and fluency. It depends on children's maturity of experience, their range of concepts, the quality and range of their vocabulary and their general linguistic maturity, as well as the emphasis given to it in teaching.

With regard to this first conclusion, Downing (1967) also recognises that since the research has not yet followed the children into the later stages of their education, it is uncertain how eventual levels of t.o. reading skills and related attainments will be affected by beginning to read with i.t.a. A study of the figures does suggest that the levels of reading of the i.t.a. and t.o. groups may well be similar later in the children's schooling. Again, Downing (1967b), in a further evaluation of the i.t.a. results, writes:

> It must also be noted that this first conclusion depends almost entirely for its evidence on the first experiment. The second experiment has produced conflicting evidence, and until the causes of this conflict can be discovered this first conclusion must be regarded as tentative.

117

Both Burt (1967) and Morgan and Proctor (1967) feel that the results and conclusions presented by Downing are still interim ones rather than final ones. Morgan and Proctor comment:

> The impression is left that it is a definitive report so far as the early stages of reading in i.t.a. are concerned: it is 'interim' so far as the transfer to t.o. in reading and writing is concerned.

Burt (1967), in similar vein, writes:

> The results reported . . . relate to the first series of experiments planned and started in 1961. This was from the outset envisaged as a longitudinal study; and for a final evaluation we should, I think, still wait until the pupils concerned have approached nearer to the end of their school careers.

However, many of the evaluers of the i.t.a. experiment, Artley (1967), Holmes (1967), Hemming (1967), Gulliford (1967) and Neale (1967), feel that although there were experimental and statistical defects they were not so serious as to invalidate the results completely, and they would agree that these results of the main i.t.a. experiment provide some positive evidence in favour of i.t.a. Some of the evaluers, for example Diack (1967), Reid (1967) and Vernon (1967), question to what extent generalisations can be made from the results, and feel Downing has generalised too freely. Vernon writes:

> Downing therefore appears to be justified in claiming the superiority of i.t.a. over t.o. *in the circumstances in which he carried out his investigations.*

Bearing in mind the difficulties in matching the experimental and control groups, the comparison of i.t.a. with a mainly eclectic approach, the possible influences of the 'Hawthorne Effect' and a 'reading drive', and the questionable statistical techniques used, Vernon's statement above seems a fair one; and as pointed out, in other circumstances, where the experiments have been designed on different lines the results have been different.

Hence with regard to Downing's first conclusion, the

author's considered view would be that it could not be accepted as it stands. If the word 'generally' was replaced by 'in the circumstances in which the investigation was carried out', then it would be acceptable.

Conclusion 2: The success of i.t.a. in improving t.o. literacy skills occurs in spite of an important setback in the growth of these basic skills at the stage of transition from i.t.a. to t.o.

When discussing this second conclusion Downing (1967a) points out that the loss in reading ability at the transfer stage could probably be reduced in two ways. Firstly, with greater experience of i.t.a., teachers' materials and methods used at the transition period could be improved; secondly, the design of some of the i.t.a. characters might be modified to help in the transition stage, or even an entirely new system devised to combine simplicity and regularity with greater facility in transfer. Artley (1967), Holmes (1967), Morgan and Proctor (1967) and Neale (1967) agree that research is needed into the medium of i.t.a. itself, and Downing (1967a) writes:

> If the device of a transitional alphabet is to be made fully efficient, then a programme of research on the shaping of the alphabet itself and on the development of teaching techniques and materials clearly should have high priority in the next stage of this line of investigation.

This second conclusion is linked with the first conclusion, and again could be accepted within the framework of the design of the experiment, but is not one which could be generalised to all situations.

Conclusion 3: The traditional orthography of English is a serious cause of difficulty in the early stages of learning to read and write.

To support this conclusion, Downing (1967a) makes the following points:

(a) t.o. slowed down the children's progress in their series of readers.

(b) t.o. caused significantly lower scores on all tests of reading, but especially word recognition and accuracy.

(c) t.o. also produced markedly inferior results in written composition.

(d) t.o. had a seriously limiting effect on the size of the children's written vocabulary.

It has been pointed out that the matched sample used for comparing composition and vocabulary was small; the matching of the groups was not so rigorous and there were certain uncontrolled factors. Hence it is questionable whether writing should be included in the third conclusion.

This third conclusion is one which most of the evaluers accept, and one which can to a certain extent be generalised. This does not mean, of course, that i.t.a. is the only, or the best, method of simplifying t.o. to make reading easier in the earlier stages. As Downing (1967a) points out, t.o. itself can be made easier in the early stages with modified teaching techniques. Well-known techniques of the simplification of t.o. are those of Bloomfield and Barnhart (1961), Daniels and Diack (1954), Gattegno (1962) and Gibson (1965). In the research literature, simplified phonic approaches to the teaching of reading are usually found to lead to quicker progress in reading than the usual eclectic approach, but it is· important to consider the definition of reading which has been accepted. For this reason Downing's i.t.a. experiment may be added to the list of those experiments which show that a simplified approach leads to quicker progress, and that the traditional orthography, as it is normally presented, is a cause of difficulty in the early stages of learning to read.

It is interesting to note that Daniels (1966) made a comparison between the i.t.a. results and results obtained in his experiment using the phonic-word method; and shows that his results were even better than the i.t.a. results. He comments:

I place no great store by these figures except to observe that the supposedly superior results of i.t.a. are by no means so very special when compared with children taught by our own method.

This final conclusion of Downing's raises the question

of whether or not our spelling should be reformed. Had the children learning i.t.a. been able to continue without any set-back at transfer, their early rapid progress would have continued, and they would have learned more easily and more quickly. But, of course, spelling reform not only affects teachers and children, but the populations of the English speaking countries; and it is a large issue upon which a decision is unlikely to be made in the foreseeable future, though, as Diack (1965) has pointed out, when the children who have learned by i.t.a. grow old enough to make their views felt, they may be more receptive to spelling reform than present adults.

A careful consideration of Downing's conclusions suggests that they could be accepted as valid within the circumstances in which he carried out his investigation, but that they cannot be generalised with true validity. All evaluers felt that the i.t.a. experiment had been a valuable one, and that research should be continued. If a number of experiments with i.t.a., but with different designs and treatments, showed similar results then, and only then, could the common findings be generalised.

Discussion of the wider implications of the i.t.a. experiment

The i.t.a. experiment and its results have brought into sharper focus the part which phonic training plays in the early stages of learning to read.

Hemming (1967) points out that, even if i.t.a. had not appeared, we would have had to re-think our reading theory in the light of new knowledge about linguistics, perception and learning, infant logic and language development in children, but the advent of i.t.a. has highlighted this need. He writes:

> The new knowledge does not cast doubt upon look-and-say as one element in teaching reading, but it does refute some of the assumptions that the early look-and-say theorists made and promulgated, and which still live on in theory and action.

He examines and skilfully refutes four assumptions which he feels have been retarding advance in reading theory. The

121

four assumptions are worth recording as they stand:

(i) That written English is not phonetic and therefore children should be encouraged to develop other cues rather than phonic cues in recognising words and differentiating one word from another.

(ii) That young children lack the auditory discrimination to deal with the phonic structure of words.

(iii) That children perceive wholes more easily than they perceive the elements of wholes; therefore the discrimination of individual letters should be avoided at the start of reading.

(iv) That swift readers deal with words and sentences at a glance, therefore we should avoid drawing attention to letters as symbols if we want children to become swift readers.

After refuting these assumptions, Hemming argues for a return to phonics in early reading, but he stresses that phonic cues should be built into the material that is read. He writes:

The child needs the experience of the discovery and reinforcement that comes from the successful application in reading attack of phonic cues as he acquires them.

Gulliford (1967) is thinking along similar lines when he writes:

The i.t.a. experiments may also have drawn attention, as Downing suggests, to other ways of circumventing the irregularities of t.o. Indeed the trend towards a more careful and systematic development of phonics instruction was apparent before the introduction of i.t.a.

In his final deliberations on the value of the i.t.a. experiment Downing (1967a) expresses a similar view that:

A regularised spelling of English, using the present Roman alphabet without the augmentations of i.t.a., has many attractions:

(i) It could justly be claimed that there would be no unlearning of the grapheme-phoneme code used in the SRWS (simplified and regularised writing systems): these would be simply the commonest t.o

122

representations of English graphemes, and the other t.o. graphemes would then be learned as additional representations only.

(ii) Transfer could be gradual without causing confusion; that is, the additional t.o. symbols could be introduced gradually.

(iii) Transfer should be more effective because a SRWS using Roman letters only would be closer to t.o.

(iv) Acceptance would be easier because the SRWS would look less strange to teachers, parents and other people.

(v) t.o. printing type-founts and t.o. typewriters would not need to be modified.

The above points have been quoted in full, as the most important outcome of the i.t.a. experiment could well be the creation of a new simplified and regularised writing system incorporating the experience of teachers using i.t.a. and the findings of laboratory experiments which Downing urgently recommends.

Diack (1967) has stated that he welcomes the amount of publicity given to i.t.a., as he feels that anything that works towards improving the system of spelling is helpful. He also feels it was short-sighted to state that teachers need not change their methods, as this implies that no re-thinking about the teaching of reading is necessary. Both Hemming (1967) and Gulliford (1967) feel that a teacher's understanding of how children learn to read is of vital importance to the children's progress. For example, Gulliford writes:

Of all the factors influencing progress in reading in schools, I believe the most important is the teacher's understanding of the processes involved in learning to read and how, on this basis, to organise instruction in large hetero-geneous classes.

Many evaluers feel that the i.t.a. experiment has encouraged teachers and educationalists to think afresh about the teaching of reading. Burt (1967) sums up this feeling when he writes about the report on the experiment:

No one can read the preceding report without recognising that we now know far more about the processes of

123

reading and of learning to read than we did before the experiments were undertaken.

In America interest in i.t.a. is strong, not only because of the improved standards of reading it is felt might result, but because it fits in with the current revolution in the curriculum in American schools. Children there are being encouraged to try new ways, new experiences, to discover and create, and to learn in a more independent, meaningful way. It is felt that i.t.a. may be helpful to the independent probing of the curious pupil. Similarly, in this country the trend is away from mechanical learning and towards 'insightful' learning, which comes through experience and discovery. This kind of learning is now common in primary schools, and learning to read with i.t.a. may be in keeping with this heuristic approach to learning.

Earlier interim reports of the i.t.a. experiment stressed that children, because their learning was more independent of the teacher, became more confident, competent and more mature in their outlook. Little was made of these earlier findings in the final report on i.t.a., though many teachers and administrators felt this was an important omission. Bartlett (1967) writes:

In spite of it not being mentioned in the report, children using i.t.a. do show improved self-confidence, greater enthusiasm for books and improved creative writing – these were not 'testable' and as such were not included by Downing, but if the evaluers will visit the schools and talk to the teachers they will find out whether or not this is so.

Hemming (1967) feels that some setback at the transfer stage is a small price to pay for the heightened self confidence the children show in the early stages.

Gulliford (1967) also feels that indirect benefits may well come from the use of i.t.a. He writes:

That i.t.a. accelerates the process of learning to read in the early stages is a strong point in its favour. Even though final achievement may not be markedly or conclusively superior, there may well be less tangible benefits such as feelings of success, the development of learning sets in reading and greater freedom in written work.

Downing (1967a) writes in similar vein that:

Happiness of infants during their stay in infants' classes is in its own right a matter of importance and if a new approach (such as i.t.a.) can make learning to read more enjoyable in these years then this new approach should be adopted even if in later years there appears to be no long term effects one way or another.

In this context it is interesting to note the enthusiasm which teachers using i.t.a. show for the new medium. Until very recently, few teachers have been known to return to teaching with t.o., and many say they would continue using i.t.a. even if it is shown that i.t.a. children eventually lose their superiority in reading; i.t.a. would be favoured because of the heightened confidence and independence generated by children learning to read with this approach. However, in very recent months the author has talked to head teachers who are either changing back to t.o. or considering doing so. The main reason given for this change of heart is that the eventual gain of using i.t.a. rather than t.o. is not sufficient to outweigh the practical difficulties of continuing with the new medium.

Another wider aspect of the i.t.a. experiment is the involvement of junior schools in the teaching of i.t.a. to those pupils coming to them from infant schools who have not transferred to t.o. Downing's (1967a) results show that the very slowest children made very little progress and no more reading progress than their t.o. counterparts. This is borne out in the teachers using i.t.a. and is understandably so, for as Gulliford (1967) points out:

Most schools have a few children who are mentally and personally immature. They are often linguistically retarded; their perceptual development is not up to the tasks of visual and auditory discrimination and their visual-motor performance is poor, as shown in immature drawings and shape copying.

In other words there were children who were not ready to read, and who, in the first stage of their school careers, could not benefit even from a simpler approach to the teaching of reading. This finding, of course, gives further weight to the view developed in Chapter 2 that the concept of reading readiness cannot be ignored.

The presence of slow learners means that the use of i.t.a. requires a longer course than is often contemplated, and for slow learners it needs to extend into the Junior School. Harrison (1967) supports this view when he comments:

> In Oldham, where every child is now taught by i.t.a., the Junior Schools expect some 25% of the children who come to them to be still reading i.t.a. by that time.

In an investigation of i.t.a. in the Junior School, Sceats' (1967) findings agreed with those of Harrison, that, on average, about 25% of children entering the Junior Schools had not transferred to t.o., but as can be seen from the figures given in Table 16 there were the widest of differences between individual schools – the percentage ranging from 0% to 100%.

TABLE 16   Adapted from Sceats (1967), showing the number of children in the First Enquiry entering Junior classes still reading i.t.a. in September 1965.

School Number	Number of children entering Junior classes in 1965 taught by i.t.a.	Number still reading i.t.a. on entry	Percentage
1,13	110	7	6
2	6	nil	nil
3	28	13	46
4	30	nil	nil
5	108	28	26
7,8	28	28	100
9	48	21	43
10, 11	18	8	44
12	41	nil	nil
14	105	8	8
15	47	5	9
16, 17	40	8	20
18, 19	32	6	19

The fact that about a quarter of the children learning to read with i.t.a. will not have transferred to t.o. when they reach their Junior Schools raises the question as to how these

126

children will be received in the Junior Schools, and what provision will be made for them to continue along the lines on which they started. Gulliford (1967) pinpoints the problem when he writes:

> In considering the use of i.t.a., steps will have to be taken to ensure that i.t.a. can be efficiently continued, otherwise it will bear hard on slow learners and reading failures whose need for improved methods of instruction is the greatest.

Harrison (1967), again referring to the Oldham Education Authority, states that there is no effort to impose t.o. on those who have not transferred when they reach the Junior School, and that all Junior School reception teachers have had instruction in i.t.a. However, as all the children in this authority are learning to read with i.t.a., provision for a continuation of method has been made; but where only a few infant schools, scattered over a wide area, are using i.t.a., then the picture is not so clear. Teachers at the conference* convened to discuss the i.t.a. report, mentioned the pressure from the Junior School for transfer to t.o. to be completed by the end of the infant school.

Goodacre (1967) points out:

> This is perhaps not surprising when one recalls that Dr Joyce Morris, in her recent book, stresses the fact that one in four of our first year Junior teachers are likely to have no training in infant methods. What are the chances of these teachers being familiar with i.t.a. and therefore able to cope with those pupils who have still to tackle the transfer from i.t.a. to t.o.?

Stott (1964) holds a similar viewpoint concerning i.t.a. in the Junior School, and comments that:

> Group methods are less used in the junior departments, and the curriculum is widened in such a way that progressively less time is devoted to basic skills and more to the use of them ... The difficulties of organisation

*Press Conference on the first national report on i.t.a. held in London, 30 January 1967.

127

which a temporary teaching medium entails would consequently bear hardest on the slowest part of any year-group.

Sceats (1967) is also aware of the difficulties which may arise when i.t.a. children still reading in i.t.a. join the Junior School. He makes the point that the continued use of i.t.a. (and he found children of eight and nine still using it) may become associated with failure and backwardness in children's minds. He writes on this point:

This is a real danger, but it may be avoided by the development of a non-competitive climate of thought in the classroom, which is desirable also on other grounds.

To create such a climate would be no easy task, and impossible if the teachers concerned were not sympathetic to i.t.a.

In trying to make a final statement about the value of the i.t.a. experiment it would be satisfactory and fitting to accept what Downing* considers to be a fair and conservative judgment, namely, that i.t.a. did not do any harm, and that if less direct factors such as i.t.a.'s role as a confidence builder are considered, then his judgment would be more positively in favour. Downing has shown that his research was worthwhile and made a good case for the continuation of research into i.t.a.

Now follows the question: In view of the research evidence should teachers be recommended to use i.t.a.? Wall's** verdict would be that teachers *should* be encouraged to use i.t.a., but it should not be pushed in any way. Nisbet*** feels that widespread adoption of i.t.a. would prevent further development of i.t.a. as a medium, as the more it was used, the more difficult it would be to improve it. On the other hand, a final recommendation of Downing's (1967a) is that:

The Initial Teaching Alphabet as at present constituted should be introduced into more schools, so that it can

*Dr J. A. Downing. **Dr W. D. Wall ***Professor J. Nisbet. Speakers at a conference held by the National Foundation for Educational Research at the Institute of Education, London, on 15 April 1967.

become more generally available to beginners learning to read and write.

The above recommendation might be reasonable if experiments to improve the writing system of i.t.a. could be carried out at once. Unfortunately, the Reading Research Unit formerly attached to the University of London has been forced to close down through lack of funds, and so the probability of the required research being carried out is very considerably reduced. This being the present situation, the author is inclined to support Nisbet's view, as the more schools which adopt i.t.a. in its present form – which has been shown to be far from ideal – the more difficult it will become to improve it both for reading and writing on the lines which Downing himself suggests.

However, Warburton and Southgate (1969), write:

... our final recommendation is in favour of the use of i.t.a. (albeit with many qualifications) ... The evidence suggests that, for most children in most schools, the use of i.t.a. as an *initial* teaching alphabet would considerably raise the children's standards of reading and their rate of scholastic progress, although it seems likely that this advantage will be lost after the transition.

Hemming (1967) believes that in the last analysis, the best method for any infant teacher to use is the one in which she believes, and perhaps in this view lies the answer to the question. If a teacher believes that the use of i.t.a. will benefit her children, and the Head is sympathetic, then she should be encouraged to use it; no pressure should be exerted from above on an unwilling teacher.

Before concluding this chapter, which brings to an end Part I, due praise must be accorded to Dr Downing for the design of, and the successful completion of, the first main i.t.a. experiment. Criticisms of various aspects of the experiment have been made, but as Wall (1967) has correctly pointed out:

Most of the contributors pay a well deserved tribute to Downing for his attempt to control these variables as far as possible, and applaud the caution with which he presents his results.

F

The author, who has followed the i.t.a. experiment with great interest from its conception and been in constant contact with the Reading Research Unit of London University Institute of Education, would like to add his own tribute to Dr Downing for his valuable work.

PART II
THE INVESTIGATION

Introduction

In Part I a review has been made of the research literatur felt to be relevant to the problem under investigation. It wa with this background of knowledge that the author decidec upon, and carried out, this particular research investigation Part II is an account of this investigation, and describes th methods and measures used and discusses the result obtained.

The author decided to make a comparison between th reading readiness and early reading progress of childre learning to read with i.t.a. and of children learning to rea with t.o. The main purpose of the study was to ascertai experimentally the difference, if any, between the readir readiness requirements necessary for the satisfactory readir progress of children learning to read with i.t.a. and t.o.

The method of approach was to enlist the co-operation sixteen schools – eight schools where the children were lear ing to read with i.t.a. and eight schools, matched as well possible with the i.t.a. schools, where the children were lear ing to read with t.o. The original total sample was 300 chi ren, 150 in each group, but family removals and the matchi of the two groups reduced these numbers to 119 in each gro during the first two years of experiment and to 102 childr in each group during the third year.

The children in the experiment were studied over a thr year period, during which time the children learning to re with i.t.a. had transferred to t.o. and been given the opp tunity to make good any setback in reading achieveme experienced after transfer. Reading readiness consideratic were the main ones in the investigation, but it was realised that true reading standards, needed for comparison with standards on reading readiness measures, are not established until the children who started to read with i.t.a. have been reading for a reasonable length of time in t.o. after the transfer. This meant testing and observing the children who were taking part in the experiment over a period of three years.

After being in school for approximately six weeks, all the children in the sample were given reading readiness tests of visual and auditory discrimination, tests of mental ability, and a test of vocabulary. At the same time the class teachers of the children were asked, firstly, to rate each child on a five point scale for a number of reading readiness evaluations including mental abilities, physical attributes, social and emotional traits and language development; and, secondly, to give the fathers' occupations and details of any homes which were other than normal. The information gained from tests, evaluations and teachers' reports enabled the later matching of the i.t.a. and t.o. groups and sub-groups to be made.

At the beginning of the children's third term in school, two of the reading readiness tests were given again to the whole sample, namely, the tests of visual and auditory discrimination constructed by the author. These two tests were given again, firstly, to measure progress made in these two skills, and secondly, to see if the children learning to read with i.t.a. had in any way developed these skills differently from the children learning to read with t.o. Also at this same time, a first reading achievement test was given to all the children. The usual form of the test was given to the t.o. group, but a transliterated version of the same test was given the i.t.a. group. In this way initial progress in learning to read was assessed.

After a further term, that is, at the beginning of the child-ren's fourth term in school, the same reading achievement test was repeated, together with a second more comprehensive reading test; transliterated versions of the tests were used with the i.t.a. children.

Reading achievement and progress was again measured at the beginning of the children's sixth term in school. At this stage it was found that many children had transferred to t.o., and where this had occurred the children concerned were tested in t.o. Those children still reading with i.t.a. were tested in both i.t.a. and t.o.; in these cases the t.o. test was given to the children first, as, being the more difficult, the taking of the t.o. test would not affect the i.t.a. scores to any great extent. A comparison of i.t.a. and t.o. scores made by the same children, at the same time, on the same test, provided interesting evidence regarding the ease of transfer from i.t.a. to t.o.

The final reading achievement tests of the investigation were given at the beginning of the children's ninth term in school, when some of the children had moved on to Junior Schools or Junior Departments. The same two reading achievement tests were given, but this time only the t.o. versions were used.

In addition to the standardized objective measures of reading achievement, the teachers of the children concerned kept records of each child's progress through the basic books of the reading scheme being used, and this gave another measure of the children's progress in reading. At the end of this introduction is a table showing the main stages in the three year testing programme with the tests used.

To make a valid study of this nature as outlined above it is important:

1. to select valid and reliable tests of all attributes to be measured;
2. to administer such tests under satisfactory test conditions to representative and well-matched groups of five year old children who have been in school the same length of time, and who are approximately the same age;
3. to give adequate statistical treatment to the data obtained in order to ensure that valid conclusions are reached regarding the relationships investigated.

A discussion and description of the tests used will be found in Chapters 1 and 2, a description of the children and schools used in Chapter 3, and a description of the statistical treatment and discussion of the results in Chapters 4 to 9, followed by the summary and conclusions.

TESTING PROGRAMME 1965–1968

First Year	Tests given and evaluations made
1st Term (Oct.–Nov. 1965)	Visual discrimination – Thackray Making visual discriminations in i.t.a. – Harrison Stroud Making visual discriminations in t.o. – Harrison Stroud Auditory discrimination – Thackray Making auditory discriminations – Harrison Stroud Wechsler Intelligence scale for children (Verbal tests only) Goodenough 'Draw-a-Man' Test Vocabulary Profile – Thackray Fathers' occupations and notes on home backgrounds Reading Readiness evaluations
3rd Term (April–May 1966)	Visual discrimination – Thackray Auditory discrimination – Thackray Schonell Graded Word Reading Test (first time given in i.t.a. in experimental schools and in t.o. control schools)

Second Year	Tests given
4th Term (Sept. – Oct. 1966)	Schonell Graded Word Reading Test (second time given in i.t.a. in experimental schools and in t.o. in control schools) Neale Analysis of Reading Ability – Form A (first time given in i.t.a. in experimental schools and in t.o. in control schools)
6th Term (April – May 1967)	Schonell Graded Word Reading Test (third time all children tested in t.o., but where i.t.a. children had not transferred they were tested also in i.t.a.) Neale Analysis of Reading Ability – Form B (second time all children tested in t.o., but where i.t.a. children had not transferred they were tested also in i.t.a.)

Third Year	Tests given
9th Term (April–May 1968)	Schonell Graded Word Reading Test (fourth time all children tested in t.o.) Neale Analysis of Reading Ability – Form A (third time all children tested in t.o.)

NB. Throughout the testing period teachers kept records of their children's progress through the basic books of the reading scheme.

Chapter 1

Discussion of the Testing Measures Selected and Constructed (I): Tests of Specific Reading Readiness Skills and Reading Achievement and Progress

In order to compare the reading readiness requirements of children learning to read with i.t.a. and the reading readiness requirements of children learning to read with t.o., three main statistical approaches were envisaged. Firstly, it was decided to give all the children in the investigation a number of reading readiness tests soon after entering school, and to correlate the scores on these early tests with the scores on the reading achievement tests given later, calculating coefficients for the i.t.a. and t.o. groups separately. A comparison of the correlation coefficients obtained would provide information about the reading readiness requirements of these two approaches to the teaching of reading.

Secondly, it was decided to take five levels of performance achieved by sub-groups of i.t.a. and t.o. children on the various reading readiness measures, and for each level to compare the mean scores attained by the same sub-groups of i.t.a. and t.o. children on the reading achievement tests given later. If it was found that similar levels of performance on the reading readiness tests led to different levels of reading achievement, then again some knowledge could be gained of the reading readiness requirements for learning to read with i.t.a. and with t.o.

Thirdly, a decision was made to compare the mean scores attained on the reading achievement measures, by sub-groups of i.t.a. and t.o. children with similar mental ages, to see if one approach to the teaching of reading required a higher level of mental ability than the other.

As there are no British reading readiness tests at present, the author had to consider American tests, particularly those which included sub-tests of visual and auditory discrimination. These two measures are central to the investigation, as it is claimed that i.t.a. is simpler than t.o. in both its visual and auditory structure, and that this relative simplicity is responsible for the quicker progress made by the children learning to read with i.t.a.

In the author's previous experiment a careful study was made of the widely used American reading readiness tests, and for a number of reasons* the Harrison-Stroud Reading Readiness Profiles were chosen. In that investigation the tests (anglicised) were found suitable for use with five year old British children, and they proved a valid measure of readiness for reading, as the results of the 183 children tested correlated at .59 with the later reading achievement results of the same children. Again, in that experiment the visual and auditory discrimination tests correlated the most highly with later reading achievement at .50 and .54, respectively.

A brief description of the two tests now follows, and the type of item in each test is given as an example.

Harrison-Stroud Reading Readiness Profiles
Test 2. Making Visual Discriminations (t.o. version)

The ability to make accurate visual discriminations with words is basic to all reading. This skill is necessary, both for the building up of a sight vocabulary, and for later rapid reading, when quick recognition of known words is essential. This test uses words common to primary reading vocabu-

*Thackray, D. V., *A study of the relationship between some specific evidence of reading readiness and reading progress in the infant school*, M.A. in Education, 1964, pp. 223–226.

laries, words commonly confused visually, such as 'horse' and 'house', and words commonly reversed, such as 'on' and 'no', 'was' and 'saw'.

An example of the type of item contained in Test 2:

book	boat	boot	book	hook

Test instructions for sample item from Test 2:
1. Move your finger down to the green box under the black box . . . Draw a line under the word in the little box . . . Slide your finger along the long box. Now draw a line under one word in the long box to show that it is like the word in the little box . . .

Harrison-Stroud Reading Readiness Profiles
Test 2. Making Visual Discriminations (i.t.a. version)

The author decided to transliterate this test into i.t.a. and to give the transliterated form of the test to all the children in the sample, irrespective of the medium to be used to teach them to read. The t.o. and i.t.a. versions of the test were identical in format, layout, size of print and test instructions; the only difference was that of transliteration.

Same example from Test 2 transliterated in i.t.a.

bʊk	bœt	bɷt	bʊk	hʊk

The two versions of the visual discrimination test were given six weeks after the children had started school, so, in general, at the stage before the children had started to read formally; this means that the tests required the matching of words rather than the reading of them. As the words used in this test are the most commonly used words in the first books of reading series, the author felt that a comparison of the mean scores on the t.o. and i.t.a. versions of the same test might indicate whether one medium was more simple visually, in the early stages, than the other.

Harrison-Stroud Reading Readiness Profiles
Test 4. Making Auditory Discriminations

The ability to make auditory discriminations is basic to the work of word analysis, which begins soon after the child has acquired a sight vocabulary and continues throughout the primary school. A child must be able to hear that two words, given orally, begin with the same sound, if he is going to develop the phonetic skills which help him to determine, independently, the pronunciation of strange words. Test 4 measures this ability to discriminate between spoken words which do, or do not, begin with identical initial consonant sounds.

An example of the type of item contained in Test 4:

Test instructions for sample item from Test 4:
1. Slide your finger along to the black box. Find a bed, a doll and a bear ... Draw a line under the bed ... The name of one of the other things begins like bed. Draw a line from the bed to the other thing in the box whose name begins like bed.

140

Use was made of two further tests of visual and auditory discrimination devised and constructed by the author especially for the purpose of this investigation; these will be described later in the chapter.

In order to understand fully the specific purpose of the author's tests, mention must first be made of a small, but very relevant, study carried out by Sister John (1966), who is interested in the problems of perceptual learning and the ways in which the development of perceptual skills in young children are influenced by the learning situation. After observing four-year old children who were learning to read with i.t.a., discriminating successfully between symbols which seemed to demand a greater awareness of finer differences than did t.o., Sister John felt that in using i.t.a. the children were not only learning to read with greater facility, but were also learning to discriminate more easily. She comments:

> The new teaching medium provides a well structured situation in which a constant association exists between different visual and auditory forms. The security which this offers should help the child to benefit from his experience. The need to make discrimination will provide training in this skill.

Sister John made two studies to test her hypothesis that, in the perceptual discrimination of visual and auditory symbols, children who are learning to read with i.t.a. will be superior to children learning with t.o. The first study attempted to measure the difference in perceptual discrimination between children who had already had experience with i.t.a. and a control group.

In a more important second experiment she attempted to isolate the effects of the teaching medium more accurately by obtaining an estimate of the improvement of perceptual discrimination during the first year at school. For this second experiment Sister John used her own tests of auditory and visual discrimination, and tested, individually, two matched groups of children, one group learning to read with i.t.a., the other with t.o. The children who had started school in September were tested a month later in November and then again with the same two tests the following May.

141

The visual discrimination test was made up of the two sub-tests of matching and recognition; the auditory discrimination test involved the recognition of initial sounds of words. In Table 17 the results of Sister John's second experiment are presented.

TABLE 17 Adapted from Sister John (1966), showing the number of children in each group who were above the mean on each of the three tasks of Matching, Recognition and Auditory Discrimination.

Group	November			May		
	Matching	Recognition	Auditory Discrim.	Matching	Recognition	Auditory Discrim.
i.t.a. (n = 19)	8	10	15	10	11	11
t.o. (n = 19)	6	10	12	7	4	4
C.R.	.45	0	1.15	.94	2.3 $P < 0.05$	2.3 $P < 0.05$

As can be seen from the figures in the above Table the performance of the children in the i.t.a. and t.o. groups were similar in November, but by May there was a reasonably marked difference in favour of the i.t.a. group. These results seemed to give confirmation to Sister John's hypothesis that the different teaching media would show differential effects on the growth of discriminative abilities.

This finding seemed very relevant to the author's investigation, as it suggests that the favourable progress made by children in the early stages of learning to read with i.t.a. could be due not only to the visual and auditory simplicity of the media, but also to the favourable effects i.t.a. has on the growth of perceptual discrimination.

As Sister John's study was with a very small sample, the author decided to carry out a similar investigation with his much larger sample; and as individual testing of large numbers is so time consuming, it was necessary to construct group tests of visual and auditory discrimination for this purpose. It was decided to give these two tests in November, a few weeks after the children in the sample had started school, and again the following May, to see to what extent, if any, the different teaching media had affected the growth of discriminative abilities. This meant that the test items finally selected had to be very carefully graded, covering a wide range of ability, so that a comparison of the initial and later scores on the same tests for each group would reflect any differential effects on the growth of perceptual abilities by the use of either i.t.a. or t.o. in the early stages of learning to read.

Now follows a description of the design and construction of the tests of visual and auditory discrimination constructed by the author.

1. Visual Discrimination of Graphic Symbols Test

When devising this test, the author's main considerations were, firstly, the kind of test material to be used, and secondly, its presentation in the form of a group test.

As already mentioned, this test was to be given in November and again the following May, by which time the children in the experiment would have been learning to read, in either i.t.a. or t.o., for some months. It was therefore realised that the test material would have to be independent of both i.t.a. and t.o. if the scores obtained were to be valid. This seemed to indicate non-verbal test material using, for example, geometrical designs. However, previous research indicates clearly that tests of visual discrimination, using non-verbal material, do not correlate as highly with later reading achievement as those tests which use letters or words.

It seemed reasonable to suppose that the answer to this problem lay in the use of alphabetic forms other than our own, which differ in their visual presentation to the extent that, whilst still recognisable as writing, they bear little, or no, resemblance to our own Roman form. A brief study of the eastern alphabets quickly showed that Chinese, with its 30,000 complicated ideogrammatic forms, and Arabic, with its extremely cursive forms and negligible differentials, were much too difficult; likewise the various Indian alphabets. Russian and Greek were also considered, but both these alphabets contained characters either identical or very similar to our own.

Sister John, who had the same problem of choosing

independent test material, used the Greek alphabet. However, the author felt that this alphabet was not sufficiently neutral, as our own Roman alphabet was developed by way of the Italo-Greek alphabet, which in turn developed from one of the later western forms of the Greek alphabet. To illustrate the similarity of the two alphabets it is interesting to note that out of the 24 characters of the Greek alphabet, in the capital form, 14 are identical to those of our own alphabet, both in their printed and written forms, namely, A, B, E, H, I, K, M, N, O, P, T, X, Y and Z. In the lower case Greek letters the resemblance is not so marked, but nevertheless it was felt that there was sufficient similarity to make it impossible to present a completely unfamiliar set of visual symbols to the child. To illustrate the similarity of the Greek lower case letters to our own Roman alphabet, a, v, o, s, p and x are identical, and b, d, e, i, k, t and u are almost so.

Because of the unsuitability of the eastern alphabets, it was decided to trace the successive stages of writing through their pictographic, ideographic and phonetic forms (i.e. syllabic signs and symbols representing primary oral sounds) to the evolution of the various alphabets, some now extinct and unsolved. One pre-alphabetic script which was of particular interest to the writer because of its clarity and simplicity was the old Persian Cuneiform ('wedge-shaped'). An example is given here of their equivalent of the word 'rain'.

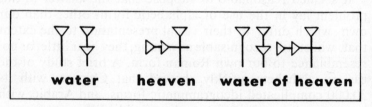

Figure 7 Showing an example of cuneiform – the equivalent of the word 'rain'.

Two other alphabetic systems were of interest to the author, as they have a special connection with the British Isles. These were the Runes and Oghams and examples are given here.

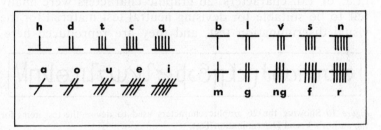

Figure 8 Showing the top line of Runic inscriptions in Anglo-Saxon on one face of a whale-bone box (8th–9th centuries) in the British Museum.

h	d	t	c	q		b	l	v	s	n

a	o	u	e	i		m	g	ng	f	r

Figure 9 Showing an example of Oghams which are of Celtic origin and date from about the fifth century.

On the above examples of Oghams it can be seen that a horizontal line is common to all the symbols, and that differing sound characters are made by adding straight lines above, below or through the common horizontal line, for example, ⊥⊥, ⊤⊤, and ╫. This positioning above and below the line, which is not used in other alphabets, seemed similar, for purposes of recognition, to the ascenders and descenders in the lower case forms of our own alphabet.

This brief analysis of the various alphabets indicated that they all had the following basic elements in common:

i) straight lines;
ii) curved lines;
iii) straight and curved lines used together.

Different characters were designed by varying these three basic elements in some or all of the following ways:

(a) length of the lines;
(b) direction of the lines, i.e. horizontal, vertical, slanting;
(c) position of the lines in relation to an imaginary horizontal line, i.e. above, below or intersecting;

145

(d) number of the lines, i.e. used singly or in multiples, to present different shapes, and attached to each other in different positions (top, bottom, right, left) and so presenting different angles.

Bearing these basic elements and their variations in mind, the author evolved a series of 47 graphic characters. Of these 47 hieratic-like characters, a number were eliminated as they were felt to be either too complex or too close to existing i.t.a. or t.o. characters. 26 graphic characters were finally felt to be suitable for devising neutral test material for the visual discrimination test, and they are reproduced here.

Figure 10 Showing the 26 graphic characters used to devise the test items for the author's Visual Discrimination Test.

From these 26 graphic symbols a group test of 90 items was devised, made up of 30 items containing single characters, 30 containing groups of two characters, and 30 containing groups of three characters, to simulate the idea of letters and words. The 30 items of a similar nature were kept together and the test booklet progressed from the one symbol items, to the two, and then to the three symbol items, as it was felt that this would prove to be the order of difficulty.

Each item was boxed by a coloured line. The boxes were coloured green, red and black consecutively in order to help the child to find the correct place in his test booklet, as the colour of the box was always referred to in the test instructions. Each item was designed so that a child could be asked to draw a line under a drawing in, for example, a 'little green box', and then asked to draw a line under the same drawing in 'the long green box'. He had to choose the right one from four drawings, and two practice items helped him to know what to do.

A pilot survey was then conducted, using a test booklet containing the 90 items described above. Over 100 children in seven representative infant schools were tested in groups of approximately 15. In the sample tested, the ages of the children ranged from 4 years 9 months to 6 years, some children being in their first term at school, some in their second term, and some in their third term. It was necessary to test for this range of ability as the test in its final form had to be given to children in their first and, later, third terms in school.

The results of this pilot survey were analysed carefully and showed that:

(i) Young testees (1st term) found it a little difficult to match the first practice items, and so it was decided in the final form to include a third very simple practice item using clear geometrical symbols which were within the child's experience.

(ii) Minor alterations would have to be made to the verbal instructions, and these were subsequently made.

(iii) Some of the items involving single characters appeared to be more difficult than some two and three character combinations, and so in the final form the items were arranged in the apparent order of difficulty.

(iv) Some items were too easy and some too difficult, and these were eliminated.

(v) The 90 item test took about an hour to administer, though, of course, the children taking part were given frequent breaks.

(vi) The children quickly realised what was expected of them, and after about six items had been completed altogether they were able to do the rest of the items on their own. It was noticed that some children failed to turn over a page, and some children missed out pages, and these points were duly noted in the final test instructions.

Using the results of the pilot survey, the test was revised and the final form contained 34 items roughly graded in difficulty and taking about 25 minutes to administer. Below is a sample test item, with the appropriate instructions.

Sample Test Item:

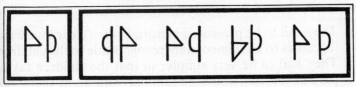

Move your finger down to the red box under the green box here ... Draw a line under the drawing in the little box ... (Slide your finger along the box as you say.) Now draw a line under one drawing in the long box to show it is like the drawing in the little box.

2. Auditory Discrimination of Sounds in Words Test

When devising this test of auditory discrimination, again, the main considerations were the kind of test material to be used and how to present the material in the form of a group test. As with the Visual Discrimination Test, items were required which could be given to the same children both in their first and third terms in school, and so had to test for this skill over a wide range of ability.

Most reading specialists and authors of reading schemes suggest the stages in which they feel auditory and phonic training should be introduced to the child as his reading ability increases. A careful study of the many phonic schemes available indicated that the majority of specialists feel that, at some stage or other, short and long vowels, initial consonants, double consonants, digraphs and blends should be included in a scientific scheme of teaching reading.

After further analysis of the common elements in the phonic schemes, the author decided to include examples of all these elements in his test, and these elements seemed to divide naturally into three groupings as follows:

  (i) sounds at the beginnings of words;
 (ii) sounds at the ends of words;
(iii) sounds contained in the middle of words.

A list of words was built up which contained clear example of the phonic elements discussed above. However, as group tests for young children who are unable to read, must be constructed in pictorial form, two further criteria were necessary for the words selected:

(a) They had to be presented pictorially in a clear line drawing, so as to be immediately recognisable to the children
(b) They had to be very simple, so that the children taking part in the test would be familiar with all of them; thi

was felt to be an important requirement, so that the differing degrees of vocabulary development inevitable in a large group of children would not affect the validity of the test results.

The well-known vocabulary frequency lists were consulted together with phonic schemes which contained illustrations of words used to teach the various sounds, and a selection of words was made bearing in mind the criteria discussed above. It was realised that in the list of words initially selected, some of them were common to the author's Vocabulary Profile (see the next chapter). This was inevitable, as here again the words chosen had to be simple and easy to illustrate clearly, thus limiting the choice of words considerably. Because of some overlapping between the Vocabulary and Auditory Discrimination Tests, and because the pictures are named in the latter test while the children listen to the various sounds, it was decided to give the Vocabulary Profile first to avoid impairing its validity.

The next step was to decide how to present the test material selected, and in this context the Harrison-Stroud Auditory Discrimination Test and a similar test of Daniels and Diack (1958) were consulted. The Harrison-Stroud approach, described earlier in this chapter, asks the child to draw a line from a picture of a word, for example, 'book', to another picture which begins like 'book'. The author when using this test found this approach successful, but found that, as there were only two pictures in the box to which a child could draw a line, a child could score quite highly through guessing one or the other.

The Daniels and Diack test is an individual test of aural discrimination of initial sounds only, but as its main function is diagnostic it introduces the sound to be tested by isolating the sound from its word context; for example, in the case of 'sun' the child is asked, 'Which thing here has a name beginning with s-s-s?' This approach was not felt to be a suitable one for children in their first term in school. Hence, it was decided to use a similar approach to that used by Harrison-Stroud, but to give a multiple choice answer of one out of three for more valid results.

From the test material selected, a group test in booklet

form of 90 items was devised, divided into three sections, namely, beginning sounds, ending sounds and middle sounds. The items incorporated short and long vowels, single and double consonants, digraphs, blends and rhymes. It was felt that by keeping the beginning, ending and middle sounds in three separate parts of the test, the child would not be confused. Two practice items at the beginning of each section were included in the test booklet.

As with the Visual Discrimination Test, each item was boxed by a coloured line. The boxes were coloured green, red and black consecutively in order to help the child to find the correct place in his test booklet, as the colour of the box was always referred to in the test instructions. Each item was designed so that a child could be asked to draw a line under an object, or animal; for example, 'cat' in a 'little red box', and then asked to draw a line under one of the objects or animals in a 'long red box' to show it began like 'cat'. (The 'c' is stressed slightly in the oral presentation.)

The writer realised that the test instructions given for each item had to be very clear, as the beginning, ending and middle sounds comprising the test had to be emphasised slightly but not separated from the rest of the word. This required a great deal of practice, and a tape recorder proved invaluable.

A pilot survey was then conducted, using the 90 items described above. Again the same 100 children from seven representative infant schools were tested in groups of approximately 15. As before, the ages of the children tested ranged from 4 years 9 months to 6 years, some children being in their first term in school, some in their second, and some in their third term.

The results of this pilot survey were analysed carefully and showed that:

(i) this test was more difficult for the children than the Visual Discrimination Test had been, and it took time for the younger children to realise what was required of them;

(ii) the children began to tire after about 20 items, and frequent breaks were necessary;

(iii) the children found the beginning sounds the easiest

to match, then the ending sounds, but the middle sounds seemed too difficult for most of the children to distinguish;

(iv) the author found it very difficult to isolate middle sound easily in the oral presentation.

Bearing in mind the above findings it was decided to:

(i) dispense with the section on middle sounds;

(ii) reduce the number of items to 33, having 18 beginning sounds in the first section, and 15 ending sounds in the second, and to have a break between sections;

(iii) make 4 additional practice items, in the form of large charts, to be used on the blackboard as demonstration items; these were produced to conform exactly to the format of the children's own smaller copies. The charts were covered with transparent p.v.c., which enabled the author to demonstrate the responses required by the children, using a grease pencil to mark the chart, which could easily be cleaned off afterwards. The four practice items already in the booklet were retained, making eight practice items in all, four at the beginning of each of the two sections;

(iv) arrange the items in each section in the apparent order of difficulty.

The final version of the test was now prepared. Following are two of the test items with their appropriate instructions; the first is from the first section of beginning sounds, the second is from the second section of ending sounds.

Sample test item (beginning sounds):

Instructions for sample test item:

Look at the pictures in the green box under the black box. We have a <u>w</u>indow, a <u>f</u>ork, a <u>m</u>ouse, and a <u>w</u>all. Draw a line under the window. Now draw a line under the thing in the long green box which begins like window.

Sample test item (ending sounds)

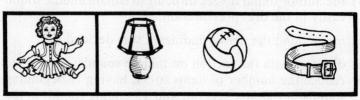

Instructions for sample test item:

Look at the pictures in the red box under the green box. We have a do<u>ll</u>, a lam<u>p</u>, a ba<u>ll</u>, and a be<u>lt</u>. Draw a line under the do<u>ll</u> ... Now draw a line under the thing in the long red box which ends like do<u>ll</u>.

Measures of Reading Achievement

The author decided to use the same three measures of reading achievement used in the main i.t.a. experiment, for the following reasons:

1. The measures had been selected carefully for the main i.t.a. experiment and their use would enable the author to make more realistic comparisons.
2. The author had a great deal of experience in the administration of these same measures.
3. Transliterated versions of the measures were readily available.

The three measures used were Schonell's **Graded** **W**ord Reading Test, Neale's Analysis of Reading Ability, and the 'primer criterion' evaluation devised by Morris (1959).

1. Schonell's Graded Word Reading Test

This is not a reading test in the true sense, but simply a word recognition test. Although this test is used widely by teachers and has been for many years, the standardization and validation of the test are not fully accepted by today's standards. Georgiades (1968) makes this point when quoting from the Mental Measurement Yearbook of 1965, as follows:

The test was standardized on a sample of 60 children per

year in the age range 5–15. The one hundred words used were selected from 300 words, the source of which is not indicated, and for a word to be included, it was necessary that 55% of the children, aged 5 years, got the easiest words correct, and 48% of those aged 14–15, the more difficult. This means that only 33 children had to respond correctly to the easier words for them to be included in this test. No indication was found of the areas from which the standardization sample had been drawn, no coefficients of reliability or validity are given, although the test itself does have a considerable amount of face validity.

However, as only raw scores were required, and it was a test to measure progress in reading from the very first stages, it was satisfactory for the purpose of this experiment.

The point has been made, and rightly so, that transliterated versions of tests are not truly valid for purposes of comparison. This fact was borne in mind when interpreting results.

The Schonell test consists of a hundred words starting very simply in large print; for example, 'tree', 'little', 'milk', and gradually increasing in difficulty and decreasing in print size; for example, words 51–53 are 'physics', 'campaign', 'choir', and words 98–100 are 'somnambulist', 'bibliography' and 'idiosyncrasy'. Reading ages between five and fifteen years can be calculated from the raw scores, but only the raw scores were used in the statistical procedures leading to the main conclusions. However, it was possible to make a comparison of average reading ages attained by the two groups towards the end of their third year in school, as by then both groups were reading in t.o.

2. Neale Analysis of Reading Ability

This test is a fairly recent one, and was devised to fulfil the twin needs of a diagnostic measure and a measure yielding scores to give a child's reading achievement. The Neale Analysis, which is an individual test, gives norms for accuracy, rate of reading, and comprehension, and so it is a more sophisticated and comprehensive measure of reading ability than the Schonell test. A measure of comprehension was felt to be important, as reading involves understanding as well as word recognition, and any discrepancy found between the

153

scores for accuracy and comprehension, in either the i.t.a. or the t.o. group, would warrant further investigation. However, the author did realise from his own experience, and that of others, that when examining the scores for comprehension he would have to bear in mind that the accuracy score sets the ceiling to the comprehension score. It has also been pointed out that the comprehension test is more a measure of recall than of understanding.

The author decided not to measure the rate of reading, which in the design of the test is scored at the same time as the accuracy test, as this speed test has been criticised by some teachers and administrators and has already been mentioned in Part I, Chapter 5.

Reading age norms are provided for accuracy and comprehension, but in the main, raw scores have been used for purposes of comparison. However, as with the Schonell test, towards the end of the children's third year in school, when nearly all the i.t.a. children had transferred to t.o., a comparison of average reading ages was possible.

Bearing in mind its limitations, the Neale Analysis of Reading Ability seemed a very suitable test for the following reasons:

1. There are three parallel forms of the test.
2. Each passage is a complete narrative suited to the interests of the age level for which it is designed and as each passage has a picture, the test material resembles a book of stories. The pictures also help the child to move easily from one train of thought to the next. It must be pointed out that no details are given as to how the passages have been selected.
3. The reliability and validity coefficients given are very satisfactory. The parallel forms were used to test reliability, and correlations between Forms A and B and Forms A and C were identical, being .98 in each case. The average validity coefficient, obtained by comparing the Neale with other well-known tests, such as the Vernon Word Reading Scale and the Holborn Scale for Oral Comprehension, was .95.

On the opposite page is a sample test item, with illustration and matching text in both t.o. and i.t.a.

Sample test item

Father gave Pam a big box.
Pam put it on the table.
She looked in the box for a doll.
Then out jumped a white rabbit.

father gæv pam a big boks.
pam pʊt it on the tæbl.
ʃhεε lʊkt in the boks for a doll.
then out jumpt a whiet rabbit.

3. Primer Criterion Evaluation

The third measure of the reading achievement and reading progress of the children in the investigation was that of the 'primer criterion' evaluation used by Morris (1959) in her reading survey in Kent, and by the author in his previous investigation.

The class teachers of the children concerned in the investigation were issued with a single sheet for each child, entitled 'Reading Progress Chart', on which they were asked to fill in the titles of the basic books read by their children, and the date when each book was started and finished. Only the basic books in a reading series were asked for, as it would have been impossible to take into consideration the many little books of all kinds read by children in the first stages of learning to read. It has been pointed out earlier that this measure is rather crude, there being no common standard to indicate when a basic book has been 'read', but it was used to provide supplementary, rather than basic, information about the children's reading ability and progress.

Chapter 2

Discussion of the Testing Measures Selected and Constructed (II): Measures of General Ability and Home Environment

The research literature has shown that the factors of general ability and home background are important factors in readiness to read, though not as important as the perceptual skills of visual and auditory discrimination. In order to compare the reading readiness requirements of children learning to read with i.t.a., and children learning to read with t.o. as fully as possible, it was felt that measures of these two important factors should also be given to children in the sample. These measures were either selected or constructed by the author.

General ability

Some investigators in the field of reading readiness have shown that general intelligence, or general ability, is the most important single factor in learning to read, and all investigators have stressed its importance. In order to measure this important factor three measures* were selected, and will be discussed on the following pages.

*See Appendix for details of tests

157

1. The Wechsler Intelligence Scale for Children.

Psychologists are generally agreed that, in order to obtain valid results when testing young children, an individual test is desirable, and for this reason the Wechsler Intelligence Scale for Children (WISC) was chosen. This test, which has gained in popularity with British educational psychologists during the last decade, is in two parts; a group of verbal tests form one part and a group of performance tests the other. Psychologists have found a very high correlation between results on the verbal tests alone, and on the complete tests (.9), and for a general appraisal of the level of mental ability of a child it is generally felt that the verbal part of the test alone is satisfactory. As the giving of both the verbal and performance tests to approximately 300 children would have been far too time-consuming, the author decided to use the verbal part of the test only.

The WISC has grown up logically out of the Wechsler-Bellevue Intelligence Scales used with adolescents and adults, but it has been independently standardized with exceptional care over a five year period. The test is interesting in that it renounces completely the concept of mental age as a basic measure of intelligence for the following reasons:

(i) Mental Age (MA) has become accepted as a measure of mental level, but a five year old with a MA of seven has not the same kind of mind as a ten year old with a MA of seven.

(ii) Intelligence quotient (IQ) is usually worked out from a MA, but the IQ notation unaccompanied by a statement of the age at which the IQ is attained does not eliminate the age factor.

(iii) MA has almost disappeared in the field of adolescent and adult testing, as it is not possible to state where the adult mental age should be set, and it varies, with the test used, from 16 to over 20.

In WISC, IQs are obtained by comparing each subject's test performance, not with a composite age group, but exclusively with the scores earned by individuals in a single age group. Each child is assigned an IQ which at his age represents his relative intelligence rating. This IQ, and all others similarly obtained, are deviation IQs, since they indicate the amount by which a subject deviates above or below the average performance of individuals of his own age group. A mean of 100 and a standard deviation of 15 have been chosen, which is in keeping with many other standardized tests. Reliability coefficients have been calculated by the split half technique and average at about .91; no information is given in the manual concerning validity.

There are five tests of verbal ability measuring information, comprehension, arithmetic, knowledge of similarities, and vocabulary. Questions in all five tests were designed to cover the 5–15 age range, so the five year olds tested could not attempt to answer very many of the questions. Below are sample items from each test;

Sample items from WISC
(General Information)

1. How many ears have you?
5. What must you do to make water boil?
10. How many things make a dozen?
15. Why does oil float on water?

Sample items from WISC
(General Comprehension)

1. What is the thing to do when you cut your finger?
5. What should you do if you see a train approaching a broken track?
10. Why is it generally better to give money to an organised charity than to a street beggar?
15. Why should a promise be kept?

Sample items from WISC
(Arithmetic)

1. Place nine blocks in a row before the subject and say, 'Count these blocks with your fingers'.
4. If I cut an apple in half, how many pieces will I have?
7. A boy had 12 newspapers and sold 5. How many did he have left?

Sample items from WISC
(Similarities)

> Test 4a
> 1. Lemons are sour but sugar is –
> 4. A knife and a piece of glass both –
> Test 4B
> 5. In what ways are a plum and peach alike?
> 6. In what ways are a pound and a yard alike?

Sample items from WISC
(Vocabulary)

> Instruction: 'I want to see how many words you know. Listen carefully and tell me what these words mean.'
> 1. Bicycle
> 5. Umbrella
> 15. Brave
> 18. Gamble

The method of scoring the answers for each test is explained carefully in the manual, and raw scores can be converted into standardized scores. All the answers given by each child were written down verbatim, so that careful and accurate scoring could be made later by the author. Questioning in each test stopped after the child had given a certain number of consecutive wrong answers, according to the instructions in the manual.

2. Goodenough-Harris Draw-a-Man Test

Although this test has been recently revised and extended, research reports by Yule, Lockyer and Noone (1967), and Strümpter and Mienie (1968), made the author realise that this general ability test is not as reliable or valid as the WISC. In this revision of the Goodenough test by Harris (1963) reliability is evaluated in two ways:

(a) the consistency with which scorers evaluate a particular

160

set of drawings. Intercorrelation figures range from .8–.96.

(b) the consistency of children's performances in the drawing task as evaluated by the scale. Intercorrelation figures range from .6–.7. The validity figures, showing the relationship of the Goodenough test to other measures, range from .16–.78.

These figures suggested that the Goodenough test would be valuable only in so far as providing supplementary evidence on the mental abilities of the children in the investigation.

The instructions for administering the test are simple and are as follows:

I want you to make a picture of a man. Make the very best picture that you can. Take your time and work very carefully. Try hard, and see what a good picture of a man you can make.

Points are allocated for various parts of the body which have been included in the drawing, and norms based on 2,975 children in the USA are provided.

3. Class Teachers' Rating of General Ability

In addition to the two standardized measures of general ability, the class teachers were asked to rate their children for general ability on a five point scale. With these three measures it was felt that a valid appraisal of the children's general mental ability could be made.

Home Environment

Home environment, or background, is a broad factor including many environmental aspects which affect the total experience the child brings to the reading situation. Many writers agree that the more important aspects are opportunities for play and social experience, the nature of the speech and language patterns, and the cultural level of the home.

Knowing that matched groups of i.t.a. and t.o. children had to be compared, the author selected t.o. schools which

161

were situated in similar environments to the i.t.a. schools which had agreed to help him in his investigation. In this way a preliminary matching of schools was carried out, details of which will be found in Chapter 3.

Information about the home background of each child, which was necessary for assessing the importance of this factor, was collected by means of the following three measures:

1. Notes on fathers' occupations

With this information it is possible to make social class groupings, according to the Registrar General's list* in which the following classification of social classes is made:

a) professional   d) semi-skilled
b) clerical   e) unskilled
c) skilled

By grouping the children into these social classes according to their fathers' occupations it is possible to match the i.t.a. and t.o. groups on this criterion.

2. Teachers' ratings on certain aspects of home environment

The respective class teachers were asked to rate their children on a five point scale for the following attributes:

(a) estimate of experiential background
(b) extent and quality of play
(c) extent of vocabulary
(d) accuracy of speech

3. A Vocabulary Profile constructed by the author.

A child's vocabulary reflects both his opportunities for play and social experiences, and the cultural level of the home; and in order to measure the vocabulary development of the children in his previous investigation, the author designed and constructed a multiple-choice picture vocabulary test. This test was constructed as a group test, as individual tests

---

*Appendix C of the General Report in the 1957 Census of England and Wales HMSO.

are time-consuming and there were no published group vocabulary tests for five year old children. The author decided to use his own vocabulary test again in the present investigation, but this test was revised to make it a more reliable measure.

The revised form of the Vocabulary Profile was now given by the author to 200 children from 12 representative infant schools. The average age of the children was 5 years 3 months, and they were all at the beginning of their second term in school. The children were tested in groups of approximately fifteen, the test taking approximately twenty-five minutes to administer.

The scores were subjected to the chi-square test and the observed results formed a normal distribution, so this revised form of the Vocabulary Profile was used in the investigation.

The 50 items are enclosed in boxes coloured red, green or black, and as there are only three items to each page, both the colour and the position (top, middle, bottom) of the item could be referred to in the test instructions. During the revision of the test a further opportunity to improve upon the instructions was afforded, and below are sample items from the test with the appropriate instructions.

Sample practice item:

Instructions for practice item (above):

Put the page in front of you with the red box at the top. (Demonstrate and check.) Look at the drawings in the red box. Remember I am going to say a word and I want you to draw a clear line through what I say. Pencils ready ... cup ... (Pause) ... cup. Have you all drawn a clear line through what I said? Look at mine again. I said 'cup', so I draw a line through the cup. (Draw a line through the cup on your booklet and check the booklets of the children.)

Sample test item:

Instructions for test item above:

Look at the *green* box at the bottom of the page. Pencil ready . . . fawn . . . fawn. (Repeat the word *once* only, after a short pause.) Hold your pencils up when you are ready for the next one . . .

It was felt that the results on the Vocabulary Profile together with the teachers' notes on fathers' occupations, and ratings on various home circumstances would enable the author to investigate the factor of home environment satisfactorily.

Measures of physical and social and emotional factors

Research into reading readiness, both in this country and in America, indicates that physical, social and emotional factors are of much less importance than those of specific readiness skills, mental ability and home background. For example, in the author's first experiment emotional and personal attitudes were found to be relatively unimportant, giving correlation figures with later reading progress of .10–.36.

However, in order to complete the reading readiness profiles of the children being studied, teachers were asked to rate their children on a five point scale for their ability to listen, for their attitudes towards books and learning, and finally for their readiness to read. They were also asked

164

note any social and emotional traits which might affect a child's readiness to read, and to indicate whether the physical attributes of vision, hearing, energy and attendance of their children were normal or below normal.

In this way the reading readiness profiles of the children in the experiment were completed as fully as possible.

Chapter 3

Discussion of the Children and
Schools Selected

Number of children and the timing of the tests

With regard to the number of children to be tested, there wer
three factors which had to be considered. Firstly, it wa
realised that the reliability of any correlation coefficient, o
mean score obtained, increases with the number of case
examined. Secondly, the author had to consider the tim
factor, as he decided to do all the testing himself to avoid an
variations in the testing procedures. Thirdly, the auth
realised from previous experience that the total number
children in the sample would be steadily reduced througho
the three year investigation by illness and family remova
and by the need to match the i.t.a. and t.o. groups as well
possible. It was decided to test approximately 300 childr
initially, 150 children in each group.

Very careful thought, based on the results of small sca
individual and group testing, was given to the age or sta
at which to test the children. It was felt that a suitable time
administer the initial tests of reading readiness, intelligen
and vocabulary would be, firstly, when the children we
fully settled into the school routine and secure enough
tackle a number of tests; and secondly, when the pre-read
programme was coming to an end, but before formal read
instruction had begun.

Vernon (1960) has pointed out that if certain reading readiness skills are necessary for reading, then the activity of reading will probably develop these skills. This means that if the testing of reading readiness skills is carried out when the children can read already, and if the resultant scores correlate positively with later results on reading achievement tests, it will not be possible to claim that competence in reading readiness skills leads to reading progress, as these skills might have been developed in learning to read. In other words, it would be difficult to distinguish between cause and effect.

In the author's previous experiment with t.o. children only, it was found that testing at the beginning of the children's second term in school was the most suitable time. However, the testing of small groups of i.t.a. children at the beginning of their second term showed that many of them had already been started by their teachers on a series of basic readers. Hence, it was finally decided to test all the children in the present investigation during the second half of their first term in school, that is, 6–8 weeks after entering school. The average age of both the i.t.a. and the t.o. groups of children tested at this time was 5 years 3 months.

Selection and matching of the schools

Approximately 300 children were required for the initial testing, and as some of the tests to be given were group tests, the number of schools enlisted was determined by the number of children who could be successfully tested together in one group. Preliminary administrations of the group tests indicated that, with the class teacher as helper, eighteen was the maximum number of children who could be tested successfully in one group. Hence, it was decided to enlist the co-operation of 16 schools, taking up to eighteen children from each school. Where there were more than eighteen in the group who had started school together, the author asked the class teachers concerned for eighteen children who constituted a good cross section of the class; any children who could already read, or who seemed so much below average that their responses to testing would be negligible, were among those excluded.

It was realised from the outset that matched groups of i.t.a. and t.o. children would eventually have to be established; this being so, the initial matching of eight i.t.a. schools with eight t.o. schools was a very important consideration.

The author was fortunate to secure the help of the Adviser to Primary Schools in the single County area from which all his schools were drawn. This Adviser, who was sympathetic to the aims of the author's experiment and who knew the schools and their environments well, carefully selected i.t.a. and t.o. schools from urban and rural areas, and schools within these types of area which differed as widely as possible in environment. i.t.a. and t.o. schools were also matched in pairs for size, type (infant or primary) and certain social class factors such as type of housing and typical occupations.

While the vital matching considerations mentioned above were influencing the selection of schools, both the Primary Advisor and the author were aware of the additional need to match, if at all possible, the competency and the approach to reading of the teachers in each pair of i.t.a. and t.o. schools.

This proved very difficult, though to the best of the Adviser's knowledge the reception class teachers concerned were all competent, and she knew of no great variations in the ways of teaching reading among the schools finally selected. The author made notes on the methods of teaching reading used by each class teacher, on three occasions during the testing period, and in particular recorded the differing emphases placed on phonic training and school organisation. However, during the three year period the children in the experiment had changes of teacher, firstly, because of moving up to another class in the same school, and secondly, because of teachers leaving and being replaced by others. Although such changes made it difficult to account for teacher competency and method of teaching reading, nevertheless these changes are usual in schools today, and any findings recorded and results obtained in the experiment are from normal representative school situations.

This particular experiment was carried out during the years 1965–68, a period when i.t.a., no longer new, was accepted as yet another approach to the teaching of reading

Hence, certain effects felt to be present in the main i.t.a. experiment, such as the 'Hawthorne Effect', and the effects of a 'reading drive', were not operative in the author's experiment. For example, a few of the teachers using i.t.a. were adopting it in the spirit of enquiry rather than conviction. One infants teacher had been reluctant to change to i.t.a., but had been encouraged to do so by the head teacher. In another i.t.a. school, the teacher who had been trained to use i.t.a. left and a supply teacher, with little knowledge of i.t.a., replaced her. Although these circumstances contrast rather sharply with those typical of the main i.t.a. experiment they are typical of the normal school situation.

Description of the schools selected

The following notes on each of the 16 schools indicate the widely differing environments from which the children were drawn. The schools are paired to indicate similarities of size, type, and social background, and each pair of schools is described in turn. One letter is used for each matched pair; number 1 is used for the i.t.a. school and number 2 for the t.o. school.

School A1 (Infants' School)

This school is situated in a good housing area of a small dormitory town, and although there are some council houses most of the children come from privately owned semi-detached houses. On the whole, the children are well cared for and their parents, many of whom are professional people, are very interested in the work of the school and most willing to co-operate with the teachers to help their children at home. The children generally are bright and receptive to learning, and over the past few years there have been few non-readers by any method. The approach to reading is mainly 'look and say', but the i.t.a. sounds are taught fairly systematically. It was in this school that the class teacher, trained in i.t.a., left to be replaced by a supply teacher. The 'Janet and John' scheme, transliterated into i.t.a., was used.

School A2 (Infants' School)

This school is situated in a very pleasant housing area in

green surroundings on the outskirts of a large town. Practically all the semi-detached houses are privately owned, and the children well cared for in every way. The parents generally are interested in their children's progress at school and willing to help them at home. The approach to reading is mainly 'look and say', with initial sounds being introduced incidentally rather than systematically. The reading scheme in use was the 'Happy Venture' scheme.

Schools A1 and A2 are well matched in a number of important respects, and, in the final analysis, 16 children came from each of these two schools.

School B1 (Primary School)

This school is situated in a working class area in a small town which, in the main, manufactures hosiery and boots and shoes. The housing consists of semi-detached council houses and pre-fabricated houses. Many of the children's mothers as well as their fathers work in the factories in the town, as women are needed in the hosiery trade. The parents care for their children adequately but are not really interested in their children's progress at school. Much money is spent on material acquisitions for the home and on enjoyment, but the cultural levels of the homes are low, and the children seem below average ability. The approach to reading is the 'look and say' approach using the Downing scheme. Sounds are introduced incidentally rather than systematically. Although i.t.a. had been taught for two years in this school, the reception class teacher was a married woman returner, who was teaching with i.t.a. for the first time, knowing very little about it and not at all convinced of its efficacy.

School B2 (Primary School)

This school is a fairly new one situated on the outskirts of a small town which contains a number of factories making mainly boots and shoes, boxes and engineering products.

These factories attract quite a number of unskilled workers, which makes for a rather unstable school population. Most of the children come from semi-detached council houses which surround the school, and the parents put material considerations before educational ones, and so are not very interested in their children's progress at school.

The approach to reading is 'look and say' initially, but after half a term, phonic training is introduced and treated systematically. A composite reading series has been devised, using the 'Happy Venture', 'Happy Trio' and 'Keywords' reading schemes.

Schools B1 and B2 are reasonably well matched for social class background, but in the teaching of reading, phonic training was more systematically treated in the t.o. school than in its i.t.a. counterpart. In the final analysis 17 children came from B1 and 16 children from B2.

School C1 (Primary School)

This school is situated in a mixed housing area in a dormitory village. Most of the houses are new and detached or semi-detached, but there are a few pre-fabricated houses and a few cottages also. The children are well cared for in every way, and their parents are very interested in their children's progress at school. The class teacher of the children tested was a very experienced and able teacher, but it was the first time she had taught with i.t.a. Her approach was the usual 'look and say' approach and the Downing reading scheme was used. The classroom was a very exciting one, and the author felt the children would learn to read quickly whatever medium was used.

School C2 (Primary School)

This school is situated in another dormitory village, and surrounded by a mixture of houses, mostly semi-detached but some detached houses and some very old terrace houses. The main occupations for both men and women are to be found in the hosiery and boot and shoe factories in the town. The children are well cared for, but not a great deal of interest is shown by the parents in the work of the school. There is much intermarriage in the village and the children do not seem to be particularly bright. The approach to reading is the usual 'look and say' approach and 'Janet and John' and 'Gay Way' readers are the two schemes used. Initial sounds are taught incidentally, and there is no systematic phonic training.

Schools C1 and C2 are not too well matched as, although environments are similar, the interest shown by the parents and the skill of the teacher seemed to favour the i.t.a. school. In the final analysis 14 children came from C1 and 15 from C2.

School D1 (Infants' school)

This school is situated in a working class area of a small town and the children come mainly from council house estates, though some come from the few private houses in the area. Fathers mainly work in the engineering industries of the nearby large town or in the two hosiery factories in the town. Many mothers also work in the hosiery factories. The parents are more interested in material than educational standards, and do not show a great deal of interest in the work done in the school. The reading approach is 'look and say' but simple phonic instruction is introduced early. The scheme used is the 'Janet and John' scheme.

School D2 (Infants' School)

This school is situated in a working class area similar to that where D1 is situated, and in the same small town. Again the children's fathers work in motor engineering or hosiery. Parents seem a little more interested in the life of the school than those whose children attend school D1, but not greatly so. This particular school organises its work round the integrated day, and reading is one of the many educational activities, though children are expected to do some reading each day. A number of schemes are in use, such as 'Janet and John', 'Happy Venture', 'Keywords' and 'Gay Way'.

These two schools are well matched in many respects, though different approaches to the teaching of reading are apparent. In the final analysis 14 children came from D1, and 16 children from D2.

School E1 (Infants' School)

This school is situated in a working class area in a medium-sized town. The children's fathers work mainly in the local engineering works as skilled and semi-skilled workers. The council housing is mainly terrace, but with some semi-detached. Parents seem to be reasonably interested in their children's progress at school. The approach to reading is a 'look and say' approach with incidental attention to phonics, and the Downing scheme is used. The class teacher seemed very able and keen on the teaching of reading.

School E2 (Infants' School)

This school is situated in a rather depressed working class area in the same town as school E1. The houses in the area are nearly all council terrace houses, with a very few semi-detached. There are local engineering factories in the area, and the children's fathers have skilled or semi-skilled jobs in these factories. Immigrants are beginning to move into the area and out of the 128 children in the school 22 are immigrant children. Basically the parents are interested in their children's schooling. The reading approach is 'look and say' with incidental attention to phonics at first, but later more regular phonic drill is practised. The 'Happy Venture' scheme is in use.

Schools E1 and E2 are well matched, though E2 is situated in a rather more depressed area than E1. In the final analysis, 16 children came from E1 and 15 children from E2.

School F1 (Primary School)

This school is situated in a mining village, though quarrying and agriculture provide other occupations. The children's parents are average working class people, living mainly in council houses and cottages. No particular interest is shown by the parents in the work of the school, and standards tend to be below average. The approach to reading is a 'look and say' approach with incidental attention given to the sounds in words. The scheme used is the Downing scheme. It was in this school that the class teacher did not wish to change to i.t.a., but because of the head teacher's enthusiasm she agreed to try.

School F2 (Primary School)

This school is also situated in a village and the local industries are mining, quarrying and agriculture. The children's parents are mainly working class, living in council houses and cottages, though a few private houses are now being built in the area. The children's material needs are catered for, but little interest is shown in the work done by the school. The approach to reading is the usual 'look and say' approach with incidental phonic training, and the 'Happy Venture' scheme is used.

Schools F1 and F2 are very well matched in many respects, and in the final analysis 11 children came from F1 and 10 children from F2.

School G1 (Infants' School)

This school is situated not far from the centre of a small market town. The children's fathers form a good cross section of the community, as some are professional and some are skilled and semi-skilled. Some of the mothers work, but usually on a part-time basis, so they can help their children. The housing is mixed, council and private, semi-detached and terrace. The approach to reading is very different from all the other schools taking part in the investigation; it is a phonic approach, and the children are taught the i.t.a. characters with their appropriate sounds from the very beginning. The standard of reading is very high in the early stages and the standards reached made the author aware of the influence of a particular approach to reading on reading results. The Downing scheme is used in this school.

School G2 (Infants' School)

This school is situated not far from the centre of another small market town. The children's fathers again form a good cross section of the community, as some have professional occupations and others work in skilled and semi-skilled occupations in the factories in the town. The school serves a large council estate and a fairly new private housing estate. The children are well cared for and a reasonable interest in, and support for, the work of the school is evident. The approach to reading is the usual 'look and say' approach with incidental phonic training at first.

Schools G1 and G2 are quite well matched in many ways, but there is a wide difference in the approaches of the two schools to reading, the former having a clear cut phonic approach, the latter a 'look and say' approach. In the final analysis 15 children came from G1 and 17 children from G2.

School H1 (Infants' School)

The school is situated in a large village. Some of the children's fathers have professional occupations, live in private houses and work in nearby large towns; other fathers have skilled and semi-skilled occupations, live on council estates and work locally. Professional fathers are interested in their children's progress, but other parents show little interest. The approach to reading is a 'look and say' approach with incidental phonic training. The Downing scheme is used.

School H2 (Infants' School)

This school is situated in a large village, and like School H1, some fathers travel to nearby large towns, others work locally. Again the housing is mixed, as there are private houses, council houses and a number of flats. Generally, the parents are interested in their children's education. The approach to reading is 'look and say', though a systematic treatment of phonics quickly develops. The general working atmosphere of the school is fairly formal, but not repressive in any way, and the children always seem to be working very hard. The reading results in this school were particularly good, which made the author aware of the possible influence on reading results of the formal or informal organisation of the school.

Schools H1 and H2 are well matched, apart from the more formal approach evident in school H2. In the final analysis 16 children came from school H1 and 14 children from H2.

Testing techniques with young children

During the preliminary testing of five year old children in small groups and in his previous experiments, the author realised fully that the way in which young children are tested is a very important consideration. The following testing techniques, which the author developed from personal experience, were noted for consideration and use in the later investigation:

1. Gardner's (1942) observation that:

> a slight difference in the wording of a test ... the pace of speaking, the tone and inflections of the voice, can make a test considerably harder, or easier, for the children.

was verified; the author realised that he must speak clearly and slowly without any undue emphasis, must strictly observe the form of wording to be used, and observe carefully all the pauses decided upon.

2. It was found that the children were more relaxed when tested in their own classrooms, so whenever possible it was decided to test the children in familiar surroundings.

3. It was noticed that afternoon testing was not as satisfactory as morning testing; the children were fresher in the morning and could concentrate more easily. Hence, most of the testing was confined to mornings, and where a second short test had to be taken the same morning, a good break in the open air was allowed between the two tests.

4. It helped the author to establish a relaxed atmosphere if he saw and talked to the children to be tested on at least one occasion before the actual testing. This ensured that the children became used to the tester's voice and manner of speaking, and also to the presence of a male teacher in the classroom. It was also found that the children enjoyed the test when it was suggested that they were playing a 'new game', and when they were consistently praised.

5. It was found that children of this age look round a great deal, and copy freely, even altering a right answer to a wrong one to be the same as the next child's. As no mention could be made of copying if the atmosphere of enjoyment was to be preserved, it was realised that the children would have to sit one to a table, and the tables separated sufficiently so that no effective copying could take place. When this was done it was found that, after the first question or two, the children settled down to their own papers.

Chapter 4

Discussion of the Results Obtained by the Statistical Methods Selected (I): Tests Carried out in the Children's First Term at School, and the Matching of the i.t.a. and t.o. Groups

If valid conclusions are to be reached from the data collected, adequate statistical treatment of this data is necessary. Realising this, the author gave careful thought to, and sought advice on, the best statistical methods for the purpose in hand.

On examining the tests used, it was seen that the Harrison-Stroud Reading Readiness Profiles and the Wechsler Scale of Intelligence for Children are standardized for American children; the Schonell Graded Word Reading Test and the Goodenough Draw-A-Man Test are standardized for British children; the three tests of Visual Discrimination, Auditory Discrimination and Vocabulary constructed by the author are at present unstandardized, and the various teachers' ratings were asked for on a five point scale.

Hence, for many of the comparisons between the i.t.a. and t.o. groups only the raw scores from the various tests could be used. However, in order to compare scores from the various tests and from the teachers' ratings, all the raw scores were converted to standardized scores with a mean of 100 and a standard deviation of 15, and for some calculations standardized scores were used.

As can be seen from the Testing Programme at the end of the introduction to Part II, both the i.t.a. and the t.o. groups were given the same battery of tests after being in school for about six weeks. The tests were designed to measure visual and auditory discrimination; general intelligence and vocabulary development; and, in addition, the class teachers concerned were asked to furnish notes for each child on father's occupation and home background and to make certain reading readiness evaluations. With the information gained from this initial testing programme, it was possible to match the i.t.a. and t.o. groups of children on a number of variables. The matching of the two groups, which finally contained 119 children in each, will be discussed later in the chapter.

Now follows in tabulated form the relevant information obtained from the tests given, and the evaluations made in the children's first term in school. In all the Tables in Part II, the following abbreviations are used:

N   = number of children in the group
S.D. = standard deviation
S.E. = standard error
C.R. = critical ratio
N.S. = not significant

(i) *Measures of visual discrimination: the author's*
    Visual Discrimination Test and the Harrison-Stroud
    Visual Discrimination Test (i.t.a. and t.o. versions)

From Tables 18, 19, and 20 it can be seen that there are no significant differences between the mean scores of the i.t.a. and t.o. groups for visual discrimination, as measured by the author's test and the Harrison-Stroud test.

Table 21 indicates that there is no significant difference between the mean scores of both i.t.a. and t.o. groups together, on the i.t.a. and t.o. versions of the Harrison-Stroud Visual Discrimination Test. It was pointed out earlier that the only difference between these two tests was that of transliteration, and the transliterated test was given to see

178

TABLE 18 Showing a comparison between the mean scores of the i.t.a. and t.o. groups on the author's Visual Discrimination Test given for the first time.

Group	N	mean score	S.D.	diff. in means	S.E. of diff.	C.R.	statis. signif.
i.t.a.	119	18.16	7.47	1.17	1.02	1.15	N.S.
t.o.	119	19.33	8.25				

TABLE 19 Showing a comparison between the mean scores of the i.t.a. and t.o. groups on the Harrison-Stroud Visual Discrimination Test (i.t.a. version).

Group	N	mean score	S.D.	diff. in means	S.E. of diff.	C.R.	statis. signif.
i.t.a.	119	20.65	7.62	.69	.96	.72	N.S.
t.o.	119	21.34	7.17				

TABLE 20 Showing a comparison between the means scores of the i.t.a. and t.o. groups on the Harrison-Stroud Visual Discrimination Test (t.o. version).

Group	N	mean score	S.D.	diff. in means	S.E. of diff.	C.R.	statis. signif.
i.t.a.	119	20.65	7.92	1.05	.96	1.09	N.S.
t.o.	119	21.7	6.81				

TABLE 21 Showing a comparison between the mean scores of both i.t.a. and t.o. groups (238) on the i.t.a. and t.o. versions of the Harrison-Stroud Visual Discrimination Test.

Test	N	mean score	S.D.	diff. in means	S.E. of diff.	C.R.	statis. signif.
Visual Discrim. I.S. i.t.a.	238	21.01	7.41	.18	.68	.26	N.S.
Visual Discrim. I.S. t.o.	238	21.19	7.41				

if either i.t.a. or t.o. was simpler, visually, to children who had not yet learned to read. The results give a clear indication that, to the children tested, the one test was no more difficult visually than the other.

At this point it seems convenient and relevant to judge to what extent the author was successful in his design and construction of a test of visual discrimination. Now follows the frequency distribution of the standardized scores of both i.t.a. and t.o. groups presented by means of a Table and a corresponding histogram.

TABLE 22   Showing the distribution of the standardized scores of 238 children on the author's Visual Discrimination Test (Mean 100, Standard Deviation 15).

Scores	Frequencies
120–129	17
110–119	63
100-109	48
90–99	41
80–89	35
70–79	24
60–69	10

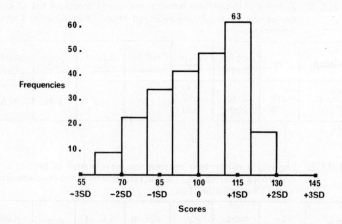

Figure 11 Showing distribution of standardized scores on the author's Visual Discrimination Test.

The distribution of the standardized scores on the author' test of Visual Discrimination was reasonably normal, though showing a negative skew; this latter indicating that the tes was rather on the easy side for the children concerned. Th distribution also indicated a fairly wide range of ability in this particular skill.

To gain a measure of the validity of the author's Visual Discrimination Test the standardized scores of both the i.t.a. and t.o. groups of 238 children were correlated, by the product moment method, with the standardized scores of the same 238 children on the t.o. version of the Harrison-Stroud Visual Discrimination Test, which is a published test widely used in America. The coefficient of correlation was .79$\pm$ .025, which denotes a very high relationship and indicates that a reasonably valid test of visual discrimination had been constructed by the author.

(ii) *Measures of auditory discrimination: the author's Auditory Discrimination Test, and the Harrison-Stroud Auditory Discrimination Test.*

TABLE 23 Showing a comparison between the mean scores of the i.t.a. and t.o. groups on the author's Auditory Discrimination Test given for the first time.

Group	N	mean score	S.D.	diff. in means	S.E. of diff.	C.R.	statis. signif.
i.t.a.	119	11.47	6.66	.15	.83	.18	N.S.
t.o.	119	11.32	6.15				

TABLE 24 Showing a comparison between the mean scores of the i.t.a. and t.o. groups on the Harrison-Stroud Auditory Discrimination Test.

Group	N	mean score	S.D.	diff. in means	S.E. of diff.	C.R.	statis. signif.
i.t.a.	119	9.9	3.18	.62	.41	1.51	N.S.
t.o.	119	10.52	3.32				

From Tables 23 and 24 it can be seen that there are no significant differences between the mean scores of the i.t.a. and t.o. groups for auditory discrimination, as measured by the author's test and the Harrison-Stroud test.

Again, at this point it is convenient and relevant to judge to what extent the author was successful in designing and constructing his test of auditory discrimination. Now follows the frequency distribution of the standardized scores of both i.t.a. and t.o. groups, presented by means of a Table and a corresponding histogram.

TABLE 25   Showing the distribution of the standardized scores of 238 children on the author's Auditory Discrimination Test (Mean 100, Standard Deviation 15).

Scores	Frequencies
130–139	7
120–129	21
110–119	34
100–109	53
90–99	57
80–89	44
70–79	22

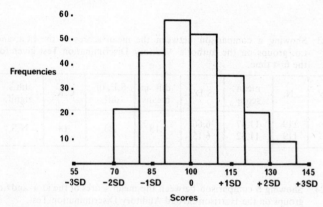

Figure 12. Showing distribution of standardized scores on the author's Auditory Discrimination Test.

The distribution of the standardized scores on the author's Auditory Discrimination Test was fairly normal, apart from a slight positive skew; this latter indicating that the test was a little on the difficult side for the children concerned. The distribution also indicated a wide range of ability in this particular skill.

Again, to gain a measure of the validity of the author's Auditory Discrimination Test, the standardized scores o.

182

both the i.t.a. and t.o. groups of 238 children were correlated, by the product moment method, with the standardized scores of the same 238 children on the Harrison-Stroud Auditory Discrimination Test, which is a published test widely used in America. The coefficient of correlation was $.56 \pm .045$, which denotes a substantial relationship, and indicates that a reasonably valid test had been constructed. It must be borne in mind that these two tests of auditory discrimination were not measuring exactly the same skills, as the author's test measured both beginning and ending sounds, whereas the Harrison-Stroud Test was only testing for beginning sounds. If the author's test had also only measured beginning sounds, the coefficient of correlation between the two tests might well have been higher.

(iii) *Measures of general intelligence: Wechsler Scale of Intelligence for Children, Goodenough Draw-A-Man Test, teachers' estimates on a five point scale.*

TABLE 26 Showing a comparison between the mean scores of the i.t.a. and t.o. groups on the Wechsler Scale of Intelligence (Verbal Tests only).

Group	N	mean score	S.D.	diff. in means	S.E. of diff.	C.R.	statis. signif.
i.t.a.	119	96.5	12.5	.7	1.77	.39	N.S.
t.o.	119	97.2	14.8				

TABLE 27 Showing a comparison between the mean scores of the i.t.a. and t.o. groups on the Goodenough Draw-A-Man Test.

Group	N	mean score	S.D.	diff. in means	S.E. of diff.	C.R.	statis. signif.
i.t.a.	119	94.75	14.6	1.65	1.81	.91	N.S.
t.o.	119	96.4	13.3				

TABLE 28 Showing a comparison between the mean scores of the i.t.a. and t.o. groups for mental ability as estimated by the class teachers on a five point scale.

Group	N	mean score	S.D.	diff. in means	S.E. of diff.	C.R.	statis. signif.
i.t.a.	119	2.99	.71	.41	.08	4.94	.1% level
t.o.	119	3.4	.66				

From Tables 26 and 27 it can be seen that, on the two standardized objective tests of general ability, there were no significant differences between the mean scores of the i.t.a. and t.o. groups. With regard to Table 28, the subjective estimate of the teachers showed a very highly significant difference (.1% level) between the mean scores of the two groups, in favour of the t.o. group. The author considered that the estimates of mental ability furnished by the class teachers would provide additional rather than key information about the children's general intelligence, being a rather cruder measure than either the Wechsler or the Goodenough test.

Relevant to this discussion of the validity of the measures of general intelligence, is a comparison made between the Wechsler Scale of Intelligence for Children and the Goodenough Draw-A-Man Test. The coefficient of correlation between the scores of both the i.t.a. and t.o. groups on these two tests was $.27^{\pm}$ .06. This figure indicates only a slight relationship between the two tests, and is in keeping with the correlation coefficients of other investigators who have examined the validity of the Goodenough Draw-A-Man Test. Hence, for the purposes of this investigation, the author felt that the Wechsler test of general intelligence was the most valid of the three measures.

(iv) *Measures of home background: the author's Vocabulary Profile, distribution of social class, and teachers' estimates of accuracy of speech, extent of vocabulary, extent and quality of play, and experiential background.*

TABLE 29 Showing a comparison between the mean scores of the i.t.a. and t.o. groups on the author's Vocabulary Profile.

Group	N	mean score	S.D.	diff. in means	S.E. of diff.	C.R.	statis. signif.
i.t.a.	119	31.1	8.1	1.4	.97	1.44	N.S.
t.o.	119	32.5	6.8				

In order to compare the distribution of social class between the i.t.a. and t.o. groups, the information provided by the teachers concerning the fathers' occupations was used. Since the 1911 Census it has been customary, as an aid to certain kinds of statistical analysis, to arrange the large number of unit groups of the occupational classification into a small number of broad based categories called Social Classes, as follows:

I   Professional Occupations
II   Clerical Occupations
III   Skilled Occupations
IV   Semi-skilled Occupations
V   Unskilled Occupations

The unit groups, included in each of these categories, have been selected so as to secure that, as far as is possible, each category is homogeneous in relation to the basic criterion of the general standing within the community of the occupation concerned. This criterion is naturally correlated with, and the application of the criterion conditioned by, other factors such as education and economic environment, but it has no direct relationship to the average level of remuneration of particular occupations. Each occupational unit group has been assigned as a whole to a social class, and it is not a specific assignment of individuals based on the merits of a particular case. The occupations of the fathers of children in the i.t.a. and t.o. groups were carefully considered and then, by referring to the classifications of occupations*, were assigned to one of the five Social Classes mentioned above. Table 30 resulted.

TABLE 30   Showing the distribution of Social Class in i.t.a. and t.o. groups according to fathers' occupations.

Group	Social Class					N
	I	II	III	IV	V	
i.t.a.	4 3.3%	13 10.8%	72 60.3%	24 20.3%	6 5.3%	119
t.o.	5 4.2%	15 12.8%	74 62.0%	20 16.8%	5 4.2%	119

*General Register Office: Classifications of Occupations. London: HMSO 1966.

TABLE 31 Showing a comparison between the mean scores of the i.t.a. and t.o. groups for accuracy of speech as estimated by the class teachers on a five point scale.

Group	N	mean score	S.D.	diff. in means	S.E. of diff.	C.R.	statis. signif.
i.t.a.	119	2.86	.62	.33	.08	3.97	.1% level
t.o.	119	3.19	.71				

TABLE 32 Showing a comparison between mean scores of the i.t.a. and t.o. groups for extent of vocabulary, as estimated by the class teachers on a five point scale.

Group	N	mean score	S.D.	diff. in means	S.E. of diff.	C.R.	statis. signif.
i.t.a.	119	2.87	.75	.43	.1	4.3	.1% level
t.o.	119	3.3	.82				

TABLE 33 Showing a comparison between the mean scores of the i.t.a. and t.o. groups for extent and quality of play, as estimated by the class teachers on a five point scale.

Group	N	mean score	S.D.	diff. in means	S.E. of diff.	C.R.	statis. signif.
i.t.a.	119	2.83	.73	.46	.09	4.84	.1% level
t.o.	119	3.29	.75				

TABLE 34 Showing a comparison between the mean scores of the i.t.a. and t.o. groups for experiential background, as estimated the class teachers on a five point scale.

Group	N	mean score	S.D.	diff. in means	S.E. of diff.	C.R.	statis. signif.
i.t.a.	119	3.02	.84	.27	.1	2.7	1% level
t.o.	119	3.29	.74				

A chi-square test showed that there were no significant differences between the numbers of i.t.a. and t.o. fathers in each of the five broad occupational groupings.

When comparing the i.t.a. and t.o. groups with regard to the broad factor of home background, we see from Table 29 that there was no significant difference between the mean scores on the author's Vocabulary Profile, and from Table 30, that no significant differences were found between the numbers of i.t.a. and t.o. fathers in each of the five broad occupational groupings. However, a comparison of the i.t.a. and t.o. groups on accuracy of speech, extent of vocabulary, extent and quality of play, and experiential background, as estimated by the class teachers on a five point scale, shows in all these aspects very highly (.1%) or highly (1%) significant differences in favour of the t.o. group (see Tables 31, 32, 33 and 34, respectively).

When studying the teacher's estimates on the various aspects of home background, the author felt that here was evidence of the often experienced 'halo' effect. Each child tended to receive the same rating on all or most of the qualities being considered. The fact that on very varied qualities the same significant differences in favour of t.o. are established seems to lend support to the presence of the 'halo' effect.

At this point it is convenient and relevant to judge to what extent the author was successful in constructing his revised version of the Vocabulary Profile. Now follows the frequency distribution of the standardized scores of both i.t.a. and t.o. groups, presented by means of a table and a corresponding histogram.

The distribution of the standardized scores on the author's revised Vocabulary Profile looked normal, but a chi-square test showed a significant difference between the observed and expected results, which indicated that a normal distribution had not been obtained.

TABLE 35   Showing the distribution of the standardized scores of 238 children on author's revised Vocabulary Profile (Mean 100, Standard Deviation 15).

Scores	Frequencies
120–129	13
110–119	53
100–109	76
90–99	52
80–89	22
70–79	15
60–69	7

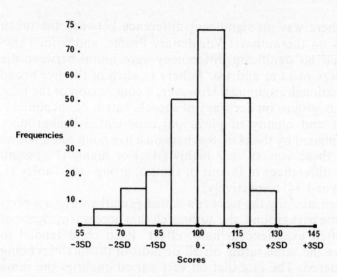

Figure 13 showing distribution of standardized scores on the author's revised Vocabulary Profile.

(v) *Measures of physical, social and emotional factors by means of class teachers' notes and estimates: ability to listen, attitudes towards books and learning, readiness to read, social and emotional traits worth noting and physical attributes.*

TABLE 36 Showing a comparison between the mean scores of the i.t.a. and t.o. groups for ability to listen, as estimated by the class teachers on a five point scale.

Group	N	mean score	S.D.	diff. in means	S.E. of diff.	C.R.	statis. signif.
i.t.a.	119	3.02	.89	.36	.1	3.6	.1% level
t.o.	119	3.38	.78				

TABLE 37 Showing a comparison between the mean scores of the i.t.a. and t.o. groups for attitudes to books and learning to read, as estimated by the class teachers on a five point scale.

Group	N	mean score	S.D.	diff. in means	S.E. of diff.	C.R.	statis. signif.
i.t.a.	119	2.93	.9	.26	.1	2.6	1% level
t.o.	119	3.19	.73				

TABLE 38 Showing a comparison between the mean scores of the i.t.a. and t.o. groups for readiness to read, as estimated by the class teachers on a five point scale.

Group	N	mean score	S.D.	diff. in means	S.E. of diff.	C.R.	statis. signif.
i.t.a.	119	2.91	.96	.3	.1	3	1% level
t.o.	119	3.21	.82				

From Table 36 it can be seen that there is a very highly significant difference (.1%) between the mean scores of the i.t.a. and t.o. groups for ability to listen, in favour of t.o.; from Tables 37 and 38 it can be seen that there are highly significant differences (1%) between the mean scores of the i.t.a and t.o. groups for attitudes to books and learning to read, and for readiness to read, again both in favour of t.o.

Again we see that all the significant differences favour the t.o. group, and this fact lends support to the possibility of a general 'halo' effect resulting from the class teachers' estimates.

With regard to the physical and social and emotional aspects which could have some bearing on a child's readiness for reading, a careful study of all the comments made by the class teachers showed that:

(i) the majority of the children in both i.t.a. and t.o. groups were marked normal in all respects.

(ii) Some children in both groups had weak eyesight which had been corrected by the wearing of spectacles.

(iii) Some children in both groups had hearing defects, and either wore hearing aids or were placed at the front of the classroom by the class teachers.

(iv) One or two children from both i.t.a. and t.o. groups came from disturbed or broken homes, and it was felt by the class teachers concerned that these children's attitudes towards school in general, and towards reading in particular, might be affected.

However, as the difficulties of all kinds mentioned by the class teachers were few in number and seemed to be fairly equally distributed between the two groups, the author felt that these relatively unimportant variables balanced themselves out.

189

The matching of the i.t.a. and t.o. groups

It has been already pointed out that with the help of the Primary Adviser of the county area from which all the 16 schools were drawn, the selection of the schools was made very carefully. Each i.t.a. school was carefully matched with a t.o. school with regard to the type of school (infant or primary), the environment of the school, and the social class backgrounds of the parents. The schools selected were drawn from small and large villages, and from small and large towns, so as to be as representative as possible.

A description of each matched pair of schools was given in Chapter 3, and the pairs were matched quite well, though it was pointed out that matching for teaching ability, methods of teaching reading, and time spent on the teaching of reading was not possible; to the best of the Adviser's knowledge, however, there were no obvious differences between each pair of schools in any of these respects at the outset of the experiment.

During the course of the first two years of the author's investigation, the original number of 150 children in each group was reduced to 119 as a result of absences, removals and the need to maintain equal numbers in the i.t.a. and t.o. groups. Whilst continually balancing the two groups the author endeavoured firstly to keep approximately the same number of children from each pair of matched schools; secondly, to keep an approximately equal number of boys and girls in each group; and thirdly, when children had to be withdrawn from the experiment to keep the numbers balanced, to keep in mind the matching of the two groups on the scores of the initial reading readiness measures.

In addition to the matching of each pair of i.t.a. and t.o. schools, the two final groups with 119 children in each, were found to be matched in the following ways:

(i) Age – Average age of the children in the i.t.a. group was 5 years 3.2 months.

Average age of the children in the t.o. group was 5 years 3.6 months.

All the children in the experiment started school at the same time, in September, 1965.

(ii) Sex – In the i.t.a. group there were 59 girls and 60 boys. in the t.o. group there were 61 girls and 58 boys.

TABLE 39

i.t.a. schools	t.o. schools
A1–16 children	A2–16 children
B1–17 children	B2–16 children
C1–14 children	C2–15 children
D1–14 children	D2–16 children
E1–16 children	E2–15 children
F1–11 children	F2–10 children
G1–15 children	G2–17 children
H1–16 children	H2–14 children

(iii) Numbers from each pair of matched schools were as shown in Table 39.

(iv) Social class – No significant differences were found between the i.t.a. and t.o. groups when the occupations of the children's fathers were distributed over five social classes.

(v) Visual discrimination – No significant differences were found between the two groups on either the author's test of Visual Discrimination or the Harrison-Stroud Test of Making Visual Discriminations.

(vi) Auditory discrimination – No significant differences were found between the two groups on either the author's test of Auditory Discrimination or the Harrison-Stroud Test of Making Auditory Discriminations.

(vii) Intelligence – No significant differences were found between the two groups on either the Wechsler Scale of Intelligence for Children, or the Goodenough Draw-A-Man Test. On the teacher's estimates of mental abililty there was a highly significant difference in favour of the t.o. group. However, this was rather a crude measure and the author feels the two groups were well matched for intelligence.

(viii) Home background – No significant differences were found between the two groups on the author's Vocabularly Profile. However, on teachers' estimates of accuracy of speech, extent of vocabularly, extent and quality of play, and experiential background, there were significant differences between the two groups in favour of the t.o. group. Here the evidence is conflicting, but the author feels that the teachers' estimates showed evidence of the 'halo' effect.

(ix) Physical, social and emotional factors – The difficulties mentioned under this heading were few in number, and equally distributed between the two groups.

On the foregoing evidence the author feels justified in claiming that the i.t.a. and t.o. groups, with 119 in each group, were well-matched for a considerable number of important variables.

Chapter 5

Discussion of the Results Obtained by the Statistical Methods Selected (II): Tests Carried out in the Children's Third Term at School

All the children in both the i.t.a. and t.o. groups were given the following three tests in the first few weeks of their third term in school:

  (i) the author's Visual Discrimination Test
 (ii) the author's Auditory Discrimination Test
(iii) the Schonell Graded Word Reading Test

The Visual and Auditory Discrimination Tests constructed by the author were given again, to enable him to compare earlier scores on these tests made by the i.t.a. and t.o. groups with later scores made by the same groups. This comparison was carried out to test Sister John's (1966) hypothesis, referred to in Chapter 1, that the different teaching media would show differential effects on the growth of discriminative abilities. Her small scale experiment suggested that learning to read with i.t.a. had more favourable effects on the growth of perceptual discrimination than learning to read with t.o.

The Schonell Graded Word Reading Test was given to compare the early reading progress made by the i.t.a. and t.o. groups, at the beginning of the children's third term in school. The t.o. version of the test was transliterated into i.t.a. for the

H

children in the i.t.a group, but apart from the transliteration the two versions of the test were identical in every way.

Now follows, in tabulated form, the relevant information obtained from the three tests given:

(i) *Measure of visual discrimination: the author's Visual Discrimination Test.*

TABLE 40   Showing a comparison between the mean scores of the i.t.a. and t.o. groups on the author's Visual Discrimination Test given for the second time.

Group	N	mean score	S.D.	diff. in means	S.E. of diff.	C.R.	statis. signif.
i.t.a.	119	24.01	6.51	1.41	.86	1.64	N.S.
t.o.	119	25.42	6.69				

Table 18 from Chapter 4, which gives the same information but for the first administration of the author's Visual Discrimination Test when the children were in their first term at school, follows for purposes of comparison.

(Table 18 from Chapter 4)

Group	N	mean score	S D	diff. in means	S.E. of diff.	C.R.	statis. signif.
i.t.a.	119	18.16	7.47	1.17	1.02	1.15	N.S.
t.o.	119	19.33	8.25				

As can be seen when comparing Tables 18 and 40, there were no significant differences between the mean scores on either the first or the second administration of the author's Visual Discrimination Test. The mean score of the i.t.a. group increased by 5.85 marks after approximately a term and a half of practice in reading; the mean score of the t.o. group increased by 6.09 marks during the same period. These increases show that the skill of visual discrimination developed as a result of the differing teaching media, but by a similar amount. There were no significant differences between the mean scores of the two groups, so as far as the author's larger sample is concerned, the hypothesis suggested by Sister John, that i.t.a. has more favourable effects than t.o. on the growth of the visual discrimination skill, is disproved.

(ii) *Measure of auditory discrimination: the author's Auditory Discrimination Test.*

TABLE 41 Showing a comparison between the mean scores of the i.t.a. and t.o. groups on the author's Auditory Discrimination Test given for the second time.

Group	N	mean score	S.D.	diff. in means	S.E. of diff.	C.R.	statis. signif.
i.t.a.	119	17.5	7.65	.57	.97	.59	N.S.
t.o.	119	18.07	7.14				

Below, for purposes of comparison, is Table 23 from Chapter 4, which gives the same information, but for the first administration of the author's Auditory Discrimination Test when the children were in their first term at school.

(Table 23 from Chapter 4)

Group	N	mean score	S.D.	diff. in means	S.E. of diff.	C R	statis. signif.
i.t.a.	119	11.47	6.66	.15	.83	.18	N.S.
t.o.	119	11.32	6.15				

As can be seen when comparing Tables 23 and 41 there were no significant differences between the mean scores on either the first or the second administration of the author's Auditory Discrimination Test. The mean score of the i.t.a. group increased by 6.03 marks after approximately a term and a half of practice in reading; the mean score of the t.o. group increased by 6.75 marks during the same period. Again, as far as the author's larger sample is concerned, the hypothesis suggested by Sister John that i.t.a. has more favourable effects than t.o. on the growth of the auditory discriminative skill, is disproved.

195

(iii) *Measures of reading achievement: the Schonell Graded Word Reading Test, and individual progress through the reading scheme*

TABLE 42   Showing a comparison between the mean scores of the i.t.a. and t.o. groups on the Schonell Graded Word Reading Test given for the first time (given in i.t.a. to the i.t.a. children; given in t.o. to the t.o. children).

Group	N	mean score	S.D.	diff. in means	S.E. of diff.	C.R.	statis. signif.
i.t.a.	119	6.8	9.55	3.25	.94	3.46	.1% level
t.o.	119	3.55	3.6				

It can be seen from Table 42 that in the children's third term in school, when they had started to read formally using either i.t.a. or t.o., there was a very highly significant difference (.1% level) between the mean scores of the i.t.a. and t.o. groups, in favour of i.t.a. One must draw conclusions from this fact with caution, bearing in mind the criticism that scores made by i.t.a. children, on a transliterated test, cannot be compared with scores made on the t.o. version of the same test by t.o. children, as a transliterated test becomes a uniformly easier test, and the i.t.a. group would therefore have the advantage. However, this criticism lends support to the conclusion which can be drawn from this result, namely, that as the two groups were well matched, children in the author's sample learned to read more easily with i.t.a. than with t.o., when used with a mainly eclectic approach. Conversely, this means that, in the author's sample, the traditional alphabet and spelling of English used with an eclectic approach was a more difficult medium for the teaching of reading than was i.t.a.

If children can learn to read more easily with i.t.a. than they can with t.o., this means that the reading readiness level for leaning to read with i.t.a. will be lower than that for learning to read with t.o. The truth, or otherwise, of this hypothesis was the central problem of the investigation, and further statistical methods were used to examine this hypothesis more thoroughly. These are dealt with later in the chapter.

Relevant to a comparison of the mean reading scores of the i.t.a. and t.o. groups, is the analysis of the class teacher records of their children's progress through the basic books of the particular reading scheme being used.

A very careful analysis of the mass of information concerning the reading progress of each child who took part in the experiment made the author realise that no valid results could be obtained from using this kind of information, for the following reasons:

(a) In the main i.t.a. experiment all the schools involved agreed to use the same reading scheme – the 'Janet and John' scheme – either in its t.o. or i.t.a. version. In the author's experiment no control could be exercised over the reading schemes in use, and it was found that many reading schemes were represented, namely, the 'Downing Readers' (i.t.a.), 'Janet and John' (i.t.a. and t.o. versions), 'Happy Venture', 'Happy Trio', 'Gayway' and the 'Keywords'.

(b) Two schools used the books from two or three different schemes and combined them in their own devised sequence, to ease their children from book to book.

(c) The Reading Progress Charts were not filled up satisfactorily by the class teachers, apart from one or two exceptions. Often, the dates when children completed the reading of particular basic books were omitted; often the forms were filled up retrospectively with many omissions; often single forms were lost, and when one teacher left a school, the whole set of forms was lost.

(d) There was no objective standard regarding what was meant by 'completing a book satisfactorily'. Some teachers moved children on to the next book the moment they had struggled to the end of the current one; other teachers felt the children ought to be able to read the current one easily before moving them on.

For the above reasons the author felt that it was not possible to use the 'primer criterion' to obtain valid comparisons between the i.t.a. and t.o. groups of progress through the reading schemes, though the author's subjective impression from studying the returns was that the i.t.a. children were making more rapid progress than the t.o. children.

In order to compare more rigorously the reading readiness

197

requirements for learning to read with i.t.a. and t.o., the following statistical analyses were carried out:

(i) A study of the relationship between the earlier results on the battery of reading readiness measures, and the results on the Schonell Graded Word Reading Test, for both the i.t.a. and t.o. groups separately.

(ii) A comparison of the mean scores achieved on the Schonell Graded Word Reading Test between subgroups of i.t.a. and t.o. children who attained similar levels of performance on each of the earlier reading readiness measures.

(iii) A comparison of the minimum mental age levels required for learning to read successfully with i.t.a. and t.o.

(i) *To study the relationship between the earlier reading readiness results and the later reading achievement results:*
the author changed the raw scores to standardized scores with a mean of 100 and a standard deviation of 15, and correlated, for each group separately, the two sets of scores.

This method of approach follows one that is often used by American research workers in the field of reading readiness, but which, to the author's knowledge, has not been used with British children except by the author himself in his previous investigation. In many American investigations, reading readiness tests are given to children upon entering the first grade of the primary school. Then six months and/ or a year later, the same children are given reading achievement tests, and the scores on these later reading tests are correlated with the earlier scores on the reading readiness tests. The predictive value of the reading readiness tests, and of individual sub-tests, is assessed by the degree of correlation between the two sets of scores.

From the correlation figures obtained in this present investigation, the author has compared the correlation figures obtained by the i.t.a. and t.o. groups to see if there are any significant differences between them. When examining correlation coefficients, the level of significance tells whether the correlation indicates a true relationship, or whether i is probably due to chance. The degree of relationship of a significant correlation is more difficult to ascertain. Garrett (1958) says that:

> there is a fairly good agreement among workers with psychological and educational tests that
>
> r from .00 to $\pm$.20 denotes indifferent or negligible relationship.
>
> r from .20 to $\pm$.40 denotes low correlation; present but slight.
>
> r from .40 to $\pm$.70 denotes substantial or marked relationship.
>
> r from .70 to $\pm$1.00 denotes high to very high relationship.

These broad divisions will be used for interpreting the correlations calculated in this investigation, and for purposes of valid comparison the coefficients of correlation – the Pearson 'r's – have been changed into corresponding Fisher 'z's.

From Table 43 it can be seen that there are no significant differences between the correlation coefficients of six of the reading readiness measures and the Schonell Graded Word Reading Test; this indicates that these six measures were of similar importance for reading progress in both i.t.a. and t.o. during the children's first two terms at school.

However, on the Harrison-Stroud Visual Discrimination Test in t.o. there is a highly significant difference (1% level) between the correlation coefficients of the i.t.a. and t.o. groups, in favour of t.o. This result indicates that even though the two groups of i.t.a. and t.o. children had not started to read formally, the pre-reading activities designed to introduce learning to read with a particular medium together with the classroom environment of words and pictures, again in either i.t.a. or t.o., had had a measurable effect. This is shown by the fact that there was a high correlation between the Harrison-Stroud Visual Discrimination Test in t.o. and the later reading achievement of the t.o. group, whereas with the i.t.a. group the same test did not bear a marked relationship with later reading progress, as an i.t.a. pre-reading environment would have been created in the first few weeks of schooling.

Again, with the author's Auditory Discrimination Test

TABLE 43 Showing a comparison of the correlations, calculated for the i.t.a. and t.o. groups separately, between the initial tests of reading readiness abilities and the Schonell Graded Word Reading Test given for the first time (given in i.t.a. to the i.t.a. children; given in t.o. to the t.o. children.)

Tests of Reading Readiness Abilities	Schonell Graded Word Reading Test 1st. time – May, 1966						
	Group	r	z	diff. in 'z's	S.E. of diff.	C.R.	statis. signif.
Visual Discrim. Thackray	i.t.a.	.39	.41	.04	.13	.31	N.S.
	t.o.	.35	.37				
Visual Discrim. in i.t.a. Harrison-Stroud	i.t.a.	.43	.46	.08	.13	.57	N.S.
	t.o.	.36	.38				
Visual Discrim. in t.o. Harrison-Stroud	i.t.a.	.37	.39	.34	.13	2.6	1% level
	t.o.	.62	.73				
Auditory Discrim. Thackray	i.t.a.	.51	.56	.26	.13	2.0	5% level
	t.o.	.29	.30				
Auditory Discrim. Harrison-Stroud	i.t.a.	.44	.47	.05	.13	.38	N.S.
	t.o.	.40	.42				
Wechsler Scale of Intelligence	i.t.a.	.29	.30	.17	.13	1.31	N.S.
	t.o.	.44	.47				
Goodenough Draw-A-Man Test	i.t.a.	.32	.33	.11	.13	.45	N.S.
	t.o.	.22	.22				
Vocabulary Profile Thackray	i.t.a.	.34	.35	.03	.13	.23	N.S.
	t.o.	.31	.32				

we see a significant difference (5% level) between the correlation coefficients of the i.t.a. and t.o. groups, this time in favour of i.t.a. This result might reflect the fact that at least one i.t.a. teacher started teaching the letters and sounds from the moment the children entered school, and that more stress was likely to be placed on a phonic approach in the i.t.a. group as a whole, than with the t.o. group.

(ii) *To compare the reading readiness level required on each of the reading readiness measures necessary for children to learn to read successfully using i.t.a. and t.o.*:
the mean reading scores, achieved on the Schonell Graded Word Reading Test by sub-groups of i.t.a. and t.o. children who attained similar levels of performance on each of the earlier reading readiness measures, were calculated and compared. To obtain the five levels of performance used in this analysis the range of marks was divided by five, so the groupings throughout the range were equal.

Where the numbers of i.t.a. and t.o. children at each level of performance could be classed, for statistical purposes, as large samples (i.e. over 25), the appropriate formula for finding the standard error of the difference between the means was used, as in large samples we can assume that the distribution of the difference between sample means is normal. Where the numbers were small (i.e. under 25) the appropriate formula for small samples was used to find the standard error of the difference between the means, as in small samples we cannot assume that the distribution of the difference between sample means is normal.

To obtain significance levels with the larger samples, those commonly accepted for a normal distribution were used as follows:

5% of a normal distribution lies outside the range of -1.96 SDs to $+1.96$ SDs.

1% of a normal distribution lies outside the range of -2.58 SDs to $+2.58$ SDs.

.1% of a normal distribution lies outside the range of -3.29 SDs to $+3.29$ SDs.

To obtain significance levels with the small samples, the 't' Table was consulted, using ($n_1 + n_2 - 2$) degrees of freedom.

Now follows a series of Tables presenting the information obtained from this statistical approach. When the information has been presented for each particular aspect of reading readiness – for example, visual discrimination – a discussion of that aspect follows.

TABLE 44   showing a comparison of the mean scores attained on the Schonell
Graded Word Reading Test, by sub-groups of i.t.a. and t.o. children
who attained similar levels of performance on the author's Visual
Discrimination Test.

Visual Discrim. Thackray			Schonell Graded Word Reading Test 1st time, May 1966					
range of scores	Group	N	mean score	S.D.	diff. in means	S.E. of diff.	C.R.	statis. signif.
28–34	i.t.a. t.o.	8 24	24.00 4.25	15.81 3.74	19.75	3.61	5.47	.1% level
21–27	i.t.a. t.o.	53 33	7.92 3.88	9.27 5.39	4.04	1.58	2.56	5% level
14–20	i.t.a. t.o.	26 27	4.96 2.30	6.40 2.83	2.66	1.37	1.94	N.S.
7–13	i.t.a. t.o.	23 28	1.87 1.29	2.50 1.90	.58	.63	.92	N.S.
0–6	i.t.a. t.o.	9 7	1.33 .29	.95 .46	1.04	.41	2.54	5% level

TABLE 45   Showing a comparison of the mean scores attained on the Schonell
Graded Word Reading Test, by sub-groups of i.t.a. and t.o. children
who attained similar levels of performance on the Harrison-Stroud
Visual Discrimination Test in i.t.a.

Visual Discrim. in i.t.a.-Harrison-Stroud			Schonell Graded Word Reading Test 1st time, May 1966					
range of scores	Group	N	mean score	S.D.	diff. in means	S.E. of diff.	C.R.	statis. signif.
25–30	i.t.a. t.o.	51 54	12.23 3.67	13.19 4.00	8.56	1.93	4.43	.1% level
19–24	i.t.a. t.o.	29 31	4.34 2.87	5.48 4.8	1.47	1.33	1.11	N.S.
13–18	i.t.a. t.o.	18 19	1.83 1.21	2.1 2.45	.62	.75	.83	N.S.
7–12	i.t.a. t.o.	14 8	2.43 1.00	2.9 1.5	1.43	1.15	1.24	N.S.
0–6	i.t.a. t.o.	7 7	1.28 .29	.89 .46	.99	.4	2.47	5% level

TABLE 46 Showing a comparison of the mean scores attained on the Schonell Graded Word Reading Test, by sub-groups of i.t.a. and t.o. children who attained similar levels of performance on the Harrison-Stroud Visual Discrimination Test in t.o.

Visual Discrim. in t.o.-Harrison-Stroud			Schonell Graded Word Reading Test 1st time, May 1966					
range of scores	Group	N	mean score	S.D.	diff. in means	S.E. of diff.	C.R.	statis. signif.
25–30	i.t.a.	48	10.15	11.62	6.40	1.75	3.65	.1% level
	t.o.	56	3.75	3.87				
19–24	i.t.a.	31	6.55	7.72	3.42	1.64	2.08	5% level
	t.o.	31	3.13	4.90				
13–18	i.t.a.	19	2.89	3.32	1.77	.90	1.97	N.S.
	t.o.	16	1.12	1.54				
7–12	i.t.o.	13	1.08	.91	.67	.33	2.03	N.S.
	t.o.	12	.42	.63				
0–6	i.t.a.	8	1.37	.86				
	t.o.	4	0	0				

From Tables 44, 45 and 46, the following results can be seen:

(a) For each level of performance, on all three tests of visual discrimination, the mean scores attained by the i.t.a. sub-groups on the Schonell reading achievement test are greater than the mean scores attained by the t.o. sub-groups.

(b) On all three tests of visual discrimination the i.t.a. sub-groups, at the highest level of performance, attained mean reading scores which were very highly significantly (.1% level) greater than the mean reading scores of the t.o. sub-groups with the same highest level of performance on the visual discrimination tests.

(c) On two out of the three tests of visual discrimination, the i.t.a. sub-groups with the second highest level of performance, attained mean reading scores which were significantly (5% level) greater than the mean reading scores of the t.o. sub-groups with the second highest level of performance, on the two visual discrimination tests.

TABLE 47 Showing a comparison of the mean scores attained on the Schonell Graded Word Reading Test, by sub-groups of i.t.a. and t.o. children who attained similar levels of performance on the author's Auditory Discrimination Test.

range of scores	Group	N	mean score	S.D.	diff. in means	S.E. in diff.	C.R.	statis. signif.
27–33	i.t.a. t.o.	1 1	30.0 20.0	0 0				
20–26	i.t.a. t.o.	15 12	18.0 4.75	9.7 5.75	13.25	8.5	1.56	N.S.
14–19	i.t.a. t.o.	26 29	8.04 4.66	10.77 4.36	3.38	2.26	1.49	N.S.
7–13	i.t.a. t.o.	43 52	5.0 1.85	6.4 2.83	3.15	1.05	3.0	1% level
0–6	i.t.a. t.o.	34 25	2.12 1.6	2.24 2.65	.52	.66	.79	N.S.

TABLE 48 Showing a comparison of the mean scores attained on the Schonell Graded Word Reading Test, by sub-groups of i.t.a. and t.o. children who attained similar levels of performance on the Harrison-Stroud Auditory Discrimination Test.

range of scores	Group	N	mean score	S.D.	diff. in means	S.E. of diff.	C.R.	statis. signif.
13–16	i.t.a. t.o.	23 30	14.91 6.2	14.12 5.39	8.71	2.69	3.42	1% level
10–12	i.t.a. t.o.	31 40	6.97 2.05	9.17 2.83	4.92	1.71	2.88	1% level
7–9	i.t.a. t.o.	53 39	3.92 1.22	5.83 1.73	2.7	.71	3.8	.1% level
4–6	i.t.a. t.o.	11 8	2.45 1.71	2.65 2.24	.74	1.27	.58	N S
0–3	i.t.a. t.o.	1 2	2 0					

(d) On two out of the three tests of visual discrimination, the i.t.a. sub-groups with the lowest level of performance obtained mean reading scores which were significantly (5% level) greater than the mean reading scores of the t.o. sub-groups with the lowest level of performance on the two visual discrimination tests.

These results indicate that, given i.t.a. and t.o. sub-groups with similar levels of performance on visual discrimination tests, the i.t.a. sub-groups have mean reading scores greater, and sometimes significantly greater, than their t.o. counterparts. This fact means that some i.t.a. sub-groups with lower levels of performance in visual discrimination than some t.o. sub-groups, can reach similar levels of reading achievement to those t.o. sub-groups, after six months of reading. An example from Table 44 might make this point clear. From this Table it can be seen that to attain a mean reading score of approximately 4.5 the i.t.a. sub-groups would need a level of performance in visual discrimination ranging from 14–20, whereas the t.o. sub-group needs a level of performance ranging from 28–34. Such figures indicate quite clearly that less skill is required in visual discrimination for children learning to read in i.t.a. than is required for children learning to read in t.o., and therefore that i.t.a. is an easier medium from the standpoint of visual discrimination.

From Tables 47 and 48 the following results can be seen:

(a) For each level of performance, on both tests of auditory discrimination, the mean scores attained by the i.t.a. sub-groups on the Schonell reading achievement test are greater than the mean reading scores attained by the t.o. sub-groups.

(b) On the author's test of auditory discrimination, the i.t.a. sub-group at the second lowest level of performance attained a mean reading score which was highly significantly (1% level) greater than the mean reading score of the t.o. sub-group with the same level of performance on the author's test.

(c) On the Harrison-Stroud Test of auditory discrimination, the i.t.a. sub-groups at the three highest levels of performance, attained mean reading scores which were significantly (1% level) greater than the mean reading scores of the t.o. sub-groups with the same level of performance, on the Harrison-Stroud Test.

Although there is not complete agreement between the results given in Tables 47 and 48, it would seem reasonable to state that some evidence exists to show that, given i.t.a. and t.o. sub-groups with similar levels of performance on auditory discrimination tests, the i.t.a. sub-groups have mean reading scores greater, and sometimes significantly greater, than their t.o. counterparts. Again, this fact means that some i.t.a. sub-groups with lower levels of performance in auditory discrimination than some t.o. sub-groups, can reach similar levels of reading achievement to those t.o. sub-groups after six months of reading. This means that less skill is required in auditory discrimination for children learning to read in i.t.a., and therefore i.t.a. is an easier medium from the standpoint of auditory discrimination.

From Tables 49 and 50 the following results can be seen:

(a) With one exception, for each level of performance on

TABLE 49   Showing a comparison of the mean scores attained on the Schonell Graded Word Reading Test, by sub-groups of i.t.a. and t.o. children who attained similar levels of performance on the Wechsler Scale of Intelligence for Children.

Wechsler Scale of Intelligence			Schonell Graded Word Reading Test 1st time, May 1966					
range of scores	Group	N	mean score	S.D.	diff. in means	S.E. of diff.	C.R.	statis. signif.
113–125	i.t.a. t.o.	6 19	13.68 6.0	11.14 6.24	7.68	3.77	2.04	N.S.
100–112	i.t.a. t.o.	52 35	8.58 3.26	11.79 3.32	5.32	1.73	3.08	1% level
87–99	i.t.a. t.o.	35 36	5.03 1.78	9.11 2.83	3.25	1.61	2.02	5% level
74–86	i.t.a. t.o.	20 22	6.7 1.82	2.45 2.24	4.88	.72	6.78	.1% level
60–73	i.t.a. t.o.	6 7	1.67 .14	2.0 .35	1.53	.84	1.82	N.S.

TABLE 50　Showing a comparison of the mean scores attained on the Schonell Graded Word Reading Test, by sub-groups of i.t.a. and t.o. children who attained similar levels of performance on the Goodenough Draw-A-Man Test.

Goodenough Draw-A-Man Test			Schonell Graded Word Reading Test 1st time, May 1966					
range of scores	Group	N	mean score	S.D.	diff. in means	S.E. of diff.	C.R.	statis. signif.
120–133	i.t.a.	5	17.8	13.56	13.13	9.3	1.41	N.S.
	t.o.	3	4.67	4.47				
106–119	i.t.a.	19	10.95	14.46	8.01	3.74	2.14	5% level
	t.o.	16	2.94	4.2				
93–105	i.t.a.	47	7.49	10.25	3.22	1.62	1.99	5% level
	t.o.	40	4.27	4.0				
79–92	i.t.a.	32	4.87	5.92	3.44	1.08	3.18	1% level
	t.o.	42	1.43	1.73				
65–78	i.t.a.	16	1.27	.93	.84	1.44	.58	N.S.
	t.o.	18	2.11	3.87				

both tests of general intelligence, the mean scores attained by the i.t.a. sub-groups on the Schonell reading achievement test, are greater than the mean reading scores attained by the t.o. sub-groups.

(b) On both measures of intelligence the i.t.a. sub-groups with the three middle levels of performance, attained mean reading scores which were significantly greater than the mean reading scores of the t.o. sub-groups with the same levels of performance on the measures of intelligence.

These results indicate that, given i.t.a. and t.o. sub-groups with similar levels of performance on intelligence measures, the i.t.a. sub-groups have mean reading scores greater, and sometimes significantly (.1%, 1% and 5% levels) greater than their t.o. counterparts. This fact provides evidence that some i.t.a. sub-groups with lower levels of performance in intelligence measures than some t.o. sub-groups, can reach similar levels of reading achievement to those t.o. sub-groups after six months of reading. This means that a lower level of

TABLE 51 Showing a comparison of the mean scores attained on the Schonell Graded Word Reading Test, by sub-groups of i.t.a. and t.o. children who attained similar levels of performance on the author's Vocabulary Profile.

| Vocabulary Profile Thackray | | | Schonell Graded Word Reading Test 1st time, May 1966 | | | | | |
range of scores	Group	N	mean score	S.D.	diff. in means	S.E. of diff.	C.R.	statis. signif.
41–50	i.t.a.	10	11.6	11.83	5.6	4.5	1.24	N.S.
	t.o.	10	6.0	6.32				
31–40	i.t.a.	65	9.03	11.92	5.66	1.55	3.65	.1% level
	t.o.	68	3.37	4.0				
21–30	i.t.a.	29	3.24	4.0	2.19	.8	2.74	.1% level
	t.o.	36	1.05	1.73				
11–20	i.t.a.	13	2.46	3.0				
	t.o.	3	0	0				
0–10	i.t.a.	2	0	0				
	t.o.	2	1.5	1.41				

intelligence is adequate for children learning to read in i.t.a. than is required for children learning to read in t.o. and therefore that the problems to be solved in reading with i.t.a. are of a simpler nature than those to be solved in reading with t.o.

From Table 51 the following results can be seen:

(a) With one minor exception, for each level of performance the mean reading scores obtained by the i.t.a. sub-groups are greater than the mean reading scores obtained by the t.o. sub-groups.

(b) The i.t.a. sub-groups at the two intermediate levels of performance attained mean reading scores which were significantly (.1% and 1% levels) greater than the mean reading scores of the t.o. sub-groups with the same levels of performance on the author's Vocabulary Profile. Again the conclusions to be drawn from these results are the same in regard to this measure as those drawn from all the results from this particular statistical approach.

This second statistical approach has shown quite clearly that i.t.a. sub-groups could attain similar reading achievement levels to t.o. sub-groups, but with lower levels of reading readiness abilities, thus proving experimentally that i.t.a. is simpler than t.o. in its visual and auditory structure and that the problems to be solved in learning to read with i.t.a. are of a simpler nature than those of t.o. Assuming that, in most cases, the reading readiness abilities which have been discussed develop with age, that is, the older a child is the more developed will be these skills, then it follows that a child who is going to learn to read with i.t.a. will be ready to start reading at an earlier age. The third statistical approach looks further into this question.

(iii) *In order to make a comparison of the minimum mental age levels required for learning to read successfully with i.t.a. and t.o.:*
the 119 children in each of the i.t.a. and t.o. groups were grouped according to their mental ages, worked out from the scores on the Wechsler Scale of Intelligence for Children, with group intervals of six months. For each mental age group, the raw scores of the children on the Schonell reading achievement test were averaged, and comparisons between the mean scores of the i.t.a. and t.o. sub-groups were made.

TABLE 52 Showing a comparison between the mean scores attained on the Schonell Graded Word Reading Test, given for the first time, by sub-groups of i.t.a. and t.o. children with similar mental ages.

Mental ages (Years, months)	below 3–6	3–6 3–11	4–0 4–5	4–6 4–11	5–0 5–5	5–6 5–11	6–0 6–5	6–6 6–11
no. of i.t.a. chn. in each mental age group	2	5	15	23	36	30	7	1
no. of t.o. chn. in each mental age group	4	7	14	20	25	27	20	12
mean score of i.t.a. chn. on Schonell	.5	2	3.13	3.69	6.69	10.93	11.71	20
mean score of t.o. chn. on Schonell	0	1.71	1.8	1.65	2.24	3.0	5.22	12

Table 52 shows that:

(a) For the i.t.a. group, a mental age range of 5 years to 5 years 5 months gives a mean score of 6.69, and is a relatively reasonable advance on the mean scores at lower mental ages.

(b) For the t.o. groups, the nearest similar mean score of 5.22, which is a relatively reasonable advance on the mean scores at lower mental ages, requires a mental age range of 6 years to 6 years 5 months.

This analysis is only a crude one, but does suggest that in the author's sample the i.t.a. children were able to learn to read successfully with a mental age of 5 years to 5 years 5 months, whereas with the t.o. children mental ages of 6 years to 6 years 5 months seemed to be necessary for learning to read successfully. This is not to say that in this particular example the i.t.a. children were reading as well as the t.o. children, as it has been pointed out that scores on a transliterated test cannot be compared with scores on the t.o. version of the same test. However, the evidence does suggest that children learning to read with i.t.a. can do so with a lower mental age level than can their t.o. counterparts, and that i.t.a. is an easier medium than t.o.

Chapter 6

Discussion of the Results Obtained by the Statistical Methods Selected (III): Tests Carried out in the Children's Fourth Term at School

At the beginning of the children's second year in school (fourth term) the i.t.a. and t.o. groups were given the following two reading achievement measures:

(i) Schonell Graded Word Reading Test – 2nd time;
(ii) Neale Analysis of Reading Ability – 1st time. The subtests of Accuracy of reading and Comprehension of reading were used.

On these two measures the children in the i.t.a. group were all tested with the i.t.a. versions, although at this stage ten children were on the point of transfer to t.o. or had just been transferred by their teachers. It was felt to be fairer to take the i.t.a. scores of these ten children, as lower reading scores are usually made on the t.o. version of a test by i.t.a. children just after the transfer. The children in the t.o. group were given the t.o. versions of the same tests.

Now follows, in tabulated form, the relevant information obtained from the two measures given:

(i) *Schonell Graded Word Reading Test*

TABLE 53   Showing a comparison between the mean scores of the i.t.a. and t.o. groups on the Schonell Graded Word Reading Test given for the second time (given in i.t.a. to the i.t.a. children; given in t.o. to the t.o. children).

Group	N	mean score	S.D;	diff. in means	S.E. of diff.	C.R.	statis. signif.
i.t.a.	119	16.0	9.45	10.7	1.03	10.39	.1% level
t.o.	119	5.3	6.1				

Table 53 shows that after a year of schooling there was a very highly significant difference (.1% level) between the means scores of the i.t.a. and t.o. groups in favour of the i.t.a. group. This result is a similar one to that obtained when giving the Schonell test in the children's third term at school but again it must be considered with caution, bearing in mind that it may not be valid to compare scores made on a trans literated test with scores made on the t.o. version of that same test, particularly when there are no contextual clues given in the test. However, as the two groups were well-matched on a number of important variables, this result would seem to indicate that in the author's sample children learned to read more easily with i.t.a., than with t.o. used with a mainly eclectic approach.

(ii) *Neale Analysis of Reading Ability*

TABLE 54   Showing a comparison between the mean scores of the i.t.a. and t.o. groups on Reading Accuracy as measured by the Neale Analysis of Reading Ability (Form A), given for the first time (given in i.t.a. to the i.t.a. children; given in t.o. to the t.o. children).

Group	N	mean score	S.D.	diff. in means	S.E. of diff.	C.R.	statis. signif.
i.t.a.	119	9.55	10.30	3.6	1.16	3.13	1% level
t.o.	119	5.95	7.35				

From Table 54 we again see a highly significant difference (1% level) between the mean scores of the i.t.a. and t.o. groups in favour of i.t.a., for Reading Accuracy. This partic lar measure of reading accuracy is based on a child's reading of continuous prose, and so this result supports the conclusion to be drawn from all the reading results discussed so far, namely, that i.t.a. is a simpler medium through which to teach reading than is the usual 'look and say' approach using t.o. If children can learn to read more easily with i.t.a. than they can with t.o., this means that the reading readiness level for learning to read with i.t.a. will be lower than that for learning to read with t.o. As before, further statistical analyses will be made to study this central problem more thoroughly.

TABLE 55 Showing a comparison between the mean scores of the i.t.a. and t.o. groups on Reading Comprehension as measured by the Neale Analysis of Reading Ability (Form A), given for the first time.

Group	N	mean score	S.D.	diff. in means	S.E. of diff.	C.R.	statis. signif.
i.t.a.	119	2.62	2.96	.34	.37	.92	N.S.
t.o.	119	2.28	2.94				

Table 55 shows there is no significant difference between the mean scores of the i.t.a. and t.o. groups on Reading Comprehension. It is interesting to compare these results with those of the Reading Accuracy results. It could be argued that the discrepancy here indicates that, although the i.t.a. children could read more easily and gain higher mean scores, they were not understanding all they were reading, as the Reading Comprehension of both groups was of a similar standard. The criticism has been made concerning i.t.a. that children can read difficult prose quite easily and correctly but do not understand what they are reading, and the Reading Comprehension result lends support to this criticism. However, the Comprehension figures must be treated with caution, as firstly, the Accuracy score sets a ceiling to the Comprehension score, and secondly, difficult words in a passage are supplied by the tester, and some of these words may be answers to the questions asked in the test. For this reason it has been said that the test is one of recall rather than comprehension, and in this context the author, on a

213

number of occasions, asked for the meaning of a word a child had given correctly, to find the child did not know what the word meant. It would seem then that in the author's sample there was some evidence to suggest that in the i.t.a. reading, accuracy was outstripping understanding of the words read, but the nature of the test precludes any definite conclusion being reached.

Again, in order to compare more rigorously the reading readiness requirements for learning to read with i.t.a. and t.o., the same three statistical analyses, which are described in detail in Chapter 5, were carried out.

TABLE 56 Showing a comparison of the correlations, calculated for i.t.a. and t.o. groups separately, between the initial test of reading readiness abilities and the Schonell Graded Word Reading Test given for the second time (given in i.t.a. to the i.t.a. children; given in t.o. to the t.o. children).

Tests of Reading Readiness Abilities	Schonell Graded Word Reading Test 2nd time, September 1966						
	Group	r	z	diff. in 'z's	S.E. of diff.	C.R.	statis. signif.
Visual Discrim. Thackray	i.t.a.	.47	.51	.12	.13	.92	N.S.
	t.o.	.31	.39				
Visual Discrim. in i.t.a. Harrison-Stroud	i.t.a.	.52	.58	.25	.13	1.92	N.S.
	t.o.	.32	.33				
Visual Discrim. in t.o. Harrison-Stroud	i.t.a.	.45	.48	0	.13	0	N.S.
	t.o.	.45	.48				
Auditory Discrim. Thackray	i.t.a.	.57	.65	.34	.13	2.62	1% level
	t.o.	.30	.31				
Auditory Discrim. Harrison-Stroud	i.t.a.	.51	.56	.11	.13	.85	N.S.
	t.o.	.42	.45				
Wechsler Scale of Intelligence	i.t.a.	.37	.39	.12	.13	.92	N.S.
	t.o.	.47	.51				
Goodenough Draw-A-Man Test	i.t.a.	.31	.32	.04	.13	.31	N.S.
	t.o.	.27	.28				
Vocabulary Profile Thackray	i.t.a.	.37	.39	.08	.13	.57	N.S.
	t.o.	.30	.31				

(i) *A study of the relationship between the earlier results on the battery of reading readiness measures and the results on the two reading achievements measures* given at the beginning of the children's fourth term in school, for both the i.t.a. and the t.o. groups separately.

From Table 56 it can be seen that the only significantly different pair of correlation coefficients is that for the author's Auditory Discrimination Test (1% level). This same significant difference was found on the same test when the Schonell reading achievement test was given for the first time, and lends support to the conclusion that in the author's sample

TABLE 57   Showing a comparison of the correlations, calculated for the i.t.a. and t.o. groups separately, between the initial tests of reading readiness abilities and Reading Accuracy as measured by the Neale Analysis of Reading Ability (Form A), given for the first time. (Given in i.t.a. to the i.t.a. children; given in t.o. to the t.o. children).

Tests of Reading Readiness Abilities	Neale Analysis of Reading Ability, Form A (Accuracy) 1st time, September 1966						
	Group	r	z	diff. in 'z's	S.E. of diff.	C.R.	statis. signif.
Visual Discrim. Thackray	i.t.a.	.36	.38	.09	.13	.69	N.S.
	t.o.	.44	.47				
Visual Discrim. in i.t.a. Harrison-Stroud	i.t.a.	.51	.56	.16	.13	1.23	N.S.
	t.o.	.38	.40				
Visual Discrim. in t.o. Harrison-Stroud	i.t.a.	.48	.52	.10	.13	.77	N.S.
	t.o.	.40	.42				
Auditory Discrim. Thackray	i.t.a.	.57	.65	.36	.13	2.77	1% level
	t.o.	.29	.29				
Auditory Discrim. Harrison-Stroud	i.t.a.	.52	.58	.19	.13	1.46	N.S.
	t.o.	.37	.39				
Wechsler Scale of Intelligence	i.t.a.	.34	.35	.16	.13	1.23	N.S.
	t.o.	.47	.51				
Goodenough Draw-A-Man Test	i.t.a.	.29	.30	0	.13	0	N.S.
	t.o.	.29	.30				
Vocabulary Profile Thackray	i.t.a.	.39	.41	.07	.13	.54	N.S.
	t.o.	.33	.34				

the phonic aspects of reading were being dealt with more systematically in the i.t.a. classes than in the t.o. classes; this may have been the case in the main i.t.a. experiment, as has been suggested.

From Table 57 it can be seen that again the only significantly different pair of correlation coefficients is that for the author's Auditory Discrimination Test (1% level). This continues the pattern already established, and lends more support to the conclusion that the phonic aspects of reading were being dealt with more systematically in the i.t.a. classes than in the t.o. classes, as the author's test measuring both beginning and ending sounds was a fairly comprehensive measure of auditory discrimination.

TABLE 58   Showing a comparison of the correlations, calculated for the i.t.a. and t.o. groups separately, between the initial tests of reading readiness abilities and Reading Comprehension as measured by the Neale Analysis of Reading Ability (Form A), given for the first time.

Tests of Reading Readiness Abilities	Neale Analysis of Reading Ability, Form A (Comprehension) 1st time, September 1966						
	Group	r	z	diff. in 'z's	S.E. of diff.	C.R.	statis. signif.
Visual Discrim. Thackray	i.t.a.	.48	.52	.08	.13	.62	N.S.
	t.o.	.41	.44				
Visual Discrim. in i.t.a. Harrison-Stroud	i.t.a.	.54	.60	.29	.13	2.23	5% level
	t.o.	.30	.31				
Visual Discrim. in t.o. Harrison-Stroud	i.t.a.	.43	.46	.06	.13	.46	N.S.
	t.o.	.38	.40				
Auditory Discrim. Thackray	i.t.a.	.57	.65	.41	.13	3.15	1% level
	t.o.	.24	.24				
Auditory Discrim. Harrison-Stroud	i.t.a.	.55	.62	.21	.13	1.62	N.S.
	t.o.	.39	.41				
Wechsler Scale of Intelligence	i.t.a.	.42	.45	.10	.13	.77	N.S.
	t.o.	.50	.55				
Goodenough Draw-A-Man Test	i.t.a.	.25	.26	.03	.13	.23	N.S.
	t.o.	.23	.23				
Vocabulary Profile Thackray	i.t.a.	.37	.39	.04	.13	.31	N.S.
	t.o.	.34	.35				

It has been pointed out that the measures of Reading Accuracy and Reading Comprehension are not independent, and so the results shown in Table 58 are more for interest than for drawing conclusions. Again, we see the same pattern repeated with regard to the author's Auditory Discrimination Test (1% level).

(ii) *A comparison of the mean scores attained on the two reading achievement measures between sub-groups of i.t.a. and t.o. children who attained similar levels of performance on each of the earlier reading readiness measures:*
The Schonell Test is presented first, followed by the Neale Test. As before, when the information has been presented for each particular aspect of reading readiness, for example, visual discrimination, a discussion of that aspect follows.

(a) *The Schonell Graded Word Reading Test*

From Tables 59, 60 and 61 (overleaf) the following results can be seen:

(a) For each level of performance, except the lowest level, on all three tests of visual discrimination, the mean scores attained by the i.t.a. sub-groups on the Schonell reading achievement test are greater than the mean scores attained by the t.o. sub-groups.

(b) On all three tests of visual discrimination the i.t.a. sub-groups at the highest level of performance attained mean reading scores which were very highly significantly (.1% level) greater than the mean reading scores of the t.o. sub-groups with the same highest level of performance on the visual discrimination tests.

(c) There were no other significant differences common to all tests, but on the author's test there was a significant difference (5% level) between the mean reading scores at the second highest level of performance on visual discrimination, and on the Harrison-Stroud Test in t.o. there was a significant difference (5% level) between the mean reading scores at the second lowest level of performance.

TABLE 59   Showing a comparison of the mean scores attained on the Schonell Graded Word Reading Test, by sub-groups of i.t.a. and t.o. children who attained similar levels of performance on the author's Visual Discrimination Test.

Visual Discrim. Thackray			Schonell Graded Word Reading Test 2nd Time, September 1966					
range of scores	Group	N	mean score	S.D.	diff. in means	S.E. of diff.	C.R.	statis. signif.
28–34	i.t.a. t.o.	8 24	22.12 7.13	12.17 6.78	14.99	3.58	4.19	.1% level
21–27	i.t.a. t.o.	53 33	10.25 6.18	9.90 8.25	4.07	1.98	2.06	5% level
14–20	i.t.a. t.o.	26 27	6.04 3.81	6.78 4.0	2.23	1.49	1.5	N.S.
7–13	i.t.a. t.o.	23 28	2.48 1.64	3.1 2.24	.84	.76	1.1	N.S.
0–6	i.t.a. t.o.	9 7	1.3 1.29	.9 2.0	.01	.77	.01	N.S.

TABLE 60   Showing a comparison of the mean scores attained on the Schonell Graded Word Reading Test, by sub-groups of i.t.a. and t.o. children who attained similar levels of performance on the Harrison-Stroud Visual Discrimination Test in i.t.a.

Visual Discrim. in i.t.a. Harrison-Stroud			Schonell Graded Word Reading Test 2nd time, September 1966					
range of scores	Group	N	mean score	S.D.	diff. in means	S.E. of diff.	C.R.	statis. signif.
25–30	i.t.a. t.o.	51 54	13.16 5.98	11.27 6.56	7.18	1.81	3.97	.1% level
19–24	i.t.a. t.o.	29 31	6.14 4.42	7.35 7.42	1.72	1.9	.9	N.S.
13–18	i.t.a. t.o.	18 19	2.83 2.74	6.78 3.35	.09	1.75	.05	N.S.
7–12	i.t.a. t.o.	14 8	2.36 1.37	1.85 2.0	.99	.88	1.12	N.S.
0–6	i.t.a. t.o.	7 7	1.57 1.6	1.0 2.2	.03	.96	.03	N.S.

TABLE 61   Showing a comparison of the mean scores attained on the Schonell
Graded Word Reading Test, by sub-groups of i.t.a. and t.o. children
who attained similar levels of performance on the Harrison-Stroud
Visual Discrimination Test in t.o.

Visual Discrim. in t.o. Harrison-Stroud			Schonell Graded Word Reading Test 2nd time, September 1966					
range of scores	Group	N	mean score	S.D.	diff. in means	S.E. of diff.	C.R.	statis. signif.
25–30	i.t.a. t.o.	48 56	12.46 6.45	10.91 5.92	6.01	1.76	3.41	.1% level
19–24	i.t.a. t.o.	31 31	8.52 4.68	9.16 7.68	3.84	2.15	1.79	N.S.
13–18	i.t.a. t.o.	19 16	2.84 2.19	2.0 3.0	.65	.85	.76	N.S.
7–12	i.t.a. t.o.	13 12	1.38 .42	.85 .86	.97	.36	2.7	5% level
0–6	i.t.a. t.o.	8 4	1.25 1.75	.97 2.45	.5	1.08	.46	N.S.

TABLE 62   Showing a comparison of the mean scores attained on the Schonell
Graded Word Reading Test, by sub-groups of i.t.a. and t.o. children
who attained similar levels of performance on the author's
Auditory Discrimination Test.

Auditory Discrim. Thackray			Schonell Graded Word Reading Test 2nd time, September 1966					
range of scores	Group	N	mean score	S.D.	diff. in means	S.E. of diff.	C.R.	statis. signif.
27–33	i.t.a. t.o.	1 1	29.0 7.0	0 0				
20–26	i.t.a. t.o.	15 12	19.07 7.67	12.92 10.54	11.40	4.83	2.36	5% level
14–19	i.t.a. t.o.	26 29	8.5 8.14	10.3 7.48	.36	2.45	.15	N.S.
7–13	i.t.a. t.o.	43 52	7.0 2.94	6.93 4.47	4.06	1.22	3.33	.1% level
0–6	i.t.a. t.o.	34 25	2.79 2.64	3.61 3.32	.15	.91	.17	N.S.

TABLE 63 Showing a comparison of the mean scores attained on the Schonell
Graded Word Reading Test, by sub-groups of i.t.a. and t.o. children
who attained similar levels of performance on the Harrison-Stroud
Auditory Discrimination Test.

| Auditory Discrim. Harrison-Stroud | | | Schonell Graded Word Reading Test 2nd time, September 1966 | | | | | |
range of scores	Group	N	mean score	S.D.	diff. in means	S.E. of diff.	C.R.	statis. signif.
13–16	i.t.a. t.o.	23 30	15.96 9.3	12.04 8.54	6.66	2.7	2.47	5% level
10–12	i.t.a. t.o.	31 40	10.16 3.2	9.75 4.24	6.96	1.87	3.72	.1% level
7–9	i.t.a. t.o.	53 39	4.28 2.69	5.75 4.58	1.59	1.08	1.47	N.S.
4–6	i.t.a. t.o.	11 8	2.82 3.25	3.16 2.83	.43	3.19	.13	N.S.
0–3	i.t.a. t.o.	1 2	2 0					

These results, which are similar to those from the
Schonell test given for the first time, again indicate that
given i.t.a. and t.o. sub-groups with similar levels of performance on visual discrimination tests, some i.t.a. sub-
groups have mean reading scores greater, and sometimes
significantly greater, than their t.o. counterparts. This
also means that some i.t.a. groups with lower levels of
performance in visual discrimination than some t.o. sub-
groups, can reach similar levels of reading achievement
to those t.o. sub-groups, after one year of schooling. The
conclusion to be drawn here is that less skill is required in
visual discrimination for children learning to read successfully in i.t.a., and that i.t.a. is an easier medium than t.o. in
respect of visual discrimination.

From Tables 62 and 63 the following results can be seen:

(a) For each level of performance on both tests of auditory
    discrimination, the mean scores attained by the i.t.a.

sub-groups on the Schonell reading achievement test are greater than the mean reading scores attained by the t.o. sub-groups.

(b) On both tests of auditory discrimination the i.t.a. sub-groups with the highest level of performance attained mean reading scores which were significantly (5% level) greater than the mean reading scores of the t.o. sub-groups with the highest level of performance on auditory discrimination.

(c) There were no other significant differences common to both tests, but on the author's test there was a very highly significant difference (.1% level) between the mean reading scores at the second lowest level of performance on auditory discrimination, and on the Harrison-Stroud Test there was a very highly significant difference (.1% level) between the mean reading scores at the second highest level of performance. Both differences favoured i.t.a.

These results, which are similar to those from the Schonell test given for the first time, again indicate that given i.t.a. and t.o. sub-groups with similar levels of performance on auditory discrimination tests, the i.t.a. sub-groups have mean reading scores greater, and for some levels significantly greater than their t.o. counterparts. Again, this also means that some i.t.a. groups with lower levels of performance in auditory discrimination than some t.o. sub-groups, can reach similar levels of reading achievement to those t.o. sub-groups after one year of schooling. For example, on the author's Auditory Discrimination Test, to gain a mean reading score of 7.67, the t.o. sub-group needed a level of performance in auditory discrimination in the 20–26 range. To attain the nearest similar mean reading score (8.5) the i.t.a. sub-group needed a level of performance in auditory discrimination in the 14–19 range. Other examples of a similar kind could be given.

The conclusion to be drawn here is that less skill is required in auditory discrimination for children learning to read with i.t.a., and that with regard to auditory discrimination i.t.a. is an easier medium than t.o. in the teaching and learning of reading.

TABLE 64 Showing a comparison of the mean scores attained on the Schonell Graded Word Reading Test, by sub-groups of i.t.a. and t.o. children who attained similar levels of performance on the Wechsler Scale of Intelligence for Children.

Wechsler Scale of Intelligence			Schonell Graded Word Reading Test 2nd time, September 1966					
range of scores	Group	N	mean score	S.D.	diff. in means	S.E. of diff.	C.R.	statis. signif.
113–125	i.t.a.	6	15.33	13.23	5.54	5.39	1.03	N.S.
	t.o.	19	9.79	10.2				
100–112	i.t.a.	52	10.67	10.63	5.04	1.79	2.82	1% level
	t.o.	35	5.63	6.0				
87–99	i.t.a.	35	6.17	7.75	3.52	1.4	2.51	5% level
	t.o.	36	2.65	3.0				
74–86	i.t.a.	20	3.3	4.36	1.3	1.08	1.2	N.S.
	t.o.	22	2.0	2.45				
60–73	i.t.a.	6	2.33	2.45	.9	1.38	.65	N.S.
	t.o.	7	1.43	2.10				

TABLE 65 Showing a comparison of the mean scores attained on the Schonell Graded Word Reading Test, by sub-groups of i.t.a. and t.o. children who attained similar levels of performance on the Goodenough Draw-A-Man Test.

Goodenough Draw-A-Man Test			Schonell Graded Word Reading Test 2nd time, September 1966					
range of scores	Group	N	mean score	S.D.	diff. in means	S.E. of diff.	C.R.	statis. signif.
120–133	i.t.a.	5	18.6	11.27	10.6	3.15	1.3	N.S.
	t.o.	3	8.0	6.16				
106–119	i.t.a.	19	9.95	11.45	6.08	3.05	1.99	N.S.
	t.o.	16	3.87	4.47				
93–105	i.t.a.	47	9.47	10.05	2.76	1.92	1.44	N.S.
	t.o.	40	6.71	7.95				
79–92	i.t.a.	32	5.52	6.63	2.69	1.29	2.08	1% level
	t.o.	42	2.83	3.74				
65–78	i.t.a.	16	2.33	2.3	.78	1.58	.49	N.S.
	t.o.	18	3.11	5.95				

From Tables 64 and 65 the following results can be seen:
(a) For practically all levels of performance on the two tests, the mean scores attained by the i.t.a. sub-groups on the Schonell reading achievement test are greater than the mean scores attained by the t.o. sub-groups.
(b) There were no significant differences common to the two tests, but on the Wechsler Scale of Intelligence there was a highly significant difference (1% level) between the mean reading scores at the second highest level of performance, and a significant difference (5% level at the middle level of performance; on the Goodenough Draw-A-Man Test there was a highly significant difference (1% level) between the mean reading scores at the second lowest level of performance. Both differences favoured i.t.a.

These results are again similar to those from the Schonell test given for the first time, and again the conclusion to be drawn is that a lower level of intelligence is required for learning to read successfully with i.t.a. than is required for t.o., which suggests that the problems to be solved in reading with i.t.a., are of a simpler nature than those to be solved

TABLE 66   Showing a comparison of the mean scores attained on the Schonell Graded Word Reading Test, by sub-groups of i.t.a. and t.o. children who attained similar levels of performance on the author's Vocabulary Profile.

Vocabulary Profile Thackray			Schonell Graded Word Reading Test 2nd time, September 1966					
range of scores	Group	N	mean score	S.D.	diff. in means	S.E. of diff.	C.R.	statis. signif.
41–50	i.t.a.	10	13.0	11.0	1.9	5.42	.35	N.S.
	t.o.	10	11.1	11.83				
31–40	i.t.a.	65	10.0	10.86	4.82	1.51	3.19	1% level
	t.o.	68	5.18	5.74				
21–30	i.t.a.	29	3.62	4.24	1.98	.85	2.33	5% level
	t.o.	36	1.64	1.9				
11–20	i.t.a.	13	4.77	6.48	2.77	4.1	.68	N.S.
	t.o.	3	2.0	3.0				
0–10	i.t.a.	2	.5	.5	2.0	1.49	1.34	N.S.
	t.o.	2	2.5	1.41				

when learning to read with t.o. using an eclectic approach.

From Table 66 it can be seen that, with the exception of the lowest level of performance on vocabulary development, the i.t.a. sub-groups have mean reading scores higher than their t.o. counterparts, and at the two middle levels of performance the differences between the mean reading scores are significantly (1% and 5% levels) greater. These results conform to the familiar pattern which has emerged as a result of this particular statistical approach.

This approach has again shown quite clearly that i.t.a. sub-groups can attain similar reading achievement levels to the t.o. sub-groups, but with lower levels of reading readiness abilities, thus showing experimentally that i.t.a. is simpler than t.o. in its visual and auditory structure, and the problems to be solved in learning to read with i.t.a. are of a simpler nature. Assuming, on average, that reading readiness abilities develop with age, then it follows that a child who is going to learn to read with i.t.a. will be ready to read at an earlier age than if he were going to learn to read with t.o.

b) *The Neale Analysis of Reading Ability – Accuracy, Form A*

TABLE 67 Showing a comparison of the mean scores attained on Reading Accuracy as measured by the Neale Analysis of Reading Ability, by sub-groups of i.t.a. and t.o. children who attained similar levels of performance on the author's Visual Discrimination Test.

range of scores	Group	N	mean score	S.D.	diff. in means	S.E. of diff.	C.R.	statis. signif.
28–34	i.t.a.	8	22.37	13.49	13.95	4.28	3.3	1% level
	t.o.	24	8.42	8.5				
21–27	i.t.a.	53	11.49	11.27	4.49	2.33	1.93	N.S.
	t.o.	33	7.0	10.0				
14–20	i.t.a.	26	7.35	8.49	3.91	2.01	1.94	N.S.
	t.o.	27	3.44	5.83				
7–13	i.t.a.	23	3.04	5.1	1.93	1.16	1.66	N.S.
	t.o.	28	1.11	3.0				
0–6	i.t.a.	9	.78	1.73				
	t.o.	7	0	0				

The header spanning columns: "Visual Discrim. Thackray" over (range of scores, Group, N) and "Neale Analysis of Reading Ability, Form A (Accuracy) 1st time, September 1966" over the remaining columns.

TABLE 68 Showing a comparison of the mean scores attained on Reading Accuracy as measured by the Neale Analysis of Reading Ability, by sub-groups of i.t.a. and t.o. children who attained similar levels of performance on the Harrison-Stroud Visual Discrimination Test in i.t.a.

Visual Discrim. in i.t.a. Harrison-Stroud			Neale Analysis of Reading Ability, Form A (Accuracy) 1st time, September 1966					
range of scores	Group	N	mean score	S.D.	diff. in means	S.E. of diff.	C.R.	statis. signif.
25–30	i.t.a.	51	14.82	12.37	8.59	2.06	4.17	.1% level
	t.o.	54	6.23	8.2				
19–24	i.t.a.	29	7.0	7.81	2.16	2.15	1.0	N.S.
	t.o.	31	4.84	8.83				
13–18	i.t.a.	18	2.33	4.7	.67	1.66	.4	N.S.
	t.o.	19	3.0	5.39				
7–12	i.t.a.	14	2.36	3.2	1.86	1.23	1.51	N.S.
	t.o.	8	.5	1.3				
0–6	i.t.a.	7	.57	.9				
	t.o.	7	0					

TABLE 69 Showing a comparison of the mean scores attained on Reading Accuracy as measured by the Neale Analysis of Reading Ability, by sub-groups of i.t.a. and t.o. children who attained similar levels of of performance on the Harrison-Stroud Visual Discrimination Test in t.o.

Visual Discrim. in t.o. Harrison-Stroud			Neale Analysis of Reading Ability, Form A (Accuracy) 1st time, September 1966					
range of scores	Group	N	mean score	S.D.	diff. in means	S.E. of diff.	C.R.	statis. signif.
25–30	i.t.a.	48	13.85	12.0	6.87	2.04	3.37	.1% level
	t.o.	56	6.98	8.12				
19–24	i.t.a.	31	9.61	10.49	4.9	2.47	1.98	5% level
	t.o.	31	4.71	8.89				
13–18	i.t.a.	19	3.42	4.0	2.17	1.32	1.64	N.S.
	t.o.	16	1.25	3.74				
7–12	i.t.a.	13	.92	2.2				
	t.o.	12	0	0				
0–6	i.t.a.	8	.25	.66				
	t.o.	4	0	0				

225

I

From Tables 67, 68 and 69, the following results can be seen:

(a) For practically all levels of performance on the three visual discrimination tests, the mean scores attained by the i.t.a. sub-groups on the Neale Reading Accuracy Test are greater than the mean scores attained by the t.o. sub-groups.

(b) On all tests of visual discrimination, the i.t.a. sub-groups with the highest level of performance attained mean reading scores which were highly or very highly significantly (.1% and 1% levels) greater than the mean reading scores of the t.o. sub-groups with the highest level of performance on visual discrimination.

(c) On the Harrison-Stroud Visual Discrimination Test in t.o., there was a significant difference (5% level) between the mean reading scores at the second highest level of performance, in favour of i.t.a.

Here again we have supporting evidence from a different kind of reading test to show that a lower level of skill in visual discrimination is required for learning to read with i.t.a., than is required for t.o. used with the usual eclectic approach.

TABLE 70   Showing a comparison of the mean scores attained on Reading Accuracy as measured by the Neale Analysis of Reading Ability, by sub-groups of i.t.a. and t.o. children who attained similar levels of performance on the author's Auditory Discrimination Test.

range of scores	Group	N	mean score	S.D.	diff. in means	S.E. of diff.	C.R.	statis. signif.
27–33	i.t.a.	1	27.0	0				
	t.o.	1	10.0	0				
20–26	i.t.a.	15	21.47	13.15	13.39	5.17	2.59	5% level
	t.o.	12	8.08	12.25				
14–19	i.t.a.	26	10.5	11.92	1.91	2.83	.68	N.S.
	t.o.	29	8.59	8.67				
7–13	i.t.a.	43	7.77	7.68	4.79	1.44	3.33	.1% level
	t.o.	52	2.98	6.08				
0–6	i.t.a.	34	2.82	6.0	.98	1.29	.76	N.S.
	t.o.	25	1.84	3.87				

The table header spans: "Auditory Discrim. Thackray" over (range of scores, Group, N) and "Neale Analysis of Reading Ability, Form A (Accuracy) 1st time, Septermber 1966" over the remaining columns.

TABLE 71 Showing a comparison of the mean scores attained on Reading Accuracy as measured by the Neale Analysis of Reading Ability, by sub-groups of i.t.a. and t.o. children who attained similar levels of performance on the Harrison-Stroud Auditory Discrimination Test.

Auditory Discrim. Harrison-Stroud			Neale Analysis of Reading Ability, Form A (Accuracy) 1st time, September 1966					
range of scores	Group	N	mean score	S.D.	diff. in means	S.E. of diff.	C.R.	statis. signif.
13–16	i.t.a.	23	17.96	13.38	7.51	3.05	2.46	5% level
	t.o.	30	10.45	9.8				
10–12	i.t.a.	31	12.16	10.2	8.44	2.11	4.0	.1% level
	t.o.	40	3.72	6.71				
7–9	i.t.a.	53	4.45	7.35	2.27	1.36	1.67	N.S.
	t.o.	39	2.18	5.66				
4–6	i.t.a.	11	2.36	3.32	.31	1.5	.21	N.S.
	t.o.	8	2.67	3.22				
0–3	i.t.a.	1	0					
	t.o.	2	0					

From Tables 70 and 71 the following results can be seen:

(a) For practically all levels of performance on the two auditory discrimination tests, the mean scores attained by the i.t.a. sub-groups on the Neale Reading Accuracy Test are greater than the mean scores attained by the t.o. sub-groups.

b) On both tests of auditory discrimination the i.t.a. sub-group with the highest level of performance attained mean reading scores which were significantly (5%) greater than the mean reading scores of the t.o. sub-groups with the highest level of performance on auditory discrimination.

c) On the author's Auditory Discrimination Test there was a very highly significant difference (.1% level) between the mean reading scores at the second lowest level of performance, and on the Harrison-Stroud test there was a very highly significant difference (.1% level) between the mean reading scores at the second highest level of performance. Both these differences favoured i.t.a.

Again, this evidence from a different kind of reading

TABLE 72 Showing a comparison of the mean scores on Reading Accuracy as measured by the Neale Analysis of Reading Ability, by sub-groups of i.t.a. and t.o. children who attained similar levels of performance on the Wechsler Scale of Intelligence for Children.

| Wechsler Scale of Intelligence | | | Neale Analysis of Reading Ability, Form A (Accuracy) 1st time, September 1966 | | | | | |
range of scores	Group	N	mean score	S.D.	diff. in means	S.E. of diff.	C.R.	statis. signif.
113–125	i.t.a. t.o.	6 19	12.28 10.0	12.81 10.91	2.28	5.24	.43	N.S.
100–112	i.t.a. t.o.	52 35	12.18 6.77	11.58 8.72	5.41	2.19	2.47	5% level
87–99	i.t.a. t.o.	35 36	7.57 2.64	9.9 5.2	4.93	1.88	2.62	1% level
74–86	i.t.a. t.o.	20 22	3.1 1.59	14.14 2.65	1.51	3.05	.49	N.S.
60–73	i.t.a. t.o.	6 7	3.0 0	3.61 0				

TABLE 73 Showing a comparison of the mean scores on Reading Accuracy as measured by the Neale Analysis of Reading Ability, by sub-groups of i.t.a. and t.o. children, who attained similar levels of performance on the Goodenough Draw-A-Man Test.

| Goodenough Draw-A-Man Test | | | Neale Analysis of Reading Ability, Form A (Accuracy) 1st time, September 1966 | | | | | |
range of scores	Group	N	mean score	S.D.	diff. in means	S.E. of diff.	C.R.	statis. signif.
120–133	i.t.a. t.o.	5 3	18.6 11.67	10.49 10.25	6.98	8.77	.79	N.S.
106–119	i.t.a. t.o.	19 16	9.95 4.5	11.87 7.21	5.45	3.4	1.6	N.S.
93–105	i.t.a. t.o.	47 40	11.06 7.9	11.79 9.7	3.16	2.3	1.37	N.S.
79–92	i.t.a. t.o.	32 42	7.12 2.14	8.83 4.4	4.98	1.7	2.93	1% level
65–78	i.t.a. t.o.	16 18	1.37 2.33	2.9 5.66	.96	1.56	.61	N.S.

test indicates that a lower level of skill in auditory discrimination is required for learning to read with i.t.a., than is required for learning to read with t.o. with the usual eclectic approach.

From Tables 72 and 73 the following results can be seen:

(a) For practically all levels of performance on the two measures of intelligence the mean scores attained by the i.t.a. sub-groups on the Neale Reading Accuracy Test are greater than the mean scores attained by the t.o. sub-groups.

(b) On the Wechsler Test there were significant (5% level) and highly significant (1% level) differences between the mean reading scores at the middle levels of performance, and on the Goodenough Test there was a highly significant difference (1% level) between the mean reading scores at the second lowest level of performance. Both differences favoured i.t.a.

Here again, the same evidence is seen clearly, indicating that children learning to read with i.t.a. are able to do so

TABLE 74 Showing a comparison of the mean scores on Reading Accuracy as measured by the Neale Analysis of Reading Ability, by sub-groups of i.t.a. and t.o. children who attained similar levels of performance on the author's Vocabulary Profile.

Vocabulary Profile Thackray			Neale Analysis of Reading Ability, Form A (Accuracy) 1st time, September 1966.					
Range of scores	Group	N	mean score	S.D.	diff. in means	S.E. of diff.	C.R.	statis. signif.
41–50	i.t.a.	10	15.0	10.68	3.4	5.61	.61	N.S.
	t.o.	10	11.6	12.89				
31–40	i.t.a.	65	10.95	11.92	5.2	1.76	2.95	1% level
	t.o.	68	5.75	7.87				
21–30	i.t.a.	29	4.69	7.55	3.31	1.5	2.21	5% level
	t.o.	36	1.38	3.32				
11–20	i.t.a.	13	4.15	7.48				
	t.o.	3	0	0				
0–10	i.t.a.	2	0	0				
	t.o.	2	2.5	2.45				

229

with a lower level of intelligence than would be required for learning to read with t.o. with an initial 'look and say' approach.

From Table 74 we see that at four out of the five levels of performance on the Vocabulary Profile, the mean scores attained by the i.t.a. sub-groups on the Neale Reading Accuracy Test are greater than the mean scores attained by the t.o. sub-groups; the differences between the mean scores at the middle levels of performance are significant (5% level) and highly significant (1% level) in favour of i.t.a.

As with the other reading readiness measures, these results show that children learning to read with i.t.a. are able to do so satisfactorily with a lower level of vocabulary development than would be required for learning to read satisfactorily with t.o. approached in the usual way.

The results of this particular statistical approach which has taken into account both the Schonell and the Neale tests given at the beginning of the children's fourth term in school, show quite clearly, again, that i.t.a. sub-groups can attain similar reading achievement levels as the t.o. sub-groups, but with lower levels of reading readiness abilities. From this it follows that i.t.a. is simpler in its visual and auditory structure than is t.o., and that the problems to be solved in learning to read satisfactorily with i.t.a. are of a simpler nature than those of t.o. taught with an initial 'look and say' approach.

It is an accepted fact that intelligence, in normal circumstances, increases with age, and as visual and auditory discrimination are specific intellectual abilities it can be assumed that these skills also develop with age. But it has been clearly shown that lower levels of readiness abilities are required for learning to read satisfactorily with i.t.a. compared with t.o., and so it follows that children who are going to learn to read with i.t.a are ready to read earlier, and could start learning to read at an earlier age, than their t.o. counterparts. It is not possible to determine exactly at what age i.t.a. children are ready to read and could start learning to read easily and effectually, but the third statistical approach which follows helps us to examine this question again.

(iii) *A comparison of the minimum mental age levels required for learning to read successfully with i.t.a. and t.o.*

As discussed in Chapter 5, in order to make this comparison the 119 children in each of the i.t.a. and t.o. groups were grouped according to their mental ages, with group intervals of six months. For each mental age group, the raw scores of the children on both the Schonell and the Neale reading achievement tests were averaged, and comparisons made between the mean scores of the i.t.a. and t.o. sub-groups.

(a) For the i.t.a group a mental age range of 5 years to 5 years 5 months gives a mean score of 8.2 on the Schonell test, which is a relatively clear advance on the mean scores at lower mental ages, and so indicates sure progress is being made in learning to read.

(b) For the t.o. group the nearest similar mean score of 8.4, which is a relatively clear advance on the mean scores at lower mental ages, requires a mental age range of 6 years to 6 years 5 months.

It is interesting to note that the average age of the children at the beginning of their second year in school was 6 years 2 months, and a score on the Schonell test to give a reading age of 6 years 2 months would be approximately 12. To attain such a score, we see from Table 75 that higher mental ages would be required than those quoted

TABLE 75 Showing a comparison between the mean scores attained on the Schonell Graded Word Reading Test given a second time, by sub-groups of i.t.a. and t.o. children with similar mental ages.

mental ages (years, months)	below 3–6	3–6 3–11	4–0 4–5	4–6 4–11	5–0 5–5	5–6 5–11	6–0 6–5	6–6 6–11
No. of i.t.a. chn. in each mental age group	2	5	15	23	36	30	7	1
No. of t.o. chn. in each mental age group	4	7	14	20	25	25	22	2
mean score of i.t.a. chn. on Schonell	1.5	2.4	3.0	4.5	8.2	12.8	13.4	2
mean score of t.o. chn. on Schonell	1.7	3	2.0	2.5	2.7	5.3	8.4	22

231

TABLE 76 Showing a comparison between the mean scores attained on Reading Accuracy as measured by the Neale Analysis of Reading Ability given for the first time, by sub-groups of i.t.a. and t.o. children with similar mental ages.

mental ages (years, months)	below 3–6	3–6 3–11	4–0 4–5	4–6 4–11	5–0 5–5	5–6 5–11	6–0 6–5	6–6 6–11
no. of i.t.a chn. in each mental age group	2	5	15	23	36	30	7	1
no. of. t.o. chn. in each mental age group	4	7	14	20	25	27	20	2
mean score of i.t.a. chn. on Neale	0	3.2	3.4	5.3	9.3	14.4	12.6	10
mean score of t.o. chn. on Neale	0	.7	1.8	1.2	3.93	6.6	9.0	20.5

above, but the i.t.a. sub-groups would still achieve this score with lower mental ages than would the t.o. sub-groups.

Table 76 shows that:

(a) For the i.t.a. groups a mental age range of 5 years to 5 years 5 months gives a mean score on the Neale test of 9.3, which is a clear advance on the mean scores at lower mental ages, and so indicates that sure progress is being made in learning to read.

(b) For the t.o. group a similar mean score of 9.0, which is a reasonable advance on the mean scores at lower mental ages, requires a mental age range of 6 years to 6 years 5 months.

It is again interesting to note that the average age of the children at this stage was 6 years 2 months, and a score on the Neale test to give a reading age of 6 years 2 months for reading accuracy would be 1. However, looking at Table 54, we see that the i.t.a. sub-groups would attain any given score at a lower mental age level than would the t.o. sub-group.

232

The foregoing analysis is obviously a fairly crude one, and it would be impossible to state at what mental age level children learning to read in either i.t.a. or t.o. could do so successfully. However, the evidence does suggest quite clearly that in the author's sample the i.t.a. group was able to read satisfactorily in i.t.a. with mental ages at least six months lower than the t.o. group, following the usual approach in learning to read in t.o. This is understandable, when it has been shown experimentally that lower reading readiness levels are required for learning to read satisfactorily in i.t.a. than are required for learning to read with t.o., which means, of course, that i.t.a. is a simpler medium than t.o. used with an eclectic approach.

To conclude this chapter, the author felt that a comparison should be made of the correlations between the initial tests

TABLE 77 Showing a comparison of the correlations, calculated for the i.t.a. and t.o. groups separately, between the initial tests of reading readiness abilities, and three measures of reading achievement, given in the children's fourth term at school.

Tests of Reading Readiness Abilities		Schonell 1st time May, 1966	Schonell 2nd time Sept. 1966	Neale 1st time Sept. 1966
	Group	r	r	r
Visual Discrim. Thackray	i.t.a.	.39	.47	.36
	t.o.	.35	.37	.44
Visual Discrim. in i.t.a. Harrison-Stroud	i.t.a.	.43	.52	.51
	t.o.	.36	.32	.38
Visual Discrim. in t.o. Harrison-Stroud	i.t.a.	.37	.45	.48
	t.o.	.62	.45	.40
Auditory Discrim. Thackray	i.t.a.	.51	.57	.57
	t.o.	.29	.30	.29
Auditory Discrim. Harrison-Stroud	i.t.a.	.44	.51	.52
	t.o.	.40	.42	.37
Wechsler Scale of Intelligence	i.t.a.	.29	.37	.34
	t.o.	.44	.47	.47
Goodenough Draw-A-Man Test	i.t.a.	.32	.31	.29
	t.o.	.22	.27	.29
Vocabulary Profile Thackray	i.t.a.	.34	.37	.39
	t.o.	.31	.30	.33

of reading readiness abilities and the three reading achievement tests discussed up to this point, namely, the Schonell test, given both first and second time, and the Neale test given for the first time. In this way a further study of the relative importance of the factors in reading readiness can be made.

In order to see the relevant importance in the author's experiment of the factors making for reading readiness, the correlations for each factor were averaged, with the following results.:

visual and auditory discrimination   .43
intelligence and vocabulary   .34

These figures are in keeping with those the author found in his first experiment, and so add to the growing evidence to show that visual and auditory discrimination are more important factors in reading readiness than mental ability and language development.

Chapter 7

Discussion of the Results Obtained by the Statistical Methods Selected (IV): Tests Carried out in the Children's Sixth Term at School

Towards the end of the children's second year in school (sixth term) the i.t.a. and t.o. groups were again tested on the following two reading achievement measures:

  (i) Schonell Graded Word Reading Test – 3rd time;
  (ii) Neale Analysis of Reading Ability – 2nd time.

Again the sub-tests of Accuracy of reading, and Comprehension of reading were used.

On these two tests all the children in both the i.t.a. and the t.o. groups were tested on the t.o. versions. However, at this stage in the children's sixth term in school, 50 i.t.a. children out of the 119 in the group had not transferred to t.o. These 50 children were also tested in i.t.a. after being tested in t.o. The t.o. test was given first, as being the harder test for the children. It was felt that the scores on the following i.t.a. version of the same test would not be affected to any measurable extent. By giving the i.t.a. children who had not transferred to t.o. the two versions of the same tests at this time, a study of what happens to children's reading ability at the transfer could be made.

Now follows, in tabulated form, the relevant information gained by giving the 50 i.t.a. children who had not transferred the two versions of the Schonell and Neale tests.

TABLE 78   Showing a comparison between the mean scores attained on the i.t.a. and t.o. versions of the Schonell Graded Word Reading Test by 50 i.t.a. children who had not transferred to t.o.

Schonell	N	mean score	S.D.	diff. in means	S.E. of diff.	C.R.	statis. signif.
i.t.a. version	50	12.0	10.25	5.6	1.65	3.39	.1% level
t.o. version	50	6.4	5.55				

TABLE 79   Showing a comparison between the mean score attained on the i.t.a. and t.o. versions of the Neale Analysis of Reading Ability, Form B (Accuracy), by 50 i.t.a. children who had not transferred to t.o.

Neale Accuracy	N	mean score	S.D.	diff. in means	S.E. of diff.	C.R.	statis. signif.
i.t.a. version	50	13.5	10.05	5.8	1.61	3.6	.1% level
t.o. version	50	7.7	5.5				

From Tables 78 and 79 we see that there is a very highly significant difference (.1% level) between the mean scores on the i.t.a. and t.o. versions of both the Schonell and the Neale tests, attained by the 50 i.t.a. children who had not transferred. This indicates clearly that, for these fifty children, the t.o. version of the test was much more difficult to read than the i.t.a. version, and shows that there will be a setback in reading ability and standards during the transfer stage. These results lend support to the findings of the main i.t.a. experiment, which also showed this setback in reading at transfer.

Now follows, in tabulated form, the results of the two reading achievement measures given in the children's sixth term at school. It must be borne in mind when discussing these figures that the scores used are those which were made on the t.o. versions of the test. As 50 i.t.a. children had not transferred and would have scored higher on i.t.a. versions, the advantage lies with the t.o. group.

From Tables 80, 81 and 82 it can be seen that towards the end of the children's second year in school, there are no

TABLE 80 Showing a comparison between the mean scores of the i.t.a. and t.o. groups on the Schonell Graded Word Reading Test given for the third time (given in t.o. to both i.t.a. and t.o. groups).

Group	N	mean score	S.D.	diff. in means	S.E. of diff.	C.R.	statis. signif.
i.t.a.	119	15.4	12.25	1.05	1.56	.88	N.S.
t.o.	119	14.35	11.8				

TABLE 81 Showing a comparison between the mean scores of the i.t.a. and t.o. groups for Reading Accuracy as measured by the Neale Analysis of Reading Ability (Form B) given for the second time (given in t.o. to both i.t.a. and t.o. groups).

Group	N	mean score	S.D.	diff. in means	S.E. of diff.	C.R.	statis. signif.
i.t.a.	119	18.54	14.2	1.34	1.85	.72	N.S.
t.o.	119	17.2	14.3				

TABLE 82 Showing a comparison between the mean scores of the i.t.a. and t.o. groups for Reading Comprehension as measured by the Neale Analysis of Reading Ability (Form B) given for the second time.

Group	N	mean score	S.D.	diff. in means	S.E. of diff.	C.R.	statis. signif.
i.t.a.	119	5.98	4.89	0	.62	0	N.S.
t.o.	119	5.98	4.59				

significant differences between the mean scores of the i.t.a. and t.o. groups on either the Schonell or the Neale reading achievement tests. However, this comparison is not strictly a fair one, as 50 i.t.a. children had not transferred to t.o. Even so, it is interesting to note that, taking only t.o. scores into consideration, the significantly greater reading scores made by the i.t.a. group when tested in i.t.a. in the earlier stages, have now disappeared, and the mean reading scores are similar. This suggests quite clearly that, although the i.t.a. children may be quite fluent in i.t.a., during the transfer stage t.o. is relatively harder for them to read, and the lower reading scores show the resultant setback in progress. It will be interesting to see the figures from the same tests given after the children have been in school for nearly three years, and practically all have been transferred for a considerable time. These figures are presented and discussed in the next chapter.

Once again, in order to compare more rigorously the reading readiness requirements for learning to read with i.t.a. and t.o., the same three statistical analyses were made.

(i) *A study of the relationship between the earlier results on the battery of reading readiness measures and the results on the two reading achievement measures:*
given at the beginning of the children's sixth term in school, for both the i.t.a. and t.o. groups separately.

From Tables 83 and 84 it can be seen that, with one exception, there are no significant differences between the pairs of correlation coefficients, now that the two reading achievements tests have been given in t.o. to both groups. Here is another indication of a setback in reading standards in t.o. as, now that the mean scores of the two groups are fairly close, there are no real significant differences.

TABLE 83 Showing a comparison of the correlations, calculated for the i.t.a. and t.o. groups separately, between the initial tests of reading readiness abilities and the Schonell Graded Word Reading Test given for the third time (given in t.o. to both i.t.a. and t.o. groups).

Tests of Reading Readiness Abilities	Schonell Graded Word Reading Test 3rd time, May 1967						
	Group	r	z	diff. in 'z's	S.E. of diff.	C.R.	statis. signif.
Visual Discrim. Thackray	i.t.a.	.55	.62	.16	.13	1.23	N.S.
	t.o.	.43	.46				
Visual Discrim. in i.t.a. Harrison-Stroud	i.t.a.	.61	.71	.38	.13	2.92	1% level
	t.o.	.32	.33				
Visual Discrim. in t.o. Harrison-Stroud	i.t.a.	.55	.62	.25	.13	1.92	N.S.
	t.o.	.35	.37				
Auditory Discrim. Thackray	i.t.a.	.50	.55	.17	.13	1.31	N.S.
	t.o.	.36	.38				
Auditory Discrim. Harrison-Stroud	i.t.a.	.48	.52	.02	.13	.15	N.S.
	t.o.	.46	.50				
Wechsler Scale of Intelligence	i.t.a.	.39	.41	.10	.13	.77	N.S.
	t.o.	.47	.51				
Goodenough Draw-A-Man Test	i.t.a.	.32	.33	.01	.13	.08	N.S.
	t.o.	.31	.32				
Vocabulary Profile Thackray	i.t.a.	.43	.46	.12	.13	.92	N.S.
	t.o.	.33	.34				

TABLE 84 Showing a comparison of the correlations, calculated for the i.t.a. and t.o. groups separately, between the initial tests of reading readiness abilities and Reading Accuracy as measured by the Neale Analysis of Reading Ability, given for the second time (given in t.o. to both i.t.a. and t.o. groups).

Tests of Reading Readiness Abilities	Neale Analysis of Reading Ability, Form B (Accuracy) 2nd time, May 1967						
	Group	r	z	diff. in 'z's	S.E. of diff.	C.R.	statis. signif.
Visual Discrim. Thackray	i.t.a.	.53	.59	.09	.13	.69	N.S.
	t.o.	.46	.50				
Visual Discrim. in i.t.a. Harrison-Stroud	i.t.a.	.59	.68	.24	.13	1.85	N.S.
	t.o.	.41	.44				
Visual Discrim. in t.o. Harrison-Stroud	i.t.a.	.52	.58	.10	.13	.77	N.S.
	t.o.	.45	.48				
Auditory Discrim. Thackray	i.t.a.	.54	.68	.19	.13	1.46	N.S.
	t.o.	.39	.41				
Auditory Discrim. Harrison-Stroud	i.t.a.	.50	.55	.04	.13	.31	N.S.
	t.o.	.47	.51				
Wechsler Scale of Intelligence	i.t.a.	.36	.38	.17	.13	1.31	N.S.
	t.o.	.50	.55				
Goodenough Draw-A-Man Test	i.t.a.	.33	.34	.03	.13	.23	N.S.
	t.o.	.35	.37				
Vocabulary Profile Thackray	i.t.a.	.43	.46	.11	.13	.85	N.S.
	t.o.	.34	.35				

(ii) *A comparison of the mean scores achieved on the two reading achievement measures between sub-groups of i.t.a. and t.o. children who attained similar levels of performance on each of the earlier reading readiness measures:*
The Schonell test is presented first, followed by the Neale test, and, as before, when the information has been presented for each particular aspect of reading readiness, a discussion of that aspect follows.

(a) The Schonell Graded Word Reading Test

From Tables 85, 86 and 87 the following results can be seen:

(a) The differences between the mean scores of the sub-groups at the various levels of performance on the three

239

TABLE 85 Showing a comparison of the mean scores attained on the Schonell Graded Word Reading Test, by sub-groups of i.t.a. and t.o. children who attained similar levels of performance on the author's Visual Discrimination Test.

Visual Discrim. Thackray			Schonell Graded Word Reading Test 3rd time, May 1967					
range of scores	Group	N	mean score	S.D.	diff. in means	S.E. of diff.	C.R.	statis. signif.
28–34	i.t.a.	8	31.13	11.36	9.98	4.9	2.04	5% level
	t.o.	24	21.15	11.71				
21–27	i.t.a.	53	19.79	11.92	3.23	3.08	1.05	N.S.
	t.o.	33	16.56	14.8				
14–20	i.t.a.	26	13.31	10.05	.87	2.79	.31	N.S.
	t.o.	27	12.44	10.23				
7–13	i.t.a.	23	6.3	7.15	1.66	1.91	.87	N.S.
	t.o.	28	7.96	6.0				
0–6	i.t.a.	9	2.78	4.36	6.36	3.15	2.02	N.S.
	t.o.	7	9.14	7.42				

TABLE 86 Showing a comparison of the mean scores attained on the Schonell Graded Word Reading Test, by sub-groups of i.t.a. and t.o. children who attained similar levels of performance on the Harrison-Stroud Visual Discrimination Test in i.t.a.

Visual Discrim. in i.t.a. Harrison-Stroud			Schonell Graded Word Reading Test 3rd time, May 1967					
range of scores	Group	N	mean score	S.D.	diff. in means	S.E. of diff.	C.R.	statis. signif.
25–30	i.t.a.	51	23.41	12.45	5.88	2.41	2.44	5% level
	t.o.	54	11.53	12.37				
19–24	i.t.a.	29	13.72	8.5	.5	2.77	.18	N.S.
	t.o.	31	13.22	12.65				
13–18	i.t.a.	18	5.55	7.55	6.56	3.02	2.17	5%* level
	t.o.	19	12.11	10.54				
7–12	i.t.a.	14	5.5	7.14	1.0	3.0	.33	N.S.
	t.o.	8	6.5	5.2				
0–6	i.t.a.	7	6.43	5.2	.57	3.75	.15	N.S.
	t.o.	7	7.0	7.62				

* In favour of t.o.

TABLE 87 Showing a comparison of the mean scores attained on the Schonell Graded Word Reading Test, by sub-groups of i.t.a. and t.o. children who attained similar levels of performance on the Harrison-Stroud Visual Discrimination Test in t.o.

Visual Discrim. in t.o. Harrison-Stroud		Schonell Graded Word Reading Test 3rd time, May 1967						
range of scores	Group	N	mean score	S.D.	diff. in means	S.E. of diff.	C.R.	statis. signif.
25–30	i.t.a. t.o.	48 56	22.31 18.48	12.6 12.45	3.83	3.46	1.56	N.S.
19–24	i.t.a. t.o.	31 31	17.16 12.45	10.15 11.83	4.71	2.8	1.68	N.S.
13–18	i.t.a. t.o.	19 16	7.68 9.69	7.48 10.2	2.28	2.99	.76	N.S.
7–12	i.t.a. t.o.	13 12	3.46 7.25	3.74 5.48	3.79	1.94	1.95	N.S.
0–6	i.t.a. t.o.	8 4	2.87 7.5	4.58 9.05	4.63	4.29	1.08	N.S.

visual discrimination tests are now fairly equally divided, i.e., approximately half of the differences favour i.t.a., approximately half favour t.o.

(b) On the author's Visual Discrimination Test there was a significant difference (5% level) between the mean reading scores at the highest level of performance, in favour of i.t.a.; however, this is almost balanced by a rather large difference which is nearly significant, at the lowest level of performance, in favour of t.o.

(c) On the Harrison-Stroud Visual Discrimination Test in i.t.a. there was a significant difference (5% level) between the mean reading scores at the highest level of performance, in favour of i.t.a.; however, this is balanced by a significant difference (5% level) between the mean reading scores at the middle level of performance, in favour of t.o.

These results show clearly that, now the Schonell test has been given in t.o. to both groups, a distinct change of pattern has developed. Previously, all differences between mean reading scores favoured i.t.a., indicating that for reading with i.t.a. lower levels of visual discrimination were adequate for satisfactory reading than for reading with t.o. However, now the differences between the mean reading scores of the i.t.a. and t.o. sub-groups are fairly equally balanced; and for reading with t.o. after the transfer, the results indicate that there is no difference in the level of visual discrimination required. This again shows that the transfer from i.t.a. to t.o. does result in a setback to reading progress.

From Tables 88 and 89 the following results can be seen:

(a) The differences between the mean reading scores of the sub-groups at the various levels of performance on the two auditory discrimination tests are now fairly equally divided between i.t.a. and t.o.

(b) On the author's Auditory Discrimination Test there was a very highly significant difference (.1% level) between the mean reading scores at the next to the lowest level of performance, in favour of i.t.a.; but this difference was not seen in the Harrison-Stroud results, and this was the only significant difference in the results of the two tests.

These results again show quite clearly that now the Schonell test has been given in t.o. to both groups, a distinct change of pattern has developed. The differences between the mean scores of the i.t.a. and t.o. sub-groups are fairly equally balanced, and so, for reading with t.o. through the medium of i.t.a., the results indicate that a similar level of reading readiness is required to that for reading with t.o. This change in the pattern of results shows that children can learn to read more easily with i.t.a. than with t.o. approached in the usual way, but during the transfer to t.o., which becomes a more difficult medium for the i.t.a. children, a setback in reading progress and standards results.

From Tables 90 and 91 the following results can be seen:

(a) The differences between the mean reading scores of the sub-groups at the various levels of performance on the two tests are very small, and are sometimes in favour of i.t.a., sometimes in favour of t.o.

(b) There are no significant differences between the mean reading scores of the i.t.a. and t.o. sub-groups.

TABLE 88 Showing a comparison of the mean scores attained on the Schonell Graded Word Reading Test, by sub-groups of i.t.a. and t.o. children who attained similar levels of performance on the author's Auditory Discrimination Test.

Auditory Discrim. Thackray			Schonell Graded Word Reading Test 3rd time, May 1967					
range of scores	Group	N	mean score	S.D.	diff. in means	S.E. of diff.	C.R.	statis. signif.
27–33	i.t.a.	1	32	0				
	t.o.	1	30	0				
20–26	i.t.a.	15	26.73	14.28	5.98	5.76	1.04	N.S.
	t.o.	12	20.75	14.14				
14–19	i.t.a.	26	15.54	12.77	5.46	3.53	1.55	N.S.
	t.o.	29	21.0	13.49				
7–13	i.t.a.	43	17.4	10.49	7.03	2.14	3.29	.1% level
	t.o.	52	10.37	10.58				
0–6	i.t.a.	34	6.74	8.12	3.18	1.98	1.61	N.S.
	t.o.	25	9.92	7.21				

TABLE 89 Showing a comparison of the mean scores attained on the Schonell Graded Word Reading Test, by sub-groups of i.t.a. and t.o. children who attained similar levels of performance on the Harrison-Stroud Auditory Discrimination Test.

Auditory Discrim. Harrison-Stroud			Schonell Graded Word Reading Test 3rd time, May 1967					
range of scores	Group	N	mean score	S.D.	diff. in means	S.E. of diff.	C.R.	statis. signif.
13–16	i.t.a.	23	25.83	12.96	1.43	3.4	.42	N.S.
	t.o.	30	24.4	12.96				
10–12	i.t.a.	31	17.19	12.04	4.94	2.71	1.82	N.S.
	t.o.	40	12.25	10.3				
7–9	i.t.a.	53	11.36	10.39	1.85	2.08	.89	N.S.
	t.o.	39	9.51	9.43				
4–6	i.t.a.	11	7.73	6.86	4.65	3.2	1.45	N.S.
	t.o.	8	12.38	5.83				
0–3	i.t.a.	1	0					
	t.o.	2	.5					

TABLE 91 Showing a comparison of the mean scores attained on the Schonell Graded Word Reading Test, by sub-groups of i.t.a. and t.o. children who attained similar levels of performance on the Goodenough Draw-A-Man Test.

Goodenough Draw-A-Man Test			Schonell Graded Word Reading Test 3rd time, May 1967					
range of scores	Group	N	mean score	S.D.	diff. in means	S.E. of diff.	C.R.	statis. signif.
120–133	i.t.a.	5	25.4	11.53	.31	9.99	.03	N.S.
	t.o.	3	25.09	12.37				
106–119	i.t.a.	19	17.31	13.27	2.25	4.15	.54	N.S.
	t.o.	16	15.06	10.82				
93–105	i.t.a.	47	18.4	12.77	0	2.86	0	N.S.
	t.o.	40	18.4	13.75				
79–92	i.t.a.	32	12.0	11.18	.05	2.48	.02	N.S.
	t.o.	42	12.05	9.69				
65–78	i.t.a.	16	6.87	7.07	.91	2.86	.32	N.S.
	t.o.	18	7.78	9.49				

TABLE 90 Showing a comparison of the mean scores attained on the Schonell Graded Word Reading Test, by sub-groups of i.t.a. and t.o. children who attained similar levels of performance on the Wechsler Scale of Intelligence for Children.

Wechsler Scale of Intelligence			Schonell Graded Word Reading Test 3rd time, May 1967					
range of scores	Group	N	mean score	S.D.	diff. in means	S.E. of diff.	C.R.	statis. signif.
113–125	i.t.a.	6	26.66	10.58	2.4	6.44	.37	N.S.
	t.o.	19	24.26	13.86				
100–112	i.t.a.	52	18.69	12.49	2.12	2.91	.73	N.S.
	t.o.	35	16.57	13.88				
87–99	i.t.a.	35	13.4	11.71	2.68	2.44	1.1	N.S.
	t.o.	36	10.73	8.6				
74–86	i.t.a.	20	8.25	10.39	2.02	2.86	.71	N.S.
	t.o.	22	10.27	8.25				
60–73	i.t.a.	6	8.0	8.6	2.29	4.82	.47	N.S.
	t.o.	7	5.71	7.28				

Here again we see the change in pattern from earlier results continued, and the results indicate that the level of intelligence required for reading with t.o. through the medium of i.t.a. is similar to that required for reading with t.o. The discrepancy between these and earlier results must be due to the setback of the i.t.a. children during the transfer stage, when a more difficult medium for them is being attempted.

TABLE 92   Showing a comparison of the mean scores attained on the Schonell Graded Word Reading Test, by sub-groups of i.t.a. and t.o. children who attained similar levels of performance on the author's Vocabulary Profile.

Vocabulary Profile Thackray			Schonell Graded Word Reading Test 3rd time, May 1967					
range of scores	Group	N	mean score	S.D.	diff. in means	S.E. of diff.	C.R.	statis. signif.
41–50	i.t.a.	10	23.0	11.7	2.3	6.6	.35	N.S.
	t.o.	10	25.3	15.84				
31–40	i.t.a.	65	18.57	13.32	12.55	2.86	4.39	.1% level
	t.o.	68	6.02	19.21				
21–30	i.t.a.	29	9.24	8.94	.82	2.04	.4	N.S.
	t.o.	36	8.42	7.07				
11–20	i.t.a.	13	8.31	11.09	1.02	7.44	.14	N.S.
	t.o.	3	9.33	9.9				
0–10	i.t.a.	2	.5	.5	10.0	4.47	2.24	N.S.
	t.o.	2	10.5	4.47				

From Table 92 it can be seen that there is a very highly significant difference (.1% level) between the mean scores of the sub-groups at the second highest level of performance; but three of the mean differences favour the t.o. sub-groups, though these are not significant. These results are somewhat conflicting, but certainly show a change in pattern from the earlier results on this test, and so to some extent support what has been said concerning the other reading readiness measures.

b) The Neale Analysis of Reading Ability

TABLE 93 Showing a comparison of the mean scores attained on Reading Accuracy as measured by the Neale Analysis of Reading Ability, by sub-groups of i.t.a. and t.o. children who attained similar levels of performance on the author's Visual Discrimination Test.

Visual Discrim. Thackray			Neale Analysis of Reading Ability, Form B (Accuracy) 2nd time, May 1967					
range of scores	Group	N	mean score	S.D.	diff. in means	S.E. of diff.	C.R.	statis. signif.
28–34	i.t.a.	8	36.5	19.03	11.88	6.43	1.85	N.S.
	t.o.	24	24.62	13.71				
21–27	i.t.a.	53	22.36	15.1	1.71	3.74	.64	N.S.
	t.o.	33	20.65	18.14				
14–20	i.t.a.	26	15.42	11.96	3.0	3.2	.94	N.S.
	t.o.	27	12.42	11.09				
7–13	i.t.a.	23	6.52	8.25	2.91	2.33	1.25	N.S.
	t.o.	28	9.43	8.12				
0–6	i.t.a.	9	2.78	4.5	2.36	2.75	.86	N.S.
	t.o.	7	5.14	5.92				

TABLE 94 Showing a comparison of the mean scores attained on Reading Accuracy as measured by the Neale Analysis of Reading Ability, by sub-groups of i.t.a. and t.o. children who attained similar levels of performance on the Harrison-Stroud Visual Discrimination Test in i.t.a.

Visual Discrim. in i.t.a. Harrison-Stroud			Neale Analysis of Reading Ability, Form B (Accuracy) 2nd time, May 1967					
range of scores	Group	N	mean score	S.D.	diff. in means	S.E. of diff.	C.R.	statis. signif.
25–30	i.t.a.	51	26.96	16.19	6.52	3.11	2.1	5% level
	t.o.	54	20.44	15.65				
19–24	i.t.a.	29	15.59	10.49	.28	3.32	.08	N.S.
	t.o.	31	15.87	15.04				
13–18	i.t.a.	18	6.53	9.43	5.78	1.06	5.45	.1%* level
	t.o.	19	12.31	10.82				
7–12	i.t.a.	14	5.93	8.43	.57	3.52	.16	N.S.
	t.o.	8	6.5	5.95				
0–6	i.t.a.	7	6.28	7.56	1.42	3.89	.36	N.S.
	t.o.	7	4.86	5.92				

* In favour of t.o.

246

TABLE 95 Showing a comparison of the mean scores attained on **Reading** Accuracy as measured by the Neale Analysis of Reading Ability, by sub-groups of i.t.a. and t.o. children who attained similar levels of performance on the Harrison-Stroud Visual Discrimination Test in t.o.

Visual Discrim. in t.o. Harrison-Stroud			Neale Analysis of Reading Ability, Form **B** (Accuracy) 2nd time, May 1967					
range of scores	Group	N	mean scores	S.D.	diff. in means	S.E. of diff.	C.R.	statis. signif.
25–30	i.t.a.	48	25.84	16.0	3.2	3.06	1.05	N.S.
	t.o.	56	22.64	15.2				
19–24	i.t.a.	31	18.87	12.84	5.19	3.35	1.55	N.S.
	t.o.	31	13.68	13.56				
13–18	i.t.a.	19	8.67	9.54	.45	1.07	.42	N.S.
	t.o.	16	9.12	10.39				
7–12	i.t.a.	13	3.15	4.69	2.18	2.06	1.06	N.S.
	t.o.	12	5.33	5.2				
0–6	i.t.a.	8	2.13	4.9	2.62	3.83	.68	N.S.
	t.o.	4	4.75	7.14				

From Tables 93, 94 and 95 the following results can be seen:

(a) The differences between the mean reading scores of the sub-groups at the various levels of performance on the three tests of visual discrimination are fairly equally divided between i.t.a. and t.o.

(b) On the Harrison-Stroud Visual Discrimination Test in i.t.a. there was a significant difference (5% level) between the mean reading scores at the highest level of performance in favour of i.t.a.; but this difference is balanced by a very highly significant difference (.1% level) between the mean reading scores at the middle level of performance in favour of t.o. There are no other significant differences.

These results show quite clearly that on the Neale test, which is a test using continuous prose, the same change in pattern has developed as was seen from the results of the Schonell test. Previously, all differences between mean reading scores favoured i.t.a., indicating that, for reading with

247

TABLE 96 Showing a comparison of the mean scores attained on Reading Accuracy as measured by the Neale Analysis of Reading Ability, by sub-groups of i.t.a. and t.o. children who attained similar levels of performance on the author's Auditory Discrimination Test.

| Auditory Discrim. Thackray | | | Neale Analysis of Reading Ability, Form B (Accuracy) 2nd time, May 1967 | | | | | |
range of scores	Group	N	mean score	S.D.	diff. in means.	S.E. of diff.	C.R.	statis. signif.
27–33	i.t.a.	1	36	0				
	t.o.	1	36	0				
20–36	i.t.a.	15	32.6	18.19	10.27	7.17	1.43	N.S.
	t.o.	12	22.33	17.08				
14–19	i.t.a.	26	19.08	16.0	6.64	4.46	1.49	N.S.
	t.o.	29	25.72	16.76				
7–13	i.t.a.	43	18.99	12.29	7.33	2.47	2.98	1% level
	t.o.	52	11.56	11.58				
0–6	i.t.a.	34	6.82	9.9	.7	2.9	.24	N.S.
	t.o.	25	6.12	11.75				

TABLE 97 Showing a comparison of the mean scores attained on Reading Accuracy as measured by the Neale Analysis of Reading Ability, by sub-groups of i.t.a. and t.o. children who attained similar levels of performance on the Harrison-Stroud Auditory Discrimination Test.

| Auditory Discrim. Harrison-Stroud | | | Neale Analysis of Reading Ability, Form B (Accuracy) 2nd time, May 1967 | | | | | |
range of scores	Group	N	mean score	S.D.	diff. in means	S.E. of diff.	C.R.	statis. signif.
13–16	i.t.a.	23	28.65	16.61	.52	4.14	.12	N.S.
	t.o.	20	28.13	14.87				
10–12	i.t.a.	31	20.35	14.93	6.13	3.35	1.83	N.S.
	t.o.	40	14.22	12.85				
7–9	i.t.a.	53	11.87	12.29	2.05	2.57	.8	N.S.
	t.o.	39	9.82	12.12				
4–6	i.t.a.	11	9.27	9.11	5.73	4.1	1.4	N.S.
	t.o.	8	15.0	6.86				
0–3	i.t.a.	1	0					
	t.o.	2	0					

i.t.a., lower levels of visual discrimination were adequate for satisfactory reading progress than for reading with t.o. However, the differences between the mean reading scores of the i.t.a. and t.o. sub-groups are now fairly equally balanced, and so the results indicate that the level of visual discrimination required for reading with t.o. through the medium of i.t.a. is similar to that required for reading with t.o. This shows that children can learn to read more easily with i.t.a. than with t.o. approached to the usual eclectic way, but after the transfer to t.o., which becomes a more difficult medium for the i.t.a. children, a setback in reading progress and standards results.

From Tables 96 and 97 it can be seen that the differences between the mean reading scores of the sub-groups at the various levels of performance on the two tests of auditory discrimination are fairly equally divided between i.t.a. and t.o. On the author's Auditory Discrimination test there is a highly significant difference (1% level) between the mean reading scores at the next lowest level of performance in favour of i.t.a., but this is the only significant difference.

These results again show that now the Neale test has been given in t.o. to both groups a change of pattern has developed, and the results indicate that the level of auditory discrimination required for reading with t.o. through the medium of i.t.a. is similar to that required for reading with t.o. from the start. The discrepancy between these and earlier results must be due to the setback of the i.t.a. children during the transfer stage, when a (for them) more difficult medium is being attempted.

From Tables 98 and 99 it can be seen that the differences between the mean reading scores of the sub-groups, at the various levels of performance, on the two tests of intelligence were quite small, sometimes in favour of i.t.a., sometimes in favour of t.o.; there were no significant differences. Here again, we see the new pattern continued now that the Reading Accuracy test was given to both groups in t.o., and the results indicate that a similar level of intelligence for i.t.a. and t.o. sub-groups gives similar mean reading scores.

From Table 100 it can be seen that the results conform to the newly established pattern, now the reading achievement test has been given in t.o. to both the groups.

The figures produced by the second statistical approach show quite clearly that during the children's sixth term in

TABLE 98 Showing a comparison of the mean scores attained on Reading Accuracy as measured by the Neale Analysis of Reading Ability, by sub-groups of i.t.a. and t.o. children who attained similar levels of performance on the Wechsler Scale of Intelligence for Children.

Wechsler Scale of Intelligence			Neale Analysis of Reading Ability, Form B (Accuracy) 2nd time, May 1967					
range of scores	Group	N	mean score	S.D.	diff. in means	S.E. of diff.	C.R.	statis. signif.
113–125	i.t.a.	6	31.53	12.92	4.27	7.98	.53	N.S.
	t.o.	19	27.26	17.23				
100–112	i.t.a.	52	21.67	16.46	1.78	3.61	.49	N.S.
	t.o.	35	19.89	16.37				
87–99	i.t.a.	35	14.29	13.0	2.04	2.8	.73	N.S.
	t.o.	36	12.25	10.44				
74–86	i.t.a.	20	9.25	13.08	1.44	3.45	.42	N.S.
	t.o.	22	10.69	9.38				
60–73	i.t.a.	6	9.83	10.77	4.83	5.21	.93	N.S.
	t.o.	7	5.0	6.08				

TABLE 99 Showing a comparison of the mean scores attained on Reading Accuracy as measured by the Neale Analysis of Reading Ability, by sub-groups of i.t.a. and t.o. children who attained similar levels of performance on the Goodenough Draw-A-Man Test.

Goodenough Draw-A-Man Test			Neale Analysis of Reading Ability, Form B (Accuracy) 2nd time, May 1967					
range of scores	Group	N	mean score	S.D.	diff. in means	S.E. of diff.	C.R.	statis. signif.
120–133	i.t.a.	5	29.4	14.62	4.6	12.11	.38	N.S.
	t.o.	3	34.0	13.96				
106–119	i.t.a.	19	20.89	16.86	3.64	5.22	.7	N.S.
	t.o.	16	17.25	13.34				
93–105	i.t.a.	47	21.21	15.72	1.19	3.65	.33	N.S.
	t.o.	40	20.02	18.11				
79–92	i.t.a.	32	12.87	13.42	.44	2.9	.15	N.S.
	t.o.	42	12.43	10.78				
65–78	i.t.a.	16	6.69	8.78	2.53	3.75	.67	N.S.
	t.o.	18	9.22	12.69				

TABLE 100   Showing a comparison of the mean scores attained on Reading Accuracy as measured by the Neale Analysis of Reading Ability, by sub-groups of i.t.a. and t.o. children who attained similar levels of performance on the author's Vocabulary Profile.

Vocabulary Profile Thackray			Neale Analysis of Reading Ability, Form B (Accuracy) 2nd time, May 1967					
range of scores	Group	N	mean score	S.D.	diff. in means	S.E. of diff.	C.R.	statis. signif.
41–50	i.t.a.	10	27.3	12.69	2.3	7.41	.31	N.S.
	t.o.	10	29.6	18.08				
31–40	i.t.a.	65	20.8	16.31	2.24	2.72	.82	N.S.
	t.o.	68	18.56	15.03				
21–30	i.t.a.	29	10.86	11.22	1.94	2.55	.76	N.S.
	t.o.	36	8.92	8.77				
11–20	i.t.a.	13	6.61	14.83	.94	9.45	.1	N.S.
	t.o.	3	5.67	8.0				
0–10	i.t.a.	2	0	0				
	t.o.	2	12.5	8.48				

school, when the reading tests were given in t.o. to both i.t.a. and t.o. groups, a new pattern of results has emerged. In the third and fourth term tests, the differences between the mean reading scores favoured i.t.a. almost without exception, and there were a number of significant differences in all tests to show that reading readiness levels required to learn to read with i.t.a. were lower than those required to learn to read with t.o. In the sixth term we are looking at the reading readiness requirements for learning to read with t.o. through the medium of i.t.a., compared with those for learning to read with t.o. from the start, and it has been shown that similar reading readiness levels are now required. The discrepancy between the earlier results, and those obtained in the children's sixth term in school, is added evidence to show that reading in t.o. after the transfer is more difficult than reading in i.t.a. The reading standards of the i.t.a. group can now be validly compared with those attained by the t.o. group, and they are found to be similar.

This analysis may well favour the t.o. group, as 50 i.t.a. children had not transferred to t.o., and their t.o. scores were taken. The results attained during the children's ninth term in school, to be discussed in the next chapter, will be fairer to the i.t.a. children, who will then have had time to make good the setback during the transfer stage.

(iii) *A comparison of the minimum mental age levels required for learning to read successfully with i.t.a. and t.o.*

From Tables 101 and 102 it can be seen that the mean reading scores of the i.t.a. and t.o. sub-groups in each mental age range are much closer together than they were in earlier tables giving the same information. Again, we see here, in one or two cases, the mean reading score of the t.o. sub-group is greater than that of the i.t.a. sub-group in the same mental age range. However, the changes from earlier results are not great, as, at many mental age levels, the i.t.a. sub-groups have mean reading scores greater than their t.o. counterparts, and there is some evidence to suggest that i.t.a. children who have transferred to t.o. reading can achieve similar mean reading scores to children who have read with t.o. from the start, but with slightly lower mental ages. It will

TABLE 101   Showing a comparison between the mean scores attained on the Schonell Graded Word Reading Test given a third time, by sub-groups of i.t.a. and t.o. children with similar mental ages.

mental ages (years, months)	below 3–6	3–6 3–11	4–0 4–5	4–6 4–11	5–0 5–5	5–6 5–11	6–0 6–5	6–6 6–11
no. of i.t.a. chn. in each mental age group	2	5	15	23	36	30	7	1
no. of t.o. chn. in each mental age group	4	7	14	20	25	25	22	2
mean score of i.t.a. chn. on Schonell	7.5	6.6	7.4	13	15.1	21.3	24.6	1
mean score of t.o. chn. on Schonell	8	4.3	10.3	11.8	10.0	16.6	22.8	36

252

TABLE 102 Showing a comparison between the mean scores attained on Reading Accuracy as measured by the Neale Analysis of Reading Ability given for the second time, by sub-groups of i.t.a. and t.o. children with similar mental ages.

mental ages (years, months)	below 3–6	3–6 3–11	4–0 4–5	4–6 4–11	5–0 5–5	5–6 5–11	6–0 6–5	6–6 6–11
no. of i.t.a. chn. in each mental age group	2	5	15	23	36	30	7	1
no. of t.o. chn. in each mental age group	4	7	14	20	25	25	22	2
mean score of i.t.a. chn. on Neale	6.0	7.8	8.2	15.6	16.7	23.9	28.4	2
mean score of t.o. chn. on Neale	6.0	4.8	12.6	10.8	13.7	19.1	26.0	36.5

be interesting to look at this same kind of information when the results are presented from the tests given in the ninth term at school.

Again, to conclude this chapter, a comparison has been made of the correlations between the initial tests of reading readiness abilities and the two reading achievement tests discussed in this chapter, so as further study can be made of the relative importance of the factors in reading readiness.

Again, in order to see the relevant importance in the author's experiment of the factors making for reading readiness the correlations for each factor were averaged, with the following results:

visual discrimination	.48
auditory discrimination	.46
intelligence and vocabulary	.38

As before, the correlation coefficients for visual and auditory discrimination show a substantial relationship with later reading achievement, and are more important than mental ability and language development in learning to read by either i.t.a. or t.o.

TABLE 103 Showing a comparison of the correlations, calculated for the i.t.a. and t.o. groups separately, between the initial tests of reading readiness abilities and the two measures of reading achievement given in the children's sixth term at school.

Tests of Reading Readiness Abilities	Group	Schonell 3rd time May 1967 r	Neale 2nd time May 1967 r
Visual Discrim. Thackray	i.t.a.	.55	.53
	t.o.	.43	.46
Visual Discrim. in i.t.a. Harrison-Stroud	i.t.a.	.61	.59
	t.o.	.32	.41
Visual Discrim. in t.o. Harrison-Stroud	i.t.a.	.55	.52
	t.o.	.35	.45
Auditory Discrim. Thackray	i.t.a.	.50	.54
	t.o.	.36	.39
Auditory Discrim. Harrison-Stroud	i.t.a.	.48	.50
	t.o.	.46	.47
Wechsler Scale of Intelligence	i.t.a.	.39	.36
	t.o.	.47	.50
Goodenough Draw-A-Man Test	i.t.a.	.32	.33
	t.o.	.31	.35
Vocabulary Profile	i.t.a.	.43	.43
	t.o.	.33	.34

Chapter 8

Discussion of the Results Obtained by the Statistical Methods Selected (V): Tests Carried out in the Children's Ninth Term at School

Towards the end of the children's third year in school (ninth term) the i.t.a. and t.o. groups were tested for the final time on the same two reading achievement tests of Schonell and Neale. The two groups at this stage were reduced to 102 in each group, because of family removals and the corresponding elimination needed to keep the groups as well matched as possible. Out of the 102 children in the i.t.a. groups, 66 had moved up into junior departments or junior schools. Out of the 102 in the t.o. group, 82 had moved up into junior departments or junior schools. This means that because of their birth dates 56 out of the 204 children remaining from the original sample would benefit from an extra year of schooling in the infants' school and an extra year's development of their reading skills. Four children only had not transferred to t.o. in May, 1968, when the final tests were given.

When visiting the junior schools to test the children at the end of their third year in school, the author realised quite clearly that the longer an investigation continues, the more variables there are to affect any results he may obtain. For example, two of the junior schools had remedial classes during the children's first year in the school, and another headmaster felt reading was so important he himself tested each child twice a year, and by doing this created a strong 'reading drive' throughout the school. Other junior schools placed no special emphasis on reading but approached the teaching of it in a variety of ways. All these different conditions would, of course, have some effect, though hardly measurable, on the results at the end of the third year.

At this stage, as only four children had not transferred to t.o., and as those who had would have made good any setback occurring during the transfer, the author felt that the results obtained from the Schonell and Neale tests given in t.o. would be as valid as was possible in the circumstances.

Now follows the relevant information obtained from the two tests given in t.o., for the last time:

TABLE 104 Showing a comparison between the mean scores of the i.t.a. and t.o. groups on the Schonell Graded Word Reading Test given for the fourth time (given in t.o. to both i.t.a. and t.o. groups).

Group	N	mean score	S.D.	diff. in means	S.E. of diff.	C.R.	statis. signif.
i.t.a.	102	28.15	14.15	.4	2.06	.19	N.S.
t.o.	102	27.75	15.25				

TABLE 105 Showing a comparison between the mean scores of the i.t.a. and t.o. groups on Reading Accuracy as measured by the Neale Analysis of Reading Ability (Form A) given for the third time (given in t.o. to both i.t.a. and t.o. groups).

Group	N	mean score	S.D.	diff. in means	S.E. of diff.	C.R.	statis. signif.
i.t.a.	102	32.04	17.8	.11	2.49	.04	N.S.
t.o.	102	32.15	17.8				

TABLE 106 Showing a comparison between the mean scores of the i.t.a. and t.o. groups on Reading Comprehension as measured by the Neale Analysis of Reading Ability (Form A) given for the third time.

Group	N	mean score	S.D.	diff. in means	S.E. of diff.	C.R.	statis. signif.
i.t.a.	102	9.89	6.6	.37	.94	.49	N.S.
t.o.	102	10.26	6.88				

From Tables 104, 105 and 106 it can be seen that there are no significant differences between the mean scores of the i.t.a. and t.o. groups when tested on the t.o. versions of the tests towards the end of their third year in school, and the mean scores are very close. It is interesting to note that the average age of the children when tested at this time was 7 years 9 months. The Schonell mean score of 28 gives a reading age of 7 years 9 months, and the Neale mean score of 32 for accuracy gives a reading age of 8 years 4 months. In the author's sample the norms obtained on the Schonell test seemed to be relatively lower than those given in the Neale test, but nearer the average chronological ages of the children.

These results indicate that, after three years of schooling, the i.t.a. group who learned to read first with i.t.a. and then transferred to t.o. had very similar mean reading scores to the t.o. group who started to read with t.o. from the beginning, and there were no significant differences between the mean scores.

These results do not agree with those of the main i.t.a. experiment obtained after three years of schooling. Downing (1967a) found a significant difference between the mean scores of his i.t.a. and t.o. groups on both the Schonell and the Neale tests, though it has been pointed out by Burt (1967) that, had he not used the Kolmogorov-Smirnov test, the difference may not have been significant.

However, it is encouraging to note that, after examining the verbal and research evidence on this particular aspect of i.t.a., the findings of Warburton and Southgate (1969) are in keeping with those found by the author. They write:

> Both kinds of evidence also indicate that, after about three years of schooling, the reading attainments of most children taught initially by t.o. are approximately equal to those of children whose initial medium of instruction was i.t.a.

Again, to complete the rigorous comparisons between the reading readiness requirements of learning to read with i.t.a. and t.o., the same three statistical analyses were made for the final time.

(i) *A study of the relationship between the earlier results on the battery of reading readiness measures and the results on the two reading achievement measures:*

K

given at the beginning of the children's ninth term in school, for both the i.t.a. and t.o. groups separately.

From Tables 107 and 108 it can be seen that there are no significant differences between the pairs of correlation coefficients, indicating that after nearly three years of schooling the various factors making for reading readiness are of similar importance in learning to read with t.o. through the initial medium of i.t.a., and in learning to read with t.o. from the start.

(ii) *A comparison of the mean scores attained on the two reading achievement measures between sub-groups of i.t.a. and t.o.*

TABLE 107   Showing a comparison of the correlations calculated for the i.t.a. and t.o. groups separately, between the initial tests of reading readiness abilities and the Schonell Graded Word Reading Test given for the fourth time (given in t.o. to both the i.t.a. and t.o. groups).

Tests of Reading Readiness Abilities	Schonell Graded Word Reading Test 4th time, May 1968						
	Group	r	z	diff. in 'z's	S.E. of diff.	C.R.	statis. signif.
Visual Discrim. Thackray	i.t.a. t.o.	.55 .49	.62 .54	.08	.14	.51	N.S.
Visual Discrim. in i.t.a. Harrison-Stroud	i.t.a. t.o.	.55 .50	.62 .55	.07	.14	.5	N.S.
Visual Discrim. in t.o. Harrison-Stroud	i.t.a. t.o.	.55 .50	.62 .55	.07	.14	.5	N.S.
Auditory Discrim. Thackray	i.t.a. t.o.	.47 .41	.51 .44	.07	.14	.5	N.S.
Auditory Discrim. Harrison-Stroud	i.t.a. t.o.	.40 .44	.42 .47	.05	.14	.36	N.S.
Wechsler Scale of Intelligence	i.t.a. t.o.	.36 .45	.38 .48	.1	.14	.7	N.S.
Goodenough Draw-A-Man Test	i.t.a. t.o.	.28 .36	.29 .38	.09	.14	.64	N.S.
Vocabulary Profile Thackray	i.t.a. t.o.	.48 .42	.46 .45	.01	.14	.07	N.S.

children who attained similar levels of performance on each of the earlier reading readiness measures.

As before, the Schonell Test is presented first, followed by Neale, but the author feels that only one comment on these Tables is necessary and this is given at the end of the two series of Tables.

A study of Tables 109 – 124 shows a further repetition of the new pattern established when the children were tested towards the end of their second year in school. At this stage, only four i.t.a. children had not transferred to t.o., and most of the other i.t.a. children had been transferred for a time long enough for them to make good any setback, if they were able to do this.

TABLE 108 Showing a comparison of the correlations calculated for the i.t.a. and t.o. groups separately between the initial tests of reading readiness abilities and Reading Accuracy as measured by the Neale Analysis of Reading Ability (Form A), given for the third time (given in t.o. to both the i.t.a. and t.o. groups).

Tests of Reading Readiness Abilities	Neale Analysis of Reading Ability, Form A (Accuracy) 3rd time, May, 1968						
	Group	r	z	diff. in 'z's	S.E. of diff.	C.R.	statis. signif.
Visual Discrim. Thackray	i.t.a.	.56	.63	0	.14	0	N.S.
	t.o.	.56	.63				
Visual Discrim. in i.t.a. Harrison-Stroud	i.t.a.	.57	.65	.07	.14	.5	N.S.
	t.o.	.52	.58				
Visual Discrim. in t.o. Harrison-Stroud	i.t.a.	.57	.65	.05	.14	.36	N.S.
	t.o.	.54	.60				
Auditory Discrim. Thackray	i.t.a.	.45	.48	.11	.14	.79	N.S.
	t.o.	.35	.37				
Auditory Discrim. Harrison-Stroud	i.t.a.	.34	.35	.12	.14	.86	N.S.
	t.o.	.44	.47				
Wechsler Scale of Intelligence	i.t.a.	.40	.42	.06	.14	.43	N.S.
	t.o.	.45	.48				
Goodenough Draw-A-Man Test	i.t.a.	.36	.38	.07	.14	.5	N.S.
	t.o.	.42	.45				
Vocabulary Profile Thackray	i.t.a.	.45	.48	.04	.14	.29	N.S.
	t.o.	.41	.44				

(a) The Schonell Graded Word Reading Test

TABLE 109   Showing a comparison of the mean scores attained on the Schonell Graded Word Reading Test, by sub-groups of i.t.a. and t.o. children who attained similar levels of performance on the author's Visual Discrimination Test.

Visual Discrim. Thackray			Schonell Graded Word Reading Test 4th time, May 1968					
range of scores	Group	N	mean score	S.D.	diff. in means	S.E. of diff.	C.R.	statis. signif.
28–34	i.t.a.	6	41.67	12.88	6.0	6.11	.98	N.S.
	t.o.	21	35.67	12.41				
21–27	i.t.a.	47	34.38	12.17	1.97	3.88	.51	N.S.
	t.o.	27	32.41	18.03				
14–20	i.t.a.	20	25.45	13.75	.95	3.9	.24	N.S.
	t.o.	25	26.4	12.0				
7–13	i.t.a.	21	18.24	12.92	1.54	3.7	.42	N.S.
	t.o.	23	19.78	11.27				
0–6	i.t.a.	8	16.0	9.33	1.0	5.52	.18	N.S.
	t.o.	6	15.0	11.31				

TABLE 110   Showing a comparison of the mean scores attained on the Schonell Graded Word Reading Test, by sub-groups of i.t.a. and t.o. children who attained similar levels of performance on the Harrison-Stroud Visual Discrimination Test in i.t.a.

Visual Discrim. in i.t.a. Harrison-Stroud			Schonell Graded Word Reading Test 4th time, May 1968					
range of scores	Group	N	mean score	S.D.	diff. in means	S.E. of diff.	C.R.	statis. signif.
25–30	i.t.a.	43	37.39	12.92	4.09	2.87	1.42	N.S.
	t.o.	47	33.30	14.35				
19–24	i.t.a.	24	28.17	11.05	1.17	3.64	.32	N.S.
	t.o.	27	27.0	14.93				
13–18	i.t.a.	15	15.67	10.5	7.29	4.32	1.68	N.S.
	t.o.	16	23.06	12.53				
7–12	i.t.a.	13	16.92	11.0	2.09	5.45	.38	N.S.
	t.o.	6	14.83	8.67				
0–6	i.t.a.	7	21.0	9.06	8.17	5.78	1.41	N.S.
	t.o.	6	12.83	12.0				

TABLE 111 Showing a comparison of the mean scores attained on the Schonell Graded Word Reading Test, by sub-groups of i.t.a. and t.o. children who attained similar levels of performance on the Harrison-Stroud Visual Discrimination Test in t.o.

Visual Discrim. in t.o. Harrison-Stroud			Schonell Graded Word Reading Test 4th time, May 1968					
range of scores	Group	N	mean score	S.D.	diff. in means	S.E. of diff.	C.R.	statis. signif.
25–30	i.t.a.	40	36.57	12.24	2.15	2.79	.77	N.S.
	t.o.	48	34.42	13.89				
19–24	i.t.a.	27	28.85	12.49	3.28	3.38	.97	N.S.
	t.o.	28	25.57	12.96				
13–18	i.t.a.	16	20.06	14.11	.31	5.44	.06	N.S.
	t.o.	12	19.75	14.28				
7–12	i.t.a.	12	15.64	10.34	1.62	4.2	.38	N.S.
	t.o.	11	17.27	9.27				
0–6	i.t.a.	7	14.71	9.69	3.38	8.57	.39	N.S.
	t.o.	3	11.33	13.89				

TABLE 112 Showing a comparison of the mean scores attained on the Schonell Graded word Reading Test, by sub-groups of i.t.a. and t.o. children who attained similar levels of performance on the author's Auditory Discrimination Test.

Auditory Discrim. Thackray			Schonell Graded Word Reading Test 4th time, May 1968					
range of scores	Group	N	mean score	S.D.	diff. in means	S.E. of diff.	C.R.	statis. signif.
27–33	i.t.a.	1	51.0	0				
	t.o.	1	58.0	0				
20–26	i.t.a.	13	38.0	16.43	2.0	6.9	.29	N.S.
	t.o.	11	36.0	15.68				
14–19	i.t.a.	23	29.5	12.12	7.08	3.98	1.78	N.S.
	t.o.	24	36.58	14.63				
7–13	i.t.a.	35	30.59	13.45	7.09	3.03	2.34	5% level
	t.o.	44	23.5	13.08				
0–6	i.t.a.	30	19.33	11.79	1.72	3.11	.55	N.S.
	t.o.	22	21.05	11.66				

TABLE 113 Showing a comparison of the mean scores attained on the Schonell Graded Word Reading Test, by sub-groups of i.t.a. and t.o. children who attained similar levels of performance on the Harrison-Stroud Auditory Discrimination Test.

Auditory Discrim. Harrison-Stroud			Schonell Graded Word Reading Test 4th time, May 1968					
range of scores	Group	N	mean score	S.D.	diff. in means	S.E. of diff.	C.R.	statis. signif.
13–16	i.t.a.	19	39.4	13.0	1.3	4.05	.32	N.S.
	t.o.	26	40.77	13.34				
10–12	i.t.a.	24	29.79	15.33	5.65	3.8	1.49	N.S.
	t.o.	35	24.14	13.08				
7–9	i.t.a.	48	25.04	13.23	2.76	3.13	.88	N.S.
	t.o.	33	27.8	13.5				
4–6	i.t.a.	10	22.6	10.77	4.73	4.86	.97	N.S.
	t.o.	6	27.33	4.47				
0–3	i.t.a.	1	7					
	t.o.	2	12.5					

TABLE 114 Showing a comparison of the mean scores attained on the Schonell Graded Word Reading Test, by sub-groups of i.t.a. and t.o. children who attained similar levels of performance on the Wechsler Scale of Intelligence for Children.

Wechsler Scale of Intelligence			Schonell Graded Word Reading Test 4th time, May 1968					
range of scores	Group	N	mean score	S.D.	diff. in means	S.E. of diff.	C.R.	statis. signif.
113–125	i.t.a.	4	42.0	6.71	1.82	7.64	.24	N.S.
	t.o.	17	40.18	14.07				
100–112	i.t.a.	45	33.0	13.23	2.61	3.31	.79	N.S.
	t.o.	28	30.29	14.03				
87–99	i.t.a.	30	25.17	13.89	.38	3.54	.11	N.S.
	t.o.	33	24.79	14.25				
74–86	i.t.a.	18	20.17	15.33	3.33	4.59	.72	N.S.
	t.o.	18	23.5	12.33				
60–73	i.t.a.	5	23.0	12.4	13.67	7.48	1.83	N.S.
	t.o.	6	9.33	9.9				

TABLE 115 Showing a comparison of the mean scores attained on the Schonell Graded Word Reading Test, by sub-groups of i.t.a. and t.o. children who attained similar levels of performance on the Goodenough Draw-A-Man Test.

Goodenough Draw-A-Man Test			Schonell Graded Word Reading Test 4th time, May 1968					
range of scores	Group	N	mean score	S.D.	diff. in means	S.E. of diff.	C.R.	statis. signif.
120–133	i.t.a.	4	41.75	5.92	3.25	10.4	.31	N.S.
	t.o.	3	45.0	16.31				
106–119	i.t.a.	18	30.47	14.39	.15	4.95	.03	N.S.
	t.o.	13	30.62	11.62				
93–105	i.t.a.	39	31.45	13.6	.74	3.38	.22	N.S.
	t.o.	36	32.19	15.43				
79–92	i.t.a.	26	25.08	15.43	.63	3.74	.17	N.S.
	t.o.	34	25.71	12.81				
65–78	i.t.a.	15	19.53	12.41	3.09	4.72	.65	N.S.
	t.o.	16	16.44	12.96				

TABLE 116 Showing a comparison of the mean scores attained on the Schonell Graded Word Reading Test, by sub-groups of i.t.a. and t.o. children who attained similar levels of performance of the authors Vocabulary Profile.

Vocabulary Profile Thackray			Schonell Graded Word Reading Test 4th time, May 1968					
range of scores	Group	N	mean score	S.D.	diff. in means	S.E. of diff.	C.R.	statis. signif.
41–50	i.t.a.	7	39.42	9.8	.13	8.19	.02	N.S.
	t.o.	9	39.55	18.52				
31–40	i.t.a.	57	31.85	13.56	.36	2.34	.15	N.S.
	t.o.	57	31.49	11.36				
21–30	i.t.a.	24	23.37	13.67	4.29	3.34	1.28	N.S.
	t.o.	32	19.08	10.49				
11–20	i.t.a.	12	18.83	12.96	7.5	9.04	.83	N.S.
	t.o.	3	11.33	13.93				
0–10	i.t.a.	2	3	1				
	t.o.	1	33	0				

(b) The Neale Analysis of Reading Ability

TABLE 117 Showing a comparison of the mean scores attained on Reading Accuracy measured by the Neale Analysis of Reading Ability, by sub-groups of i.t.a. and t.o. children who attained similar levels of performance on the author's Visual Discrimination Test.

Visual Discrim. Thackray			Neale Analysis of Reading Ability, Form A (Accuracy) 3rd time, May 1968.					
range of scores	Group	N	mean score	S.D.	diff. in means	S.E. of diff.	C.R.	statis. signif.
28–34	i.t.a.	6	42.86	21.71	.86	7.94	.1	N.S.
	t.o.	21	42.0	14.0				
21–27	i.t.a.	47	39.57	14.53	2.05	4.47	.46	N.S.
	t.o.	27	37.52	20.45				
14–20	i.t.a.	20	28.45	16.43	1.83	4.5	.41	N.S.
	t.o.	25	30.28	13.42				
7–13	i.t.a.	21	20.0	14.35	1.69	4.2	.4	N.S.
	t.o.	23	21.69	13.34				
0–6	i.t.a.	8	16.87	10.1	3.2	6.32	.51	N.S.
	t.o.	6	13.67	11.75				

TABLE 118 Showing a comparison of the mean scores attained on Reading Accuracy measured by the Neale Analysis of Reading Ability, by sub-groups of i.t.a. and t.o. children who attained similar levels of performance on the Harrison-Stroud Visual Discrimination Test in i.t.a.

Visual Discrim. in i.t.a. Harrison-Stroud			Neale Analysis of Reading Ability, Form A (Accuracy) 3rd time, May 1968					
range of scores	Group	N	mean score	S.D.	diff. in means	S.E. of diff.	C.R.	statis. signif.
25–30	i.t.a.	43	42.6	16.4	4.07	3.61	1.13	N.S.
	t.o.	47	38.53	17.75				
19–24	i.t.a.	24	31.87	13.0	1.91	3.8	.5	N.S.
	t.o.	27	29.96	14.18				
13–18	i.t.a.	15	18.33	12.81	7.82	4.93	1.59	N.S.
	t.o.	16	26.25	13.64				
7–12	i.t.a.	13	17.0	12.65	1.17	5.96	.2	N.S.
	t.o.	6	15.83	7.42				
0–6	i.t.a.	7	23.43	10.34	10.43	6.83	1.53	N.S.
	t.o.	6	13.0	13.42				

TABLE 119 Showing a comparison of the mean scores attained on Reading Accuracy measured by the Neale Analysis of Reading Ability, by sub-groups of i.t.a. and t.o. children who attained similar levels of performance on the Harrison-Stroud Visual Discrimination Test in t.o.

Visual Discrim. in t.o. Harrison-Stroud			Neale Analysis of Reading Ability, Form A (Accuracy) 3rd time, May 1968					
range of scores	Group	N	mean score	S.D.	diff. in means	S.E. of diff.	C.R.	statis. signif.
25–30	i.t.a. t.o.	40 48	42.5 40.42	15.26 17.11	2.08	3.46	.6	N.S.
19–24	i.t.a. t.o.	27 28	33.96 29.39	14.8 15.84	4.57	4.12	1.12	N.S.
13–18	i.t.a. t.o.	16 12	21.62 23.08	14.07 13.23	1.46	5.26	.28	N.S.
7–12	i.t.a. t.o.	12 11	15.67 17.18	10.68 11.4	1.51	4.73	.32	N.S.
0–6	i.t.a. t.o.	7 3	14.71 11.33	10.95 14.63	3.38	9.38	.36	N.S.

TABLE 120 Showing a comparison of the mean scores attained on Reading Accuracy measured by the Neale Analysis of Reading Ability, by sub-groups of i.t.a. and t.o. children who attained similar levels of performance on the author's Auditory Discrimination Test.

Auditory Discrim. Thackray			Neale Analysis of Reading Ability, Form A (Accuracy) 3rd time, May 1968					
range of scores	Group	N	mean score	S.D.	diff. in means	S.E. of diff.	C.R.	statis. signif.
27–33	i.t.a. t.o.	1 1	46.0 65.0	0 0				
20–26	i.t.a. t.o.	13 11	45.76 38.55	18.06 19.11	7.21	7.94	.91	N.S.
14–19	i.t.a. t.o.	23 24	33.26 42.42	14.32 16.7	9.16	4.6	1.99	N.S.
7–13	i.t.a. t.o.	35 44	34.57 22.25	16.6 15.3	7.32	3.64	2.01	5% level
0–6	i.t.a. t.o.	30 22	22.1 23.95	14.39 14.63	1.85	3.84	.48	N.S.

TABLE 12 Showing a comparison of the mean scores attained on Reading Accuracy measured by the Neale Analysis of Reading Ability, by sub-groups of i.t.a. and t.o. children who attained similar levels of performance on the Harrison-Stroud Auditory Discrimination Test.

Auditory Discrim. Harrison-Stroud			Neale Analysis of Reading Ability, Form A (Accuracy) 3rd time, May 1968					
range of scores	Group	N	mean score	S.D.	diff. in means	S.E. of diff.	C.R.	statis. signif.
13–16	i.t.a. t.o.	19 26	45.26 44.04	15.36 13.86	1.22	4.46	.27	N.S.
10–12	i.t.a. t.o.	24 35	32.5 28.3	17.58 15.52	4.2	4.46	.94	N.S.
7–9	i.t.a. t.o.	48 33	28.19 25.48	16.5 16.29	2.71	3.68	.74	N.S.
4–6	i.t.a. t.o.	10 6	25.7 37.83	14.0 15.49	12.13	7.95	1.53	N.S.
0–3	i.t.a. t.o.	1 2	7.0 13.0					

TABLE 122 Showing a comparison of the mean scores attained on Reading Accuracy measured by the Neale Analysis of Reading Ability, by sub-groups of i.t.a. and t.o. children who attained similar levels of performance on the Wechsler Scale of Intelligence for Children.

Wechsler Scale of Intelligence			Neale Analysis of Reading Ability, Form A (Accuracy) 3rd time, May 1968					
range of scores	Group	N	mean score	S.D.	diff. in means	S.E. of diff.	C.R.	statis. signif.
113–125	i.t.a. t.o.	4 17	49.5 46.71	8.67 17.26	2.79	9.41	.3	N.S.
100–112	i.t.a. t.o.	45 28	37.64 35.04	15.49 17.09	2.6	3.94	.66	N.S.
87–99	i.t.a. t.o.	30 33	28.23 27.94	17.12 15.39	.29	4.12	.07	N.S.
74–86	i.t.a. t.o.	18 18	21.4 26.17	17.2 12.49	4.77	4.95	.96	N.S.
60–73	i.t.a. t.o.	5 6	26.6 10.83	17.58 10.68	15.77	9.59	1.64	N.S.

TABLE 123 Showing a comparison of the mean scores attained on Reading Accuracy measured by the Neale Analysis of Reading Ability, by sub-groups of i.t.a. and t.o. children who attained similar levels of performance on the Goodenough Draw-A-Man Test.

Goodenough Draw-A-Man Test			Neale Analysis of Reading Ability, Form A (Accuracy) 3rd time, May 1968					
range of scores	Group	N	mean score	S.D.	diff. in means	S.E. of diff.	C.R.	statis. signif.
120–133	i.t.a.	4	55.0	5.38	3.67	11.55	.32	N.S.
	t.o.	3	51.33	18.63				
106–119	i.t.a.	18	35.55	19.23	15.78	7.06	2.23	5%* level
	t.o.	13	51.33	18.63				
93–105	i.t.a.	39	35.59	15.75	1.74	3.95	.44	N.S.
	t.o.	36	37.33	18.52				
79–92	i.t.a.	26	26.54	16.82	1.57	4.27	.37	N.S.
	t.o.	34	28.11	16.12				
65–78	i.t.a.	15	20.93	13.6	.33	5.54	.06	N.S.
	t.o.	16	20.6	16.06				

*In favour of t.o.

TABLE 124 Showing a comparison of the mean scores attained on Reading Accuracy measured by the Neale Analysis of Reading Ability, by sub-groups of i.t.a. and t.o. children who attained similar levels of performance on the author's Vocabulary Profile.

Vocabulary Profile Thackray			Neale Analysis of Reading Ability, Form A (Accuracy) 3rd time, May 1968					
range of scores	Group	N	mean score	S.D.	diff. in means	S.E. of diff.	C.R.	statis. signif.
41–50	i.t.a.	7	41.75	11.91	2.36	8.65	.27	N.S.
	t.o.	9	44.11	19.31				
31–40	i.t.a.	57	36.55	15.26	.36	3.37	.11	N.S.
	t.o.	57	36.19	20.3				
21–30	i.t.a.	24	25.08	15.84	3.08	3.8	.81	N.S.
	t.o.	32	22.0	11.49				
11–20	i.t.a.	12	22.42	15.2	11.09	10.36	1.07	N.S.
	t.o.	3	11.33	14.63				
0–10	i.t.a.	2	0	0				
	t.o.	1	36	0				

These results again show that the mean reading scores, attained on the two reading achievement tests by sub-groups of i.t.a. and t.o. children with similar levels of performance on the reading readiness abilities, are very similar. Out of eighty differences between mean reading scores, only three were significant, two in favour of i.t.a. and one in favour of t.o. This indicates that similar levels of reading readiness, attained initially, give similar levels of reading achievement after three years' schooling, irrespective of the differing media of i.t.a. and t.o.

Considering the figures presented in this chapter, it can be seen that there were no significant differences between the mean reading scores of the total i.t.a. and t.o. groups, the pairs of correlation coefficients obtained by comparing reading readiness scores with later reading achievement scores, and the mean reading scores attained for similar levels of performance on the reading readiness tests. This shows quite clearly that in the author's sample towards the end of the children's third year in school there were no differences in reading ability between the i.t.a. and t.o. groups. As was pointed out earlier, this is a different result from that produced by the main i.t.a. experiment.

(iii) *A comparison of the minimum mental age levels required for learning to read successfully with i.t.a. and t.o.*

From Tables 125 and 126 it can be seen that the results of the analysis made towards the end of the children's third year in school, show that i.t.a. and t.o. sub-groups with similar levels of mental ability initially have attained similar levels of reading ability, as measured by Schonell and Neale. Here again, then, we find no differences between the two groups at the end of the third year.

To conclude this chapter, a comparison has been made of the correlations between the initial tests of reading readiness abilities and the two reading achievement measures discussed in this chapter, to add further information concerning the relative importance of the factors involved in reading readiness and early reading progress.

The correlations for each reading readiness factor were

TABLE 125 Showing a comparison between the mean scores attained on the Schonell Graded Word Reading Test given a fourth time, by sub-groups of i.t.a. and t.o. children with similar mental ages.

mental ages (years, months)	below 3–6	3–6 3–11	4–0 4–5	4–6 4–11	5–0 5–5	5–6 5–11	6–0 6–5	6–6 6–11
no. of i.t.a. chn. in each mental age group	1	4	13	22	33	23	5	1
no. of t.o. chn. in each mental age group	3	5	12	18	21	22	19	2
mean score of i.t.a. chn. on Schonell	2.0	19.7	20.4	25.2	28.3	36.4	39.4	16.0
mean score of t.o. chn. on Schonell	3.0	8.4	26.5	25.2	21.9	31.3	38.3	49.5

TABLE 126 Showing a comparison between the mean scores attained on Reading Accuracy measured by the Neale Analysis of Reading Ability given for the third time, by sub-groups of i.t.a. and t.o. children with similar mental ages.

mental ages (years, months)	below 3–6	3–6 3–11	4–0 4–5	4–6 4–11	5–0 5–5	5–6 5–11	6–0 6–5	6–6 6–11
no. of i.t.a. chn. in each mental age group	1	4	13	22	33	23	5	1
no. of t.o. chn. in each mental age group	3	5	12	8	21	22	19	2
mean score of i.t.a. chn. on Neale	5.0	20.2	24.9	28.5	29.6	41.4	46.0	17.0
mean score of t.o. chn. on Neale	12.7	10.6	30.1	27.6	28.3	34.5	44.3	53.0

averaged with the following results:

visual discrimination	.58
auditory discrimination	.41
vocabulary development	.44
intelligence	.38

Again, we see that the correlation coefficients for visual and auditory discrimination show a substantial relationship with later reading achievement and progress, and are shown to be more important than mental ability.

TABLE 127 Showing a comparison of the correlations, calculated for the i.t.a. and t.o. groups separately, between the initial tests of reading readiness abilities, and the two measures of reading achievement given in the children's ninth term at school.

Tests of Reading Readiness Abilities	Group	Schonell 4th time May 1968 r	Neale 3rd time May 1968 r
Visual Discrim. Thackray	i.t.a. t.o.	.55 .49	.56 .56
Visual Discrim. in i.t.a. Harrison-Stroud	i.t.a. t.o.	.55 .50	.57 .52
Visual Discrim. in t.o. Harrison-Stroud	i.t.a. t.o.	.55 .50	.57 .54
Auditory Discrim. Thackray	i.t.a. t.o.	.47 .41	.45 .35
Auditory Discrim. Harrison-Stroud	i.t.a. t.o.	.40 .44	.34 .44
Wechsler Scale of Intelligence	i.t.a. t.o.	.36 .45	.40 .45
Goodenough Draw-A-Man Test	i.t.a. t.o.	.28 .36	.36 .42
Vocabulary Profile Thackray	i.t.a. t.o.	.48 .42	.45 .41

Chapter 9

The Comparison of Boys' and Girls' Performances on Reading Readiness and Reading Achievement Tests, and a Study of the Reading Progress Made by Children from the Different Schools

Mention was made in Part I, Chapter 1, of the studies which have examined the differences in readiness to read between boys and girls entering school, and also the difference between their respective achievements during the first year or two in school.

With regard to the comparisons which have been made between boys' and girls' performances on reading readiness measures, many of the American investigations show significant differences in favour of the girls. In the author's first experiment with British children, the scores of the girls were significantly superior to those of the boys on two of the five reading readiness measures given. This comparison, to the best of the author's knowledge, was the first that had been made with British children, and so it was decided to continue this aspect of research in the present investigation. The relevant information is presented in Table 128 following:

It can be seen from Table 128 that in this second investigation there were no significant differences between the mean scores of the boys and girls on the reading readiness measures.

Tests of Reading Readiness Abilities	Group	mean score	S.D.	diff. in means	S.E. of diff.	C.R.	statis. signif.
Visual Discrim. Thackray	boys	18.67	7.2	.1	1.02	.1	N.S.
	girls	18.77	8.58				
Visual Discrim. in i.t.a. Harrison-Stroud	boys	20.27	7.44	1.28	.96	1.33	N.S.
	girls	21.55	7.41				
Visual Discrim. in t.o. Harrison-Stroud	boys	20.8	6.99	.75	.95	.79	N.S.
	girls	21.55	7.77				
Auditory Discrim. Thackray	boys	11.02	6.27	.7	.83	.84	N.S.
	girls	11.72	6.48				
Auditory Discrim. Harrison-Stroud	boys	9.88	3.16	.05	.44	.11	N.S.
	girls	9.83	3.7				
Wechsler Scale of Intelligence	boys	96.87	12.7	.29	1.78	.16	N.S.
	girls	97.16	14.7				
Goodenough Draw-A-Man Test	boys	94.25	14.4	1.08	1.84	.59	N.S.
	girls	93.17	13.9				
Vocabulary Profile Thackray	boys	31.53	7.4	.59	.97	.61	N.S.
	girls	32.12	7.7				

These results conflict with those produced by American investigators, who have found significant differences in favour of the girls, but a possible explanation for this is the fact that American children usually begin school when they are six years of age, and this is when the tests are given. During the year before they start school, girls are more likely than boys to be engaged in sedentary activities, which are more likely to foster reading readiness and reading.

With regard to the relative performance of boys and girls on reading tests, the evidence from research workers in this country is conflicting. In the author's present investigation, the first three reading achievements tests were given in i.t.a. to the i.t.a. children, and in t.o. to the t.o. children, and so, for these three tests, a comparison has been made of the mean scores of the boys and girls in the i.t.a. and t.o. groups separately. The final three reading achievement tests were given in t.o. to both groups, and so for these three tests a comparison has been made between the mean scores of the boys in both groups and the girls in both groups. Now follows, in tabulated form, the relevant information.

TABLE 129 Showing a comparison between the mean scores of the boys and girls in the i.t.a. group on three reading achievement measures (given in i.t.a.).

Reading Test	i.t.a. group 60 boys, 59 girls						
	Group	mean score	S.D.	diff. in means	S.E. of diff.	C.R.	statis. signif.
Schonell, 1st time May 1966	boys	5.08	7.9	3.45	1.72	2.01	5% level
	girls	8.53	10.7				
Schonell, 2nd time Sept. 1966	boys	11.5	7.8	2.38	1.63	1.46	N.S.
	girls	9.12	9.9				
Neale, 1st. time Sept. 1966	boys	7.75	9.3	3.49	1.84	1.90	N.S.
	girls	11.24	10.75				

TABLE 130 Showing a comparison between the mean scores of the boys and girls in the t.o. group on three reading achievement measures (given in t.o.)

Reading Test	t.o. group 58 boys, 61 girls						
	Group	mean score	S.D.	diff. in means	S.E. of diff.	C.R.	statis. signif.
Schonell, 1st time May 1966	boys	2.6	1.9	2.02	.64	3.16	1% level
	girls	4.62	4.65				
Schonell. 2nd time Sept. 1966	boys	3.38	3.75	3.21	1.05	3.06	1% level
	girls	6.59	7.4				
Neale, 1st. time Sept. 1966	boys	3.64	4.75	4.26	1.26	3.38	.1% level
	girls	7.9	8.55				

It can be seen from Table 129 that the only significant difference between the mean reading scores of the boys and girls in the i.t.a. group is that for the Schonell test given for the first time, and this difference in favour of the girls is only just significant at the 5% level. However, the results from Table 130 show quite clearly that there are two highly significant differences (1% level) and one very highly significant difference (.1% level) between the mean reading scores of the boys and girls in the t.o. group on the same three measures of reading achievement. All three differences favour the girls.

This clear difference in results between the i.t.a. and t.o. groups indicates that boys can learn to read with i.t.a. as easily as girls, and make similar progress in reading achievement. However, boys learning to read with t.o. do not learn to read as easily as the girls, and their progress in reading is slower. This finding provides more evidence that children can learn to read more easily with i.t.a. than they can with t.o.

TABLE 131   Showing a comparison between the mean scores of the boys and girls from both i.t.a. and t.o. groups, on four reading achievement measures (given in t.o. to both groups).

Reading tests	118 boys, 120 girls						
	Group	mean score	S.D.	diff. in means	S.E. of diff.	C.R.	statis. signif.
Schonell, 3rd time May 1967	boys	11.83	11.2	6.09	1.52	4.01	.1% level
	girls	17.92	12.2				
Neale, 2nd time May 1967	boys	14.34	13.2	6.58	1.78	3.7	1% level
	girls	20.92	14.3				
Schonell, 4th time May 1968	boys	25.73	15.65	4.7	2.08	2.26	5% level
	girls	30.40	14.0				
Neale, 3rd time. May 1968	boys	29.21	17.8	5.79	2.46	2.35	5% level
	girls	35.0	17.3				

From Table 131 it can be seen that on all four reading achievement tests, given in t.o. to both groups, there are significant differences between the mean reading scores of the boys and the girls, one difference being highly significant (1% level) and another being very highly significant (.1% level). This evidence is similar to that found by the author in his first investigation, and adds to the evidence which suggests that girls learn to read more easily and make quicker progress in reading than boys.

TABLE 132 Showing a comparison of the mean scores attained by the children in sixteen schools on the four administrations of the Schonell Graded Word Reading Test (given in i.t.a. to i.t.a. schools for the first and second times; given in t.o. to the i.t.a. schools for the third and fourth times).

School	N	Schonell 1st time May 1966	Schonell 2nd time Sept. 1966	Schonell 3rd time· May 1967	N	Schonell 4th time May 1968
A_1	16	6.37	10.31	21.75	14	33.5
A_2	16	3.06	6.0	17.75	14	33.92
B_1	17	2.53	3.7	14.9	15	28.0
B_2	16	1.25	2.75	16.0	14	26.64
C_1	14	14.5	18.07	25.5	8	39.37
C_2	15	1.33	1.0	7.46	14	19.42
D_1	14	4.5	5.21	10.28	12	19.5
D_2	16	4.43	6.31	12.0	11	28.36
E_1	16	6.06	7.5	13.62	14	31.21
E_2	15	1.13	2.13	10.66	13	25.15
F_1	11	1.64	3.0	8.54	11	23.36
F_2	10	3.2	4.5	13.6	9	26.23
G_1	15	16.2	18.73	21.46	14	36.42
G_2	17	2.29	4.35	11.88	16	26.93
H_1	16	1.68	1.93	5.0	14	16.57
H_2	14	5.78	9.0	25.2	11	36.63

The author felt that it would be interesting to compare the mean scores, on the reading achievement measures given, of the sixteen schools taking part in the investigation. It was

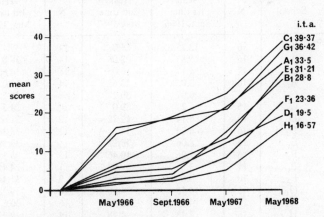

Figure 14 showing the reading progress of the chn. in the eight i.t.a. schools as measured by the Schonell Word Reading Test.

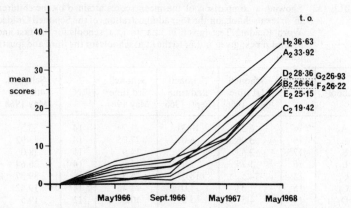

Figure 15 showing the reading progress of the chn. in the eight t.o. schools as measured by the Schonell Graded Word Reading Test.

felt that such a study would highlight mean scores which were well above and well below average in both the i.t.a. and t.o. schools, and this in turn would encourage a search for the reason or reasons for such scores. In Tables 132 and 133 and

TABLE 133   Showing a comparison of the mean scores attained by the children in sixteen schools on the three administrations of the Neale Analysis of Reading Ability (given in i.t.a. to i.t.a. schools for the first time; given in t.o. to the i.t.a. schools for the second and third times).

School	N	Neale 1st time Sept. 1966	Neale 2nd time May 1967	N	Neale 3rd time May 1968
A_1	16	12.25	25.0	14	39.42
A_2	16	5.87	22.06	14	38.0
B_1	17	4.17	16.05	15	34.86
B_2	16	2.0	13.62	14	27.07
C_1	14	20.07	30.28	8	47.5
C_2	15	.2	9.0	14	24.5
D_1	14	6.14	12.72	12	21.66
D_2	16	6.75	14.0	11	33.36
E_1	16	8.06	15.25	14	32.38
E_2	15	1.06	10.46	13	28.15
F_1	11	3.27	9.63	11	24.45
F_2	10	4.8	18.2	9	31.44
G_1	15	14.53	24.86	14	39.28
G_2	17	4.0	12.87	16	30.5
H_1	16	2.43	4.18	14	19.21
H_2	14	13.42	30.64	11	43.18

276

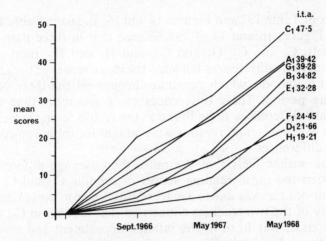

Figure 16 showing the reading progress of the chn. in the eight i.t.a. schools as measured by the Neale Analysis of Reading Ability.

Figures 14, 15, 16 and 17, the relevant information is presented and the schools are lettered and numbered in accordance with that used in Part II, Chapter 3, when they were described. The schools numbered '1' are i.t.a. schools, the schools numbered '2' are the t.o. schools; the i.t.a. and t.o. schools bearing the same letter are the ones originally matched.

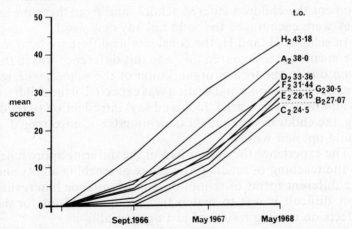

Figure 17 showing the reading progress of the chn. in the eight i.t.a. schools as measured by the Neale Analysis of Reading Ability.

277

From Table 132 and Figures 14 and 15, and from Table 133 and Figures 16 and 17, it can be seen that in three pairs of schools, C_1 and C_2, G_1 and G_2, and H_1 and H_2, there are considerable differences between the mean scores of the i.t.a. and t.o. schools which continue throughout the three year testing period. These differences are much more than the average differences to be found in the results from the other pairs of schools, and reasons were sought for these considerable differences.

The author feels that the more than average difference between the mean reading scores of schools C_1 and C_2 in favour of i.t.a. was due to a marked difference in the teaching ability of the two teachers concerned. The teacher in C_1, the i.t.a. class, was head of the infants' department and a very experienced teacher. She not only taught very ably herself, but she inspired the other teachers in the department to whom the children eventually went to do the same. On the other hand, the teacher in C_2, the t.o. class, was in her first year of teaching and as a result her work was not sufficiently well organised to be effective.

With regard to schools G_1 and G_2, where the considerable difference between the mean reading scores favoured i.t.a., the reason was most likely the systematic stress of phonic training evidenced in G_1, the i.t.a. school. In this school the letters and corresponding sounds were taught from the moment the children entered school, and from that time on they were encouraged to 'build up' any new word.

In schools H_1 and H_2 the considerable difference between the mean scores favoured t.o., and this difference was in the main due to the formal organisation of the school, where a great deal of reading and writing was expected of the children. In addition, after a brief 'look and say' introduction to reading, the children were taught their sounds and encouraged to 'build up' new words.

The experience the author had of the differing approaches to the teaching of reading, the range of teaching ability and the different forms of school organisation made him realise how difficult it was to match two groups and look for the effects on reading results of just one variable.

Relevant to the information given in Tables 132 and 133

is a questionnaire which the author asked the eight i.t.a. teachers to complete.

The questions asked were the following:

1. How long has the school been using i.t.a.?
2. Do you feel that i.t.a. is a better medium of approach for the teaching of reading?
3. If 'yes', in what ways has the reading in the school been improved?
4. When using i.t.a. do you find that the slower, average, and better readers progress differently? What differences, if any, do you find?
5. Do you still have a proportion of children leaving to the junior school unable to read? If so, is this proportion the same or less than it was with t.o.?
6. Has the use of i.t.a. affected the children's work in other areas in any way? If so, in what ways?
7. Have you found any disadvantages in using i.t.a.?
8. Would you ever consider returning to the use of t.o.?

Now follows a brief summary of the answers:

1. All eight headteachers had been using i.t.a. for at least three years.
2. Seven out of eight teachers thought i.t.a. a better approach. One said it was 'another way'.
3. The following improvements were mentioned:
   less strain on children and teachers;
   greater fluency in reading and writing;
   children learn much more quickly;
   children read with more understanding;
   children have a greater consciousness of words and vocabulary;
   children gain in confidence.
4. Here opinions varied. Some felt all groups progressed, some felt only better and average readers, some only average and slower readers.
5. Seven felt the proportion was smaller, one 'about the same'.
6. Typical comments were similar to those listed in point 3.
7. Disadvantages mentioned were as follows:

the difficulty of a child leaving to attend a t.o. school
before transfer has been made;

the setback at transfer in writing and spelling;

young teachers from college are often not trained for
i.t.a.

8. Seven teachers would not change by choice, one was uncertain.

The author found the same kind of enthusiasm for i.t.a.
that was reported in the main i.t.a. experiments, and in the
Warburton and Southgate report (1969), though it is interesting to note the very differing results attained by the i.t.a.
children in their various schools. After three years in school
the mean reading scores in the eight i.t.a. schools ranged
from 16.57–39.37 on the Schonell test, and from 19.21 –
47.5 on the Neale test. For purposes of comparison, the mean
reading scores of the t.o. group after three years ranged from
19.42 – 36.63 on the Schonell, and from 24.5 – 43.18 on the
Neale. From this comparison it can be seen that the i.t.a.
schools with the lowest mean score had a mean score lower
than the t.o. school with the lowest mean reading score, yet
this school was still enthusiastic about i.t.a. and its beneficial
effects. This indicated to the author that teachers were comparing current standards with previous standards, and were
unaware of standards in other schools, or even objective
standards. He wondered to what extent a knowledge of
standards of reading attained elsewhere would increase their
levels of expectation regarding their children's reading
ability.

Chapter 10

Summary and Conclusions

In this last chapter, the results obtained from the present investigation are summarised in points and their implications discussed.

1. There was no significant difference between the mean scores of both i.t.a. and t.o. groups together, on the i.t.a. and t.o. versions of the Harrison-Stroud Visual Discrimination Test. The only difference between these two versions was that of transliteration, so to the 238 children tested the one test was no more difficult visually than the other (Table 21, Chapter 4).

2. The distribution of the standardized scores on the author's test of Visual Discrimination was reasonably normal, though showing a negative skew. The 238 scores on this test were correlated with the scores of the same 238 children on the Harrison-Stroud Visual Discrimination Test in t.o.; the coefficient of correlation was .79, which denotes a very high relationship, and indicates a reasonably valid test of visual discrimination had been constructed by the author (Chapter 4).

3. The distribution of the standardized scores on the author's Auditory Discrimination Test are reasonably normal, though showing a slight positive skew. The 238 scores on this test were correlated with the scores of the same 238 children on the Harrison-Stroud Auditory Discrimination Test. The coefficient of correlation was .56,

which denotes a substantial relationship, though it was pointed out that the author's test measured both beginning and ending sounds, whereas the Harrison-Stroud Test measured beginning sounds only. The indications are that a reasonably valid test of auditory discrimination had been constructed by the author. (Chapter 4).

4. The scores of 238 children on the Wechsler Scale of Intelligence for Children (Verbal tests only), were correlated with the scores of the same 238 children on the Goodenough Draw-A-Man Test. The coefficient of correlation was .27, and is similar to the correlation coefficients of other investigators who have examined the validity of the Goodenough Draw-A-Man test, but with older children (Chapter 4).

5. The distribution of the standardized scores on the author's revised version of the Vocabulary Profile was considered for normality by the chi-square test of significance. The result showed the distribution was not completely normal, but it is felt that this test is ready for standardization (Chapter 4).

6. There was no significant difference between the mean scores of the i.t.a. and t.o. groups on either the first or the second administration of the author's Visual Discrimination Test, so in the author's larger sample the hypothesis proposed by Sister John, that i.t.a. has more favourable effects than t.o. on the growth of the skill of visual discrimination, is disproved (Chapter 5).

7. There was no significant difference between the mean scores of the i.t.a. and t.o. groups on either the first or second administration of the author's Auditory Discrimination Test, so in the author's larger sample the hypothesis proposed by Sister John, that i.t.a. has more favourable effects than t.o. on the growth of the skill of auditory discrimination, is disproved (Chapter 5).

8. When the children's reading achievement was tested in their third term in school by means of the Schonell Graded Word Reading Test, there was a very highly significant difference (.1%) between the mean scores of the i.t.a. and t.o. groups in favour of i.t.a. As the two groups were well-matched, the children in the author's sample learned to read more easily, and made better

initial progress with i.t.a. than with t.o.; conversely, the traditional alphabet and spelling of English used with an eclectic approach was a more difficult medium for the teaching of reading than i.t.a. (Chapter 5).

9. A comparison of the correlation coefficients, calculated for the i.t.a. and t.o. groups separately, between the initial tests of reading readiness abilities and the Schonell Graded Word Reading Test given in the children's third term at school, showed only two significant differences out of a possible eight. There was a highly significant difference (1% level) on the Harrison-Stroud Visual Discrimination Test in t.o. in favour of t.o. This result indicates that, even though the two groups of i.t.a. and t.o. children had not started to read formally, the pre-reading activities designed to introduce learning to read with either i.t.a. or t.o. had had a measurable effect, and shows the pre-reading period to be an important one. There was also a significant difference (5% level) on the author's Auditory Discrimination Test in favour of i.t.a. This result could reflect the fact that at least one i.t.a. teacher started teaching the letters and sounds from the very beginning, and that more stress was likely to be placed on a phonic approach in the i.t.a. group than in the t.o. group (Table 43, Chapter 5).

10. A comparison was made of the mean scores attained on the Schonell Graded Word Reading Test given in the children's third term by sub-groups of i.t.a. and t.o. children, who attained similar levels of performance on each of the reading readiness measures given initially. This statistical approach was carried out in order to compare the reading readiness levels required for children to learn to read satisfactorily, using i.t.a. and t.o. The results show that for nearly all levels of performance on the reading readiness tests, the mean scores attained by the i.t.a. sub-groups on the Schonell reading achievement test are greater than the mean scores attained by the t.o. sub-groups, and in many cases significantly greater (.1%, 1% and 5% levels). This pattern of results indicates that i.t.a. sub-groups with lower levels of performance on reading readiness measures than t.o. sub-groups can reach similar levels of reading achievement to those

t.o. sub-groups after six months, but in i.t.a. reading. This means that lower levels of reading readiness are required for learning to read with i.t.a. than are required for children learning to read in t.o. This, in turn, means that i.t.a. is simpler than t.o. in its visual and auditory structure, and the problems needed to be solved in reading with i.t.a. are of a simpler nature than those to be solved in reading with t.o. If children can learn to read with i.t.a. more easily than they can with t.o., children on average will be ready to read with i.t.a. at an earlier age than with t.o. (Chapter 5).

11. A comparison was made between the mean scores achieved on the Schonell Graded Word Reading Test given in the children's third term, by sub-groups of i.t.a. and t.o. children with similar mental ages initially. This analysis was a crude one, but the evidence suggested that children learning to read with i.t.a. can do so with a lower mental age level than their t.o. counterparts. The figures showed that i.t.a. children were able to learn to read satisfactorily with a mental age range of 5 years to 5 years 5 months, whereas with the t.o. children a mental age range of 6 years to 6 years 5 months seemed to be necessary for learning to read satisfactorily (Table 52, Chapter 5).

12. When the children's reading achievement was tested in their fourth term in school by means of the Schonell Graded Word Reading Test, there was a very highly significant difference (.1% level) between the mean scores of the i.t.a. and t.o. group in favour of i.t.a. As the two groups were well matched, this difference showed that the children in the author's sample learned to read more easily, and made better initial progress with i.t.a. than with t.o. Conversely, the traditional alphabet and spelling used with an eclectic approach was a more difficult medium for the teaching of reading than i.t.a. (Table 53, Chapter 6).

13. When the children's reading accuracy was tested in their fourth term in school by means of the Neale Analysis of Reading Ability, there was a highly significant difference (1% level) between the mean scores of the i.t.a. and t.o. group in favour of i.t.a. This particular measure is

based on a child's reading of continuous prose, and as this result agrees with the two other reading results already discussed, a firm conclusion must be drawn that children *can* learn to read more easily with i.t.a. than with t.o. with an initial 'look and say' approach, followed in very varying degrees by an introduction to phonics. The converse must also be accepted as a firm conclusion; namely, that the traditional orthography of English used with an eclectic approach is a more difficult medium than i.t.a. for the learning and teaching of reading. This conclusion which was reached in the main i.t.a. experiment, raises the question of spelling reform. If all children could learn to read with a simplified system of spelling, and there was no question of a later transfer, then all children would learn to read more easily, make quicker progress, and the number of reading failures would be reduced. However, a spelling reform is not likely to take place, but there are other ways of simplifying and regularising the English spelling to enable children to read more easily, and mention was made in Chapter 2 of the work of research workers who have devised simplified systems while still preserving the traditional forms of our letters and words.

The results of the main i.t.a. experiment, which are supported by the author's experiment, suggest the urgent need to experiment with simplified approaches to the teaching of reading, all of which should be based on helping the child to master the sounds of letters, as more and more it is being realised that phonics cannot be neglected or treated as merely incidental in the effective teaching of reading (Table 54, Chapter 6).

14. When the children's reading comprehension was tested by the Neale Analysis of Reading Ability in their fourth term at school, there was no significant difference between the mean scores of the i.t.a. and t.o. groups. It could be argued that the discrepancy between this result and the result from the measure of reading accuracy indicates that, although the i.t.a. group could read more easily, and gain higher mean scores than the t.o. group, they were not understanding all they were reading, as the reading comprehension of both groups was of a similar

standard. However, the nature of the comprehension test, discussed in Chapter 6, makes it impossible to draw any definite conclusion (Table 55, Chapter 6).

15. A comparison of the correlation coefficients, calculated for the i.t.a. and t.o. groups separately between the initial tests of reading readiness abilities and the Schonell and Neale reading achievement tests given in the children's fourth term at school, showed only one significant difference out of a possible eight. There was a highly significant difference (1% level) on the author's Auditory Discrimination Test in favour of i.t.a., both on the Schonell and the Neale tests. This result lends support to the conclusion suggested in point 9 that the phonic aspects of reading were being dealt with more systematically in the i.t.a. classes than in the t.o. classes. This conclusion, if valid lends support to those who stress the value of phonics in the early stages of learning to read (Tables 56 and 57, Chapter 6).

16. A comparison was made of the mean scores attained on the Schonell and Neale tests given in the children's fourth term by sub-groups of i.t.a. and t.o. children, who attained similar levels of performance on each of the reading readiness measures given initially. Again, the results show that for nearly all levels of performance on the reading readiness tests, the mean scores attained by the i.t.a. sub-groups on the two reading achievement tests are greater than the mean scores attained by the t.o. sub-groups, and in many cases significantly greater (.1%, 1% and 5% levels). This statistical approach has again shown quite clearly that i.t.a. sub-groups can attain similar reading achievement levels as the t.o. sub-groups, but with lower levels of reading readiness abilities, thus showing experimentally that i.t.a. is simpler than t.o. in its visual and auditory structure, and in the problems to be solved in learning to read. The fact that children can learn to read with i.t.a. more easily than with t.o. means that, on average, children will be ready to read with i.t.a. at an earlier age than with t.o. (Chapter 6).

17. A comparison was made between the mean scores attained on the Schonell and Neale reading achievement tests given in the children's fourth term, by sub-groups

of i.t.a. and t.o. children with similar mental ages initially. As before, the evidence suggests that children learning to read with i.t.a. can do so with a lower mental age level than their t.o. counterparts. The figures again showed that i.t.a. children were able to learn to read satisfactorily with a mental age range of 5 years to 5 years 5 months, whereas with the t.o. children a mental age range of 6 years to 6 years 5 months seemed to be necessary for learning to read satisfactorily. If this evidence, which is now shown to be consistent, is accepted, it means that the average child learning to read with i.t.a. could be taught from the moment he entered school, as happened in school G_1, whereas the average child learning to read with t.o. using an eclectic approach would need a pre-reading period of at least six months. If teachers of reading using i.t.a. taught their children to read from their first days in school, and with confidence believing this early start to be sound, the considerable lead the i.t.a. children would gain over their t.o. counterparts might be such that, even after the set-back in reading progress during the transfer period, they would continue to hold a somewhat reduced lead into their third and fourth years. If such a situation occurred, i.t.a. would prove itself a more effective method for the teaching of reading than t.o. using as eclectic approach. It is interesting to note that school G_1 did maintain its early lead over both i.t.a. and t.o. schools, and towards the end of the third year had the second highest mean reading score out of the sixteen schools (Tables 75 and 76, Chapter 6).

18. Towards the end of the children's second year in school (sixth term), a comparison was made between the mean scores attained on the i.t.a. and t.o. versions of the Schonell and Neale reading achievement tests, by 50 i.t.a. children who had not transferred to t.o. There was a highly significant difference (.1% level) between the mean scores on the i.t.a. and t.o. versions of both the Schonell and the Neale tests. This indicates quite clearly that for these 50 children the t.o. version of the test was much more difficult for them to read than the i.t.a. version, and shows that there is a setback in reading

progress during the transfer stage. This significant difference is yet another clear indication that i.t.a. is an easier medium for learning to read than t.o., as at the transfer the results are seen of a change to a more difficult medium (Tables 78 and 79, Chapter 7).

19. In the children's sixth term in school, a comparison was made between the mean scores of the i.t.a. and t.o. groups on the Schonell and Neale reading achievement tests given in t.o. to both groups. There were no significant differences between the mean scores on either test. Now the i.t.a. children are reading in the relatively more difficult medium of t.o. the average score is lowered and the i.t.a. group has lost its early lead, clearly indicating the change to a more difficult medium. It was pointed out earlier that 50 children had not transferred, and as their t.o. scores were counted, this comparison was not strictly valid (Tables 80, 81 and 82, Chapter 7).

20. A comparison of the correlation coefficients, calculated for the i.t.a. and t.o. groups separately between the initial tests of reading readiness abilities and the Schonell and Neale reading achievement tests given in the children's sixth term in school, showed only one significant difference out of a possible sixteen. These results reflect the very similar mean reading scores of the two groups, at this stage (Tables 83 and 84, Chapter 7).

21. A comparison was made of the mean scores attained on the Schonell and Neale tests, given in the children's sixth term, by sub-groups of i.t.a. and t.o. children who attained similar levels of performance on each of the reading readiness measures given initally. At this stage, when both tests were given in t.o. to both i.t.a. and t.o. groups, a new pattern of results has emerged. In the third and fourth term tests the differences between the mean reading scores favoured i.t.a., and many were significant, showing quite clearly that reading readiness levels required to learn to read with i.t.a. were lower than those required to learn to read with t.o. In the sixth term we find that the mean scores are similar when the tests are given in t.o., which means that the reading readiness requirements for learning to read t.o. through the medium of i.t.a. are similar to the reading readiness levels required

for learning to read in t.o. from the beginning (Chapter 7).

22. A comparison was made between the mean scores attained on the Schonell and Neale reading achievement tests given in the children's sixth term, by sub-groups of i.t.a. and t.o. children with similar mental ages initially. In this analysis, again, a change is seen in the pattern of results but not such a dramatic one. The mean reading scores of the i.t.a. and t.o. sub-groups in each mental age range are much closer together at this stage. In one or two cases, the mean reading score of the t.o. sub-groups is greater than that of the i.t.a. sub-group in the same mental age range, but many differences still favour i.t.a. There is, therefore, some evidence to suggest that i.t.a. children who have transferred to t.o. reading can achieve similar mean reading scores to children who have read with t.o. from the start, but with slightly lower mental ages (Tables 101 and 102, Chapter 7).

23. Towards the end of the children's third year in school (ninth term), a final comparison was made between the mean scores of the i.t.a. and t.o. groups on the Schonell and Neale reading achievement tests given in t.o. to both groups. At this stage, only four i.t.a. children had not transferred to t.o. and most of the other i.t.a. children had been reading in t.o. for some time. There were no significant differences between the mean reading scores on either test, and the mean scores were very close. These results do not agree with those produced by the main i.t.a. experiment, in which a significant difference was found between the mean scores of the i.t.a. and t.o. groups on both the Schonell and the Neale tests. It is possible that, in the main i.t.a. experiment, factors already discussed such as the 'Hawthorne Effect', a 'reading drive' and energetic, enthusiastic teaching may have resulted in the i.t.a. group developing a very considerable lead over the t.o. group, which enabled a lead to be maintained after the transfer. Again, the Kolmogorov-Smirnov test of significance is not felt to be the best test to use for significance.

On the other hand, the author carried out his experiment using normal classroom and school situations, and his results are in keeping with more recent experiments which have also been carried out in more normal circumstances than those of the main i.t.a. experiment (Tables 104, 105 and 106, Chapter 8).

24. A final comparison of the correlation coefficients, calculated for the i.t.a. and t.o. groups separately, between the initial tests of reading readiness abilities and the Schonell and Neale reading achievement tests given in the children's ninth term in school, showed no significant differences. This result indicates that after nearly three years of schooling, the various factors making for reading readiness are of similar importance in learning to read with t.o. through the medium of i.t.a., and in learning to read with t.o. form the start (Tables 107 and 108, Chapter 8).

25. A final comparison was made of the mean scores attained on the Schonell and Neale tests given in the children's ninth term, by sub-groups of i.t.a. and t.o. children who attained similar levels of performance on each of the reading readiness measures given initially. The new pattern of results, established when testing all the children in t.o. towards the end of their second year in school, has now been repeated again. At this final administration of the two reading achievement tests, the results again show that the mean reading scores, attained by sub-groups of i.t.a. and t.o. children with similar levels of performance on the reading readiness abilities, are very similar. These final results indicate quite clearly that after nearly three years of schooling the reading readiness levels required to read with t.o. through the medium of i.t.a. are similar to those required to learn to read with t.o. from the start (Tables 109–124, Chapter 8).

26. A final comparison was made between the mean score attained on the Schonell and Neale reading achievement tests given in the children's ninth term, by sub-groups of i.t.a. and t.o. children with similar mental ages. The results show that i.t.a. and t.o. sub-groups, with similar levels of mental ability initially, have similar levels of reading ability as measured by the Schonell and Neale tests given in t.o. towards the end of the children's third year in school (Tables 125 and 126, Chapter 8).

27. In order to see the relevant importance, in the authors'

experiment, of the factors making for reading readiness and early reading progress, comparisons were made throughout the experiment of the correlation coefficients, calculated for the i.t.a. and t.o. groups separately, between the initial tests of reading readiness abilities, and the two measures of reading achievement. The averaged results obtained towards the end of the children's second and third years in school when the tests were given in t.o. are as follows:

	End of 2nd year	End of 3rd year
Visual Discrimination	.48	.58
Auditory Discrimination	.46	.41
Intelligence	.38	.38
Vocabulary Development	.38	.44

The above coefficients of correlation show that visual and auditory discrimination have a substantial relationship with later reading achievement, and are more important than mental ability and language development in learning to read by t.o. through the medium of i.t.a., or in learning to read by t.o. from the start. These results are in keeping with those the author found in his first experiment, and it is therefore important for the reception class teacher to gain some estimate of her children's abilities in visual and auditory discrimination so that, if weaknesses are detected, exercises to develop these skills may be used during the pre-reading activities where necessary.

A comparison between the mean scores attained by the boys and girls on the reading readiness measures given initially showed no significant differences. This result conflicts with those produced by some American investigators who have found significant differences in favour of the girls, but a possible explanation for this is the fact that American children usually begin school when they are six, and this is when the tests are given. During the year before going to school, girls are more likely than boys to be engaged in sedentary activities, which are more likely to foster reading readiness and reading (Table 128, Chapter 9).

29. A comparison was made between the mean reading scores of the boys and girls in both the i.t.a. and t.o. groups separately, during the stage when the i.t.a. group was tested in i.t.a. The results indicate quite clearly that boys can learn to read with i.t.a. as easily as girls and make similar progress in reading achievement; however, boys learning to read with t.o. do not learn to read as easily as the girls and their progress in reading is slower. The obvious implication of these results is that with a simplified and regular medium of teaching reading, boys would learn to read as easily as girls. As the majority of our backward readers are boys, these results lend support to those who feel new approaches to the teaching of reading are required, and ones which either present simple, regular words through which the phonic elements can be taught, or present the words with colour or diacritical markings, so the child is helped to know the sounds and build up the words (Tables 129 and 130, Chapter 9).

30. A comparison was made between the mean reading scores of the boys and girls from both i.t.a. and t.o. groups during the latter stage of the experiment when all the reading tests were given in t.o.; significant differences were found in favour of the girls. This evidence was similar to that found by the author in his first investigation, and adds to the general evidence which suggests that girls learn to read more easily than boys, and make quicker progress (Table 131, Chapter 9).

31. A comparison of the mean scores attained by the children in sixteen schools on the reading achievement tests showed a similar wide range of scores in the i.t.a. and t.o. schools. It was seen that the effects of teaching ability, school organisation and the placing and intensity of the teaching of phonics *could* be greater than the effects of the use of either i.t.a. or t.o. (Tables 132 and 133, Chapter 9).

32. A questionnaire answered by the eight i.t.a. teachers indicated the same kind of enthusiasm for i.t.a. as was evident in the main i.t.a. experiment. The teachers were, in the main, comparing current standards of reading with past standards, but seemed unaware of standards attained in other similar schools or of objective standards. The

author felt that such a knowledge would, in many cases, have raised the teachers' levels of expectation with resultant higher standards of reading (Chapter 9).

Final Note

In a recent article, Southgate* has pointed out the great number of variables there are in any one particular reading situation, and which a research worker has to take into consideration when assessing the effects of a change in any one of them. She feels that in past investigations, research workers have not controlled the many variables sufficiently well for valid results to be obtained.

After completing a second experiment in the field of reading readiness and reading, the author sympathises with Southgate's point of view, but does not fully share her optimistic belief that all the many variables can be controlled. Southgate feels that the first most important variable is the beliefs and attitudes of the staff about the importance of reading, and the second most important is the teachers' competence in reading tuition. All would agree that these two variables are most important and teachers, generally, are convinced that the teacher matters more than the medium or the method, as witnessed by the recent letters to the Sunday Times from teachers of reading, published under the title of 'What matters is the teacher'.**

However, to control these variables of beliefs and attitudes of the staff and teacher competence is difficult, if not impossible. If they could be controlled at the outset of an experiment, the longer the reading experiment continued the less they could be controlled. If complete control throughout the experiment was accomplished the reading situation would become an artificial one, and a further variable would have been introduced.

For the future, the author feels that the most fruitful reading experiments will be those which examine carefully the effects on reading of the use of simplified and regular phonic

*Southgate, V., 'Formulae for beginning reading tuition', *Educational Research*, Vol. II, No. 1., November 1968, pp. 23–29.

**Article in the Sunday Times, 2 February 1969.

approaches in t.o. so that no transfer stage is necessary. Downing* has stated that even if the setback at transfer cancels out the early gains, the initial confidence building experience of learning to read with i.t.a. should recommend it to teachers. But confidence can also be engendered by using a simple and regular approach in t.o., incorporating systematic phonic training. Such an approach would avoid the difficulties during the transfer stage, not so much in reading, but in writing and spelling, which for some present-day teachers of reading in i.t.a. is a cause for concern.

When the final evaluation of i.t.a. is made, some time in the future, it may well be shown that its greatest contribution to educational development was to make it clear that learning to read can be made easier for children, and to encourage determined efforts to find the best ways of doing it.

---

*Downing, J., 'The i.t.a. – what next?', *New Education*, April 1967, p. 13.

Appendix

Lists of tests used or referred to

Daniels, J. C., and Diack, H., *The Standard Reading Tests*, London, Chatto and Windus, 1958.

Fleming, C. M., *Kelvin measurement of ability in infant classes*, Glasgow, Robert Gibson and Sons.

Gates, A. I., *Gates reading readiness tests*, New York, Bureau of Publications, Teachers' College, Columbia University, 1939.

Harris, D. B., *Children's drawings as measures of intellectual maturity. A revision and extension of the Goodenough Draw-A-Man Test*, Harcourt, Brace and World Inc., 1963.

Harrison, M. L., and Stroud, J. B., *Harrison-Stroud reading readiness profiles*, Houghton-Mifflin Co., 1950, 1956.

Hildreth, G. H., and Griffiths, N. L., *Metropolitan readiness tests*, Yonkers-on-Hudson, New York, World Book Co., 1933, 1948.

Mellone, M. A., *Moray House picture intelligence test*, University of London Press.

Monroe, M., *Monroe reading aptitude tests*, Boston, Houghton-Mifflin, Co., 1935.

Neale, M., *Neale analysis of reading ability*, London, Macmillan and Co. Ltd., 1963.

Schonell, F., *Psychology and teaching of reading*, Edinburgh, Oliver and Boyd, 1949.

Southgate, V., *Southgate group reading test 1*, University of London Press, 1959.

Wechsler, D., *The measurement and appraisal of adult intelligence*, Baltimore, Williams and Wilkins, 1958.

Wechsler, D., *Manual for the Wechsler intelligence scale for children*, New York, Psychol. Corp., 1949.

Bibliography

Abernethy, E. M. (1936), 'Relationship between mental and physical growth', *Monographs of the Society for Research in Child Development*, National Research Council.

Almy, C. (1949), 'Children's experience prior to first grade and success in beginning reading', *Contributions to Education*, No. 154, Teachers College, Columbia University.

Anderson, I. H., and Dearborn, W. F. (1951), *The Psychology of Teaching Reading*, New York, The Ronald Press Co.

Anderson, I. H., and Hughes, B. O. (1955), 'The relationship between learning to read and growth as a whole', *School of Education Bulletin*, University of Michigan.

Anderson, I. H., Hughes, B. O., and Dixon, W. R. (1957), 'The rate of reading development and its relation to age of learning to read, sex and intelligence', *Journal of Educational Research*, March, pp. 481–494.

Anderson, I. H., and Kelly, M. (1931), 'An inquiry into traits associated with reading disability', *Smith College: Studies in Social Work*, 2, pp. 46–63.

Artley, A. S. (1967), 'Evaluations – 1'. In Downing, J. A., *The i.t.a. Symposium*, National Foundation of Educational Research.

Baer, C. (1958), 'The school progress and adjustment of under-age and over-age students', *Journal of Educational Psychology*, 49, Feb., pp. 17–19.

Bartlett, D. (1967), 'The i.t.a. – how useful?', *New Education*, April, pp. 10–12.

Bremer, N. (1959), 'Do readiness tests predict success in reading?', *Elementary School Journal*, 59, Jan. pp. 222–224.

Benda, C. E. (1954), 'Psychopathology of childhood'. In Carmichael, L. (Ed.), *Handbook of Child Psychology*, London, Chapman and Hall.

Bennett, C. (1938), 'An inquiry into the genesis of poor reading',

Contributions to Education, 755, Teachers College, Columbia University.

Benton, A. L. (1969), *Right-left discrimination and finger localization*, New York, Paul B. Hoeber.

Betts, E. A. (1943), 'Factors in readiness for reading', *Educational Administration and Supervision*, Vol. 29, April, pp. 199–230.

Betts, E. A. (1946), *Foundations of reading instruction*, New York, American Book Co.

Betts, E. A. (1948), 'Remedial and corrective reading: content area approach', *Education*, 68, June, pp. 579–596.

Bigelow, E. B. (1934), 'School progress of underage children', *Elementary School Journal*, 35, Nov. pp. 186–192.

Bird, G. (1927), 'Personality factors in reading', *Personnel Journal*, pp. 56–59.

Blanchard, P. (1928), 'Reading disabilities in relation to maladjustment', *Mental Hygiene*, 12, pp. 772–788.

Bloomfield, L., and Barnhart, C. L. (1961), *Let's read*, Detroit, Wayne State University Press.

Bond, G. L. (1935), 'Auditory and speech characteristics of poor readers', *Contributions to Education*, 657, Teachers College, Columbia University.

Bond, G. L., and Tinker, M. A. (1957), *Reading difficulties: their diagnosis and correction*, Appleton-Century-Crofts Inc. New York.

Bradley, B. E. (1955–6), 'An experimental study of the readiness approach to reading', *Elementary School Journal*, 56, pp. 262–267.

Brumback, F. (1940), 'Reading expectancy', *Elementary English Review*, 17, pp. 153–155.

Brzeinski, J. E. (1964), 'Beginning reading in Denver,' *The Reading Teacher*, 18, pp. 16–21.

Burton, W. H. (1956), *Reading in child development*, The Bobbs-Merrill Co. Inc., New York.

Buswell, G. T. (1937), 'How adults read', *Supplementary Educational Monographs*, No. 45, Chicago, University of Chicago Press.

Carroll, M. W. (1948), 'Sex differences in reading readiness at first grade level', *Elementary English*, 25, Oct. 1958, pp. 370–375.

Cleator, P. E. (1959), *Lost Languages*, London, Robert Hale.

Daffon, P. (1966), 'The British scene'. In Mazurkiewicz, A., *The Initial Teaching Alphabet and the World of English*, New York, Initial Teaching Alphabet Foundation, pp. 133–137.

Dalton, M. M. (1943), 'A visual survey of 5,000 school children', *Journal of Educ. Research*, 37, Oct., pp. 81–94.

Daniels, J. C. (1966), 'The place of phonics'. In *The First International Reading Symposium*, Oxford, 1964. Ed. Downing, J. A. London: Cassell.

Daniels, J. C., and Diack, H. (1954), *The Royal Road Readers*, London, Chatto and Windus.

Daniels, J. C., and Diack, H. (1956), *Progress in reading*, University of Nottingham, Institute of Education.

Daniels, J. C., and Diack, H. (1958), *The Standard Reading Tests*, London, Chatto and Windus.

Davidson, H. P. (1931), 'An experimental study of bright, average and dull children at the four year mental level', *Genetic Psychology Monographs*, 9, No. 4, pp. 119–289.

Davidson, H. P. (1934), 'A study of reversals in young children', *Pedagogical Seminary and Journal of Genetic Psychology*, XLV, Dec., pp. 452–465.

Dean, C. D. (1939), 'Predicting first grade reading achievement', *Elementary School Journal*, 33, April 1939, pp. 609–616.

Dearborn, W. F. (1933), 'Structural factors which condition special disability in reading', *Proceedings of the American Association for Mental Deficiency*, Vol. 38., 1933, pp. 266–283.

Dearborn, W. F., and Rothney, J. W. M. (1941), *Predicting the child's development*, Sci-Art. Publications.

Delacato, C. H. (1959), *The treatment and prevention of reading problems*, Springfield LII, Thomas.

Deputy, E. C. (1930), 'Predicting first grade reading achievement', *Contributions to Education*, 426, Teachers College, Columbia University.

Dewey, J. (1898), 'The primary education fetish', *Forum*, 25, pp. 314–328.

Diack, H. (1960), *Reading and the psychology of perception*. Nottingham, P. Skinner.

Diack, H. (1965), *In spite of the alphabet*, London, Chatto and Windus Ltd.

Diack, H. (1967), 'Evaluations – 3'. In Downing, J. A., *The i.t.a. symposium*, National Foundation for Educational Research.

Dockrell, W. B. (1959), 'The relationship between socio-economic status, intelligence and attainment in some Scottish primary schools', *Alberta Journal of Education*, Vol. 5, pp. 16–22.

Dolbear, K. E. (1912), 'Precocious children', *Pedag. Seminary*, 19, pp. 461–491.

Dolch, E. W. (1950), *Teaching primary reading*, Champaign, Ill., Garrard Press.

Dolch, E. W., and Bloomster, M. (1937), 'Phonic readiness', *The Elementary School Journal*, Vol. 38, Nov. 1937.

Doll, E. (1953), 'Varieties of slow learners', *Exceptional Children*. Nov. 1953, pp. 61–64.

Doman, G. J. (1965), *Teach your baby to read*, London, Cape.

Downing, J. A. (1962), 'The relationship between reading attainment and the inconsistency of English spelling at the infants stage', *British Journal of Educational Psychology*, Vol. 32, pp. 168–177.

Downing, J. A. (1963), 'Is a "mental age of six" essential for "reading" readiness?', *Educational Research*, Vol. 6, No. 1, Nov., pp. 16–28.

Downing, J. A. (1964a), *The i.t.a. reading experiment*, London, Evans Brothers.

Downing, J. A. (1964b), *The initial teaching alphabet*, London, Cassell.

Downing, J. A. (1965), 'Current misconceptions about i.t.a.', *Elementary English*, May, pp. 492–501.

Downing, J. A. (1966), 'Reading readiness re-examined'. In the *First International Reading Symposium Oxford 1964*, London, Cassell pp. 3–23.

Downing, J. A. (1967a), *The i.t.a. symposium*, National Foundation for Educational Research.

Downing, J. A. (1967b), *Evaluating the initial teaching alphabet*, London, Cassell.

Downing, J. A. (1967c), 'Commentary on an alphabet'. Letter to *Times Educational Supplement*, 14 April, p. 1244.

Downing, J. A. (1967d), 'The i.t.a. – what next?', *New Education*, April, p. 13.

Downing, J. A. and Jones, B. (1966), 'Some problems of evaluating i.t.a. A second experiment', *Educational Research*, Vol. 8, No. 2, pp. 100–114.

Durkin, D. (1959), 'A study of children who learned to read prior to first grade', *California Journal of Educ. Research*, 10, pp. 109–113.

Durkin, D. (1961), 'Children who learned to read at home', *Elementary School Journal*, 62, pp. 14–18.

Durkin, D. (1963), 'Children who read before grade one: a second study', *Elementary School Journal*, 64, pp. 143–148.

Durkin, D. (1964), 'Early readers – reflections after six years of research', *Reading Teacher*, 18, pp. 3–7.

Durrell, D. D. (1933), 'The influence of reading ability on intelligence measures', *Journal of Educ. Psychology*, 24, pp. 412–416.

Durrell, D. D. (1940), *Improvement of basic reading abilities*, Yonkers World Book Co.

Durrell, D. D. (1956), *Improving reading instruction*, New York, World Book Co.

Durrell, D. D., and Murphy, H. A. (1953), 'The auditory discrimination factor in reading readiness and reading disability', *Education*, Vol. 73, No. 9, May, pp. 556–560.

Durrell, D. D., Murphy, H. A., and Junkins, K. M., (1941), 'Increasing the rate of learning in first grade reading', *Education*, 62, Sept. pp. 37–39.

Eames, T. H., (1932), 'A comparison of ocular characteristics of unselected and reading disability cases', *Journal of Educational Research*, 25, pp. 211–215.

Eames, T. H. (1938), 'The ocular conditions of 350 poor readers', *Journal of Educ. Research*, 32, pp. 10–16.

Edson, W. H., Bond, G. L., and Cook, W. W. (1953), 'Relationship between visual characteristics and specific silent reading abilities', *Journal of Educ. Research*, XLVI, Feb. pp. 451–457.

Ellis, A. J. (1845), *A plea for Phonotypy and Phonography*, Bath, Isaac Pitman, Phonographic Institution.

Fendrick, P. (1935), 'Visual characteristics of poor readers', *Contributions to Education*, 656. New York: T. C., Col. University.

Fendrick, P., and McGlade, C. A. (1938), 'A validation of two prognostic tests of reading aptitude', *Elementary School Journal*, Sept. pp. 41–46.

Fernald, G. M. (1943), *Remedial techniques in basic school subjects*, New York, McGraw-Hill Book Co. Inc.

Fleming, C. M. (1943), 'Socio-economic level and test performance', *British Journal of Educ. Psychology*, No. 12, pp. 74–82.

Flesch, R. (1955), *Why Johnny can't read!*, Harper Brothers.

Fowler, W. (1962), 'Teaching a two-year-old to read: an experiment in early childhood learning', *Genet. Psychol. Monograph*, 66, pp. 181–183.

Frank, H. (1935), 'A comparative study of children who are backward in reading and beginners in the infant school'. *British Journal of Educ. Psychology*, 5, Part 1, Feb.

Froebel, F. (1909), *The education of man*, translated by W. N. Hailman, New York, D. Appleton Co. p. 68.

Fry, E. B. (1967), 'First grade reading instruction using diacritical marking system, i.t.a. and basal reading system – extended to second grade', *The Reading Teacher*, Vol. 20, No. 8, May, pp. 687–693.

Furness, E. L. (1956), 'Perspective on reversal tendencies', *Elementary English*, 33, Jan., pp. 38–41.

Gaines, F. P. (1946), 'Interrelations of speech and reading disabilities', *Elementary School Journal*, XLV, Feb., pp. 326–332.

Gann, E. (1945), *Reading difficulty and personality organisation*, New York.

Gardner, D. E. M. (1948), *Testing results in the infant school*, London, Methuen.

Gardner, K. (1965), *Towards literacy*, Oxford, Basil Blackwell and Mott, p. 58.

Garrett, H. E. (1958), *Statistics in psychology and education*, Longmans Green and Co., 5th edit.

Gates, A. I. (1924), "The nature and educational significance of physical status, and of mental, physiological, social and emotional maturity', *Journal of Education Psychology*, 15, Sept., pp. 329–358.

Gates, A. I. (1937), 'The necessary mental age for beginning reading', *Elementary School Journal*, 38, Mar., pp. 497–508.

Gates, A. I. (1939), 'Basic principles in reading readiness testing', *Teachers College Record*, Vol. 11, March.

Gates, A. I. (1941), 'The role of personality maladjustment in reading disability', *Journal of Genetic Psychology*, 59, pp. 77–88.

Gates, A. I. (1949), *The improvement of reading*, 3rd edit., New York, The MacMillan Co.

Gates, A. I. (1961), 'Sex differences in reading ability', *Elementary School Journal*, May, pp. 431–434.

Gates, A. I., and Bennett, C. C., (1933), 'Reversal tendencies in reading: causes, diagnosis, prevention and correction', New York, *Bureau of Publications*, T. C., Col. University.

Gates, A. I., and Bond, G. L. (1965), 'Reading readiness: a study of factors determining success and failure in beginning reading', *Teachers College Record*, Vol. 37, May, pp. 678–685.

Gates, A. I., Bond, G. L., and Russell, D. H. (1939), *Methods of determining reading readiness*, New York, T. C., Col. University.

Gattegno, C. (1962), *Words in colour*, Reading, Berks., Educational Explorers Ltd.

Gavel, S. R. (1958), 'June reading achievement of first grade children', *Journal of Education*, Boston University, 140, Feb., pp. 30–43.

Georgiades, N. J. (1968), 'The testing of reading today'. In *The Third International Conference Reading Symposium: To-day's Child and Learning to Read*, Eds. J. Downing and A. Brown, London, Cassell.

Gesell, A., and Armatruda, C. S. (1941), 'Developmental diagnosis'. In *Normal and Abnormal Child Development*, New York, Paul B. Hoeber, Inc.

Gibson, E. J. (1963), 'Analysis of the reading process as perceptual learning'. Paper presented at the *Conference on Perceptual and Linguistic Aspects of the Reading Process*, Centre for advanced Study in the Behavioural Sciences, Stanford, California, 31 Oct. – 2 Nov.

Gibson, E. J. (1965), 'Learning to read', *Science*, 148, pp. 1066–1072.

Goodacre, E. (1967), 'Reading queries'. Letter to the *Times Educational Supplement*, 10 April.

Gray, W. S. (1937), 'The teaching of reading', *The 36th Yearbook of the National Society of the Study of Education*, Bloomington, Ill., Public School Publishing Co.

Gray, W. S. (1943), 'Growth and understanding of reading and its development among youth', *Supplementary Educ. Monographs*, No. 72, University of Chicago Press.

Gray, W. S. (1956), *Teaching of reading and writing: an international survey*, U.N.E.I.C.O.

Gulliford, R. (1967), 'Evaluations – 4'. In Downing, J. A., *The i.t.a. symposium*, National Foundation for Educational Research.

Hanna, P. R., and Moore, J. T., Jr., (1953), 'Spelling from spoken word to written symbol', *The Elementary School Journal*, Vol. 53, pp. 329–337.

Harrington, Sister M. J., and Durrell, D. D. (1955), 'Mental maturity versus perceptual abilities in primary reading', *Education*, 62, pp. 375–380.

Harris, A. J. (1961), *How to increase reading ability*, 4th edit., Longmans Green and Co. Inc.

Harris, D. B. (1963), *Children's drawings as measures of intellectual maturity. A revision and extension of the Goodenough Draw-A-Man Test*, Harcourt, Brace and World Inc.

Harrison, M. (1964), *Instant reading*, London, Sir James Pitman and Sons Ltd.

Harrison, M. (1967), 'Commentary on an alphabet'. Letter to *Times Educational Supplement*, 14 April, p. 1336.

Harrison, M. L. (1939), *Reading readiness*, New York, Houghton, Mifflin Co.

Harrison, M. L., and Stroud, J. B. (1956), *The Harrison-Stroud reading readiness profiles*, Houghton, Mifflin Co.

Hart, J. (1551), *The opening of the unreasonable writing of our English tongue*.

Hart, J. (1570), *A method or comfortable beginning for all unlearned whereby they be taught to read English, in a very short time with pleasure*.

Havighurst, R. J. (1953), *Human development and education*, Longmans Green and Co.

Hayes, E. (1933), 'Why children fail', *Educational Method*, 13, p. 25.

Hayes, R., and Nemeth, J. S. (1965), *An attempt to secure additional evidence concerning factors affecting learning to read*, V.S.O.E. Co-operative Research Project 2687, Pontiac, Michigan, Oakland Schools.

Hemming, J. (1967), 'Evaluations – 5'. In Downing, J. A., *The i.t.a. symposium*, National Foundation for Educational Research.

Henig, M. S. (1949), 'Predictive value of a reading readiness test and of teacher's forecasts', *Elementary School Journal*, Sept., pp. 41–46.

Hester, K. B. (1955), *Teaching every child to read*, New York, Harper.

Hildreth, G. (1933), 'Information tests for first grade children', *Childhood Education*, 9, May, pp. 416–420.

Hildreth, G. (1934), 'Reversals in reading and writing', *Journal of Educ. Psychology*, Vol. 25, pp. 1–20.

Hildreth, G. (1958), *Teaching reading*, Henry Holt and Co.

Hilliard, G. E., and Troxell, E. (1937), 'Informational background as a factor in reading readiness and reading progress', *Elementary School Journal*, 38, Dec., pp. 255–263.

Hinshellwood, J. (1896), 'The visual memory for words and figures', *Brit. Med. J.*, pp. 1543–1544.

Hodges, R. (1644), *The English primrose*, London, Coles.

Hollingworth, L. S. (1942), *Children above 180 I. Q.*, Yonkers, World Book Co.

Holmes, J. A. (1962), 'When should and could Johnny learn to read?' In Figure, J. A. (ed.), *Challenge and Experiment in Reading*, New York, Scholastic Magazines.

Holmes, J. A. (1967), 'Evaluations – 6'. In Downing, J. A., *The i.t.a. symposium*, National Foundation of Educational Research, pp. 123–124.

Hymes, J. L. Jr. (1958), *Before the child reads*, New York, Row, Peterson.

Inglis, W. B. (1949), 'The early stages of reading: a review of recent investigations. The Scottish Council for Research in Education' *Studies in Reading*, Vol. 1, University of London Press.

Jenson, M. B. (1943), 'Reading deficiency as related to cerebral injury and to neurotic behaviour', *Journal of Applied Psychology*, Vol. 27.

Jones, B., and Cartwright, D. (1969), 'Further report on the second i.t.a. experiment', *Educational Research*, Vol. 10, No. 1.

Jones, J. K. (1968), 'Comparing i.t.a. with colour story reading', *Educational Research*, Vol. 10, No. 3, April, pp. 226–234.

Kennedy, H. (1942), 'A study of children's hearing as it relates to reading', *Journal of Exp. Education*, Vol, 10, June, pp. 238–251.

Kennedy, H. (1954), 'Reversals, reversals, reversals', *Journal of Exp. Education*, Vol. 23, Dec., pp. 161–170.

King, I. (1941), 'Effect of age entrance into Grade one upon achievement in the Elementary School', *Elementary School Journal*, 41, April, pp. 587–596.

Kolers, P. A. (1963), 'Sequential presentation of letters for reading and naming', Paper presented at meeting of Psychonomics Society. Philadelphia, September.

Konski, V. (1955), 'An investigation into differences between boys and girls in selected reading readiness areas and in reading achievement'. Unpubl. diss., University of Missouri. Reported in Robinson, H. M., 'What research says to the teacher of reading–reading readiness', *The Reading Teacher*, 8, No. 4, April, pp. 235–237.

Kottmeyer, W. (1947), 'Readiness for reading', *Elementary English*, 24, Oct., pp. 355–360.

Ladd, M. R. (1933), 'The relation of social, economic and personal characteristics to reading ability', *Contributions to Education*, 582, Teachers College, Columbia University.

Lamoreaux, L. A., and Lee, D. M. (1943), *Learning to read through experience*, New York, Appleton-Century Crofts Inc., pp. 89–93.

Lee, W. R. (1966), *Is the irregularity with which English is spelt and important cause of reading difficulty?*, Language Division, University of London Institute of Education.

Lennon, R. (1950), 'The relation between intelligence and achievement test results for a group of communities', *Journal of Educ. Psychology*, 41, pp. 301–308.

Lichtenstein, J. (1960), 'The New Castle reading experiment in Cleveland', *Elementary English*, 37, pp. 27–28.

Lineham, E. B. (1958), 'Early instruction in letter names and sounds as related to success in beginning reading', *Journal of Education, Boston University*, 140, Feb., pp. 44–48.

Lynn, R. (1963), 'Reading readiness and the perceptual abilities of young children', *Educational Research*, Vol. 6, No. 1, Nov., pp. 10–15.

Lytton, H. (1964), *A child psychologist's view of 'reading readiness'*, University of Exeter, Institute of Education (unpublished article), pp. 1–8.

Macmeeken, A. M. (1939), *Ocular dominance in relation to developmental aphasia*, Publications of the W.H. Ross Foundation for the Study of the Prevention of Blindness, London, University of London Press.

Malmquist, E. (1958), *Factors related to reading disabilities in the first grade of the elementary school*, Stockholm.

Manolakes, G., and Sheldon, W. D. (1955), 'The relation between reading-test scores and language factors in intelligence quotients', *Elementary School Journal*, 55, Feb., pp. 346–350.

Marshall, S. (1965), 'The initial teaching alphabet – I don't agree', *Where*, No. 19, Winter.

McCarthy, D. (1935), 'Some possible explanations of sex differences in language development and disorders', *Journal of Psychology*, Jan., pp. 155–160.

McClaren, V. (1950), 'Socio-economic status and reading ability: a study in infant reading', *Studies in Reading*, Vol. 2, Publication of the Scottish Council for Research in Education, 34, pp. 1–62.

McClelland, W. (1942), 'Attainment and necessity. Selection for secondary education', *Publication No. 19 of the Scottish Council for Research in Education*, London, University of London Press, pp. 232–236.

McCracken, G. (1952), 'Have we over-emphasised the readiness factor?', *Elementary English*, 29, pp. 271–76.

McCracken, G. (1953), 'The New Castle reading experiment: a terminal report', *Elementary English*, 130, pp. 13–21.

McCracken, G. (1954), 'We must modernise reading instruction', *The Reading Teacher*, 13, pp. 100–106.

McCracken, G. (1959), 'The value of the correlated visual image', *The Reading Teacher*, 13, pp. 29–33.

McCracken, G. (1959), *The right to learn*, Chicago, Henry Regnery Co.

McLaughlin, K. L. (1928), 'First Grade readiness and retardation. Los Angeles, California', *The Research Committee of the California Kindergarten Association*.

Monroe, M. (1935), 'Diagnosis and treatment of reading disabilities'. Chapter 12 of *Educational Diagnosis. 34th Yearbook of the National Society for the Study of Education*, Chicago, University of Chicago Press, pp. 214–215.

Monroe, M. (1946), *Children who cannot read*, Chicago, University of Chicago Press.

Moorhouse, A. C. (1946), *Writing and the alphabet*, London, Cobbett Press.

Morgan, A. H., and Procter, M. (1967), 'Evaluations –8'. In Downing, J. A., *The i.t.a. symposium*, National Foundation for Educational Research.

Morphett, M. V., and Washburne, C. (1931), "When should children begin to read?' *Elementary School Journal*, 31, Mar., pp. 496–503.

Morris, J. M. (1959), 'Reading in the primary school', *Publication No. 12 of the National Foundation for Educational Research*. London Newnes.

Morris, J. M. (1966), *Standards and progress in reading*, National Foundation for Educational Research.

Morris, R. (1963), *Success and failure in learning to read*, London, Oldbourne, pp. 20–24.

Neale, M. D. (1963), *Neale analysis of reading ability*, London, Macmillan Ltd.

Neale, M. D. (1967), 'Evaluations – 9'. In Downing, J. A., *The i.t.a. symposium*, National Foundation for Educational Research.

Newman, E. B. (1966), 'Speed of reading when the span of letters is restricted'. *American Journal of Psychology*, 79, pp. 272–278.

Nicholson, A. (1958), 'Background abilities related to reading success in first grade', *Journal of Education*, Boston University, 140, Feb., pp. 7–24.

Nila, Sister M. (1940), 'An experimental study of progress in first grade reading', *Educ. Research Monographs*, Vol. 12, The Catholic University of America, June, p. 117.

Nila, Sister M. (1953), 'Foundations of a successful reading program', *Education*, Vol. 73, May, No. 9.

Olson, A. V. (1958), 'Growth in word perception abilities as it relates to success in beginning reading,' *Journal of Education*, Boston University, 140, Feb., pp. 25–36.

Olson, W. C. (1940), 'Reading as a function of the total growth of the child,' In W. S. Gray (comp. ed), *Reading and Pupil Development*, Supplementary Educational Monographs No. 51, Chicago, University of Chicago Press.

Olson, W. C. (1959), *Child development*, Boston, Mass., D. C. Heath.

Oslon, W. C., and Hughes, B. O. (1944), 'Concepts of growth–their significance to teachers', *Childhood Education*, 21, October, pp. 53–63.

Orton, S. J. (1929), 'The sight reading method of teaching reading as a source of reading disability', *Journal of Educ. Psychology*, Vol. 20, Feb., pp. 135–143.

Orton, S. J. (1937), *Reading, writing and speech problems in children*, New York, W. W. Norton & Co.

Park, G. E., and Burri, C. (1943), 'The effect of eye abnormalities on reading difficulty', *Journal of Educ. Psychology*, Vo. 34, pp. 420–430.

Patrick, G. T. (1899), 'Should children under ten learn to read and write?', *Popular Sci. Mon.*, 54, pp. 382–392.

Pestalozzi, J. H. (1907), *How Gertrude teaches her children*, translated by L. E. Holland and F. C. Turner, London, Swan Sonnenschein & Co., pp. 57—58.

Peterson, I. (1937), 'The reading readiness program of the Ironwood Public Schools', *Elementary School Journal*, 37 pp. 438–446.

Pitman, B. (1855), *First phonetic reader*, Cincinnati, American Phonetic Publishing Association.

Pitman, I. J. (1959), 'Learning to read: a suggested experiment', *Times Educational Supplement*, Friday, 29 May.

Pitman, I. J. (1961), 'Learning to read: an experiment', *Journal of Royal Society of Arts*, 109, pp. 149–180.

Pitman, I. J. (1966), 'The initial teaching alphabet in historical perspective'. In *The Initial Teaching Alphabet and the World of English*, (Ed.) Mazurkiewicz, A. J., New York, Initial Teaching Alphabet Foundation.

Potter, M. (1949), 'Perception of symbol orientation and early reading success', *Contributions to Education*, 939, Teachers College, Columbia University.

Prescott, C. A. (1955), 'Sex differences in Metropolitan readiness test results', *Journal of Educ. Research*, 48, April, pp. 605–610.

Preston, M. (1940), 'Reading failure and the child's security', *American Journal of Orthopsych.*, 10, pp. 239–252.

Raven, J. C. (1949), *Coloured progressive matrices*, London, H. K. Lewis.

Raven, J. C. (1950), *Crichton vocabulary scale*, London, H. K. Lewis.

Raybold, E. (1929), 'Reading readiness in children entering first grade,' *Third Yearbook of the Psychology and Educational Research Division*, School Publication No. 185, Los Angeles, California, pp. 98–101.

Reid, J. F. (1967), 'Evaluations – 10'. In Downing, J. A., *The i.t.a. symposium*, National Foundation for Educational Research.

Reid, J. F. (1968), 'Dyslexia: a problem of communication', *Educational Research*, Vol. 10, No. 2, pp. 126–133.

Robinson, F. P., and Hall, W. E. (1942), 'Concerning reading readiness tests', *Bulletin of the Ohio Conference on Reading*, No. 3. Mar.

Robinson, H., (1946), *Why pupils fail in reading*, Chicago, University of Chicago Press.

Roslow, S. (1940), 'Reading readiness and reading achievement in first grade', *Journal of Exp. Education*, 19, pp. 154–159.

Rousseau, J. J. (1762), *Emile*, Everyman translation, B. Foxley.

Russell, D. H. (1949), '*Children learn to read*', Ginn and Co.

Samuels, F. (1943), 'Sex differences in reading achievement', *Journal of Educ. Research*, 36, April, pp. 594–603.

Sanderson, A. E. (1963), 'The idea of reading readiness: a re-examination'. *Educational Research*, 6, pp. 3–9.

Sceats, J. (1967), *i.t.a. and the teaching of literacy*, London, The Bodley Head Ltd.

Schonell, F. J. (1940–1941), 'The relation of reading disability to handedness and certain ocular factors', *Brit. Journal of Educ. Psychology*, Vol. 10, Nov., pp. 227–237; Vol. II, Feb., pp. 20–27.

Schonell, F. J. (1942), *Backwardness in the basic subjects*, Oliver and Boyd.

Schonell, F. J., and Schonell, F. E. (1950), *Graded word reading test*, Edinburgh, Oliver and Boyd.

Schonell, F. J. (1961), *The psychology and teaching of reading*, 4th edit., Oliver and Boyd.

Scott, C. M. (1947), 'An evaluation of training in readiness classes', *Elementary School Journal*, 48, September.

Sheldon, W. D., and Carillo, L. (1952), 'Relation of parents, home and certain developmental characteristics of children's reading ability', *Elementary School Journal*, Jan., pp. 262–270.

Sister John (1966), 'The effect of the i.t.a. medium on the development of visual and auditory awareness of symbol differences'. In Downing, J. A. (Ed.), *The First International Reading Symposium*, London, Cassell, pp. 112–123.

Sister Mary of the Visitation (1929), 'Visual perception in reading and spelling', *Educational Research Bulletin*, Catholic University of America, 41.

Smith, D. E. P., and Carrington, P. M. (1959), *The nature of reading disability*, New York, Harcourt, Brace and Co.

Smith, H. P., and Dechant, V. (1961), *Psychology in teaching reading*, Prentice-Hall Inc.

Smith, N. B. (1950), 'Readiness for reading and related language arts', *A Research Bulletin of the National Committee on Research in English*, New York.

Southgate, V. (1963–64), 'Augmented roman alphabet experiment. An outsider's report', *Educational Review*, 16, pp. 32–41.

Southgate, V. (1965), 'Approaching i.t.a. results with caution', *Educational Research*, Vol. 7, No. 2, pp. 83–96.

Southgate, V. (1968), 'Formulae for beginning reading tuition', *Education Research*, Vol. 11, No. 1, November, pp. 23–29.

Spaulding, G. (1956), 'The relation between performance of independent school pupils on the Harrison-Stroud reading readiness profiles and reading achievement a year later,' *Educational Records Bulletin*, New York, No. 67, February, pp. 73–76.

Strang, R., and Bracken, D. (1957), *Making better readers*, Boston, Heath.

Stott, D. H. (1964), *The programmed reading kit*, Glasgow, Holmes.

Stott, D. H. (1964), *Roads to literacy*, Glasgow, Holmes.

Stroud, J. B. (1956), *Psychology in Education*, New York, Longmans Green & Co. Inc.

Strümpter, D. J. W., and Mienie, C. J. P. (1968), 'A validation of the Harris-Goodenough test', *British Journal of Educational Psychology*, Feb., Vol. 38, Part I, pp. 96–100.

Sutton, R. S. (1955), 'A study of certain factors associated with reading readiness in the Kindergarten', *Journal of Educational Research*, Vol. 48, March, pp. 531–538.

Swales, T. D. (1966), *The attainments in reading and spelling of children who learned to read through the initial teaching alphabet*. M. Ed. Thesis. University of Reading. April.

Swanson, D. E. and Tiffen, J. (1936), Bett's physiological approach to the analysis of reading disabilities as applied to the college level. *Journal of Educ. Research*. Vol. 29, pp. 433–448.

Tanyzer, H., Alpert, H. and Sandel, L. (1965), *Beginning reading – the effectiveness of different media*. Naussan School Development Council (sponsored by New York State Education Department).

Taylor, C. D. (1950), The effect of training on reading readiness, in Scottish Council for Research in Education. *Studies in Reading*, Vol. 11. London: University of London Press.

Teegarden, L. (1932), Tests for the tendency to reversals in reading. *Journal of Educ. Research*. Vol. 27, pp. 81–97.

Terman, L. M. (1918), An experiment in infant education. *Journal of Applied Psychology*. 2. pp. 219–228.

Terman, L. M. and Oden, M. (1947), The gifted child grows up: twenty-five years follow up of a superior group. *Genetic Studies of Genius*. 4.

Thackray, D. V. (1964), *A study of the relationship between some specific evidence of reading readiness and reading progress in the infant school*. M. A. Thesis, University of London.

Thompson, T. (1942), *The a.b.c. of our alphabet*. London: Studio Publications.

Tinker, M. (1932), Diagnostic and remedial reading. *Elementary School Journal*. 33.

Vernon, M. D. (1958), *Backwardness in reading*. London: Cambridge University Press.

Vernon, M. D. (1960), The investigation of reading problems today. *British Journal of Educational Psychology*. Vol. 30, pp. 146–54.

Vernon, M. D. (1962), Specific Dyslexia. *British Journal of Educational Psychology*, June, Vol. 32, Part 2.

Vernon, M. D. (1967), Evaluations – 11. In Downing, J. A., *The i.t.a. symposium*. National Foundation for Educational Research.

Wall, W. D. (1967), 'The evaluations – a summary'. In Downing, J. A., *The i.t.a. symposium*, National Foundation for Educational Research.

Warburton, F. W. and Southgate, V. (1969), *i.t.a.: An Independent Evaluation'*, John Murray and W. & R. Chambers.

Washburne, C. (1941), 'Individualized plan of instruction in Winnetka in adjusting reading programs to individuals', *Suppl. Educ. Monographs*, No. 52, Chicago, University of Chicago Press, pp. 90–95.

Whipple, G. (1944), 'Remedial programs in relation to basic programs in teaching', *Elementary School Journal*, 44, May, pp. 525–535.

Winch, W. T. (1925), 'Teaching beginners to read in England: its methods, results and psychological bases', *Journal of Educ. Research Monographs*, No. 8, Bloomington, Ill., Public School Publishing Co.

Witty, P. (1949), *Reading in modern education*, Boston, Heath and Co.

Witty, P., and Kopel, D. (1939), *Reading and the educative process*, Ginn and Co.

Witty, P., and Kopel, D. (1936), 'Sinistral and mixed manual-ocular behaviour in reading disability', *Journal of Educ. Psychology*, Vol. 27, pp. 119–134.

Witty, P., and Kopel, D. (1936), 'Heterophoria and reading disability', *Journal of Educ. Psychology*, Vol. 27, pp. 222–230.

Witty, P., and Kopel, D. (1936), 'Preventing reading disability: the reading readiness factor', *Ed. Admin. and Super.*, 22, pp. 401–418.

Yates, A. (1954), 'The teaching of reading from the researcher's point of view', *Child Education*, Vol. 31, No. 12.

Young, N., and Gaier, E. L. (1951), 'Implications in emotionally caused reading retardation', *Elementary English*, 28, pp. 271–275.

Yule, W., Lockyer, L., and Noone, A., (1967), 'The reliability and validity of the Goodenough-Harris drawing test', *Brit. Journal of Educ. Psychology*, Feb., Vol. 37, Part 1, pp. 110–111.